CEMETERIES AND GRAVEYARDS

FAMILY HISTORY FROM PEN & SWORD BOOKS

Birth, Marriage & Death Records
The Family History Web Directory
Tracing British Battalions on the Somme
Tracing Great War Ancestors
Tracing History Through Title Deeds
Tracing Secret Service Ancestors
Tracing the Rifle Volunteers
Tracing Your Air Force Ancestors
Tracing Your Ancestors
Tracing Your Ancestors from 1066 to 1837
Tracing Your Ancestors Through Death Records –
  Second Edition
Tracing Your Ancestors through Family
  Photographs
Tracing Your Ancestors Through Letters and
  Personal Writings
Tracing Your Ancestors Using DNA
Tracing Your Ancestors Using the Census
Tracing Your Ancestors: Cambridgeshire, Essex,
  Norfolk and Suffolk
Tracing Your Aristocratic Ancestors
Tracing Your Army Ancestors
Tracing Your Army Ancestors – Third Edition
Tracing Your Birmingham Ancestors
Tracing Your Black Country Ancestors
Tracing Your Boer War Ancestors
Tracing Your British Indian Ancestors
Tracing Your Canal Ancestors
Tracing Your Channel Islands Ancestors
Tracing Your Church of England Ancestors
Tracing Your Criminal Ancestors
Tracing Your Docker Ancestors
Tracing Your East Anglian Ancestors
Tracing Your East End Ancestors
Tracing Your Family History on the Internet
Tracing Your Female Ancestors
Tracing Your First World War Ancestors
Tracing Your Freemason, Friendly Society and
  Trade Union Ancestors
Tracing Your Georgian Ancestors, 1714–1837
Tracing Your Glasgow Ancestors
Tracing Your Great War Ancestors: The Gallipoli
  Campaign

Tracing Your Great War Ancestors: The Somme
Tracing Your Great War Ancestors: Ypres
Tracing Your Huguenot Ancestors
Tracing Your Insolvent Ancestors
Tracing Your Irish Family History on the Internet
Tracing Your Jewish Ancestors
Tracing Your Jewish Ancestors – Second Edition
Tracing Your Labour Movement Ancestors
Tracing Your Legal Ancestors
Tracing Your Liverpool Ancestors
Tracing Your Liverpool Ancestors – Second
  Edition
Tracing Your London Ancestors
Tracing Your Medical Ancestors
Tracing Your Merchant Navy Ancestors
Tracing Your Northern Ancestors
Tracing Your Northern Irish Ancestors
Tracing Your Northern Irish Ancestors – Second
  Edition
Tracing Your Oxfordshire Ancestors
Tracing Your Pauper Ancestors
Tracing Your Police Ancestors
Tracing Your Potteries Ancestors
Tracing Your Pre-Victorian Ancestors
Tracing Your Prisoner of War Ancestors: The First
  World War
Tracing Your Railway Ancestors
Tracing Your Roman Catholic Ancestors
Tracing Your Royal Marine Ancestors
Tracing Your Rural Ancestors
Tracing Your Scottish Ancestors
Tracing Your Second World War Ancestors
Tracing Your Servant Ancestors
Tracing Your Service Women Ancestors
Tracing Your Shipbuilding Ancestors
Tracing Your Tank Ancestors
Tracing Your Textile Ancestors
Tracing Your Twentieth-Century Ancestors
Tracing Your Welsh Ancestors
Tracing Your West Country Ancestors
Tracing Your Yorkshire Ancestors
Writing Your Family History
Your Irish Ancestors

CEMETERIES AND GRAVEYARDS

A Guide for Local and Family Historians in England and Wales

CELIA HERITAGE

Pen & Sword
FAMILY HISTORY

First published in Great Britain in 2022 by
PEN AND SWORD FAMILY HISTORY
An imprint of
Pen & Sword Books Ltd
Yorkshire – Philadelphia

ISBN 978 1 52670 237 1

Typeset by Mac Style
Printed and bound by CPI Group (UK) Ltd, Croydon, CR0 4YY

FSC MIX
Paper from responsible sources
FSC® C013604
www.fsc.org

Pen & Sword Books Limited incorporates the imprints of Atlas, Archaeology, Aviation, Discovery, Family History, Fiction, History, Maritime, Military, Military Classics, Politics, Select, Transport, True Crime, Air World, Frontline Publishing, Leo Cooper, Remember When, Seaforth Publishing, The Praetorian Press, Wharncliffe Local History, Wharncliffe Transport, Wharncliffe True Crime and White Owl.

For a complete list of Pen & Sword titles please contact

PEN & SWORD BOOKS LIMITED
47 Church Street, Barnsley, South Yorkshire, S70 2AS, England
E-mail: enquiries@pen-and-sword.co.uk
Website: www.pen-and-sword.co.uk

Or

PEN AND SWORD BOOKS
1950 Lawrence Rd, Havertown, PA 19083, USA
E-mail: Uspen-and-sword@casematepublishers.com
Website: www.penandswordbooks.com

To P.W. with my love.

Cover Images: Clodock Church, Herefordshire, depositum plate Emmeline Elizabeth Lugard (1887 St. Alphege, Seasalter, Kent), Cross slab, St Bees Priory, Cumbria, Brompton Cemetery (All Author's collection). Cemetery burial register book (Deceasedonline.com)

CONTENTS

ACKNOWLEDGEMENTS

Many thanks go to everyone who has helped me in the writing of this book; to my friends, and colleagues, who gave encouragement and support, and to those who helped in practical ways. Particular thanks go to the following, in no order of priority: Ivor Spencer of Cleverley and Spencer, Philip Gore of Gore Brothers Ltd, Elliott Brotherton of EB Sculpture Ltd, and also Brian Parsons for valuable help and advice. To Jake Holmes for letting me use the photograph of his great-grandmother Isabella Holmes, and Anne Powers for her blog on Isabella, and putting me in touch with Jake! To Anna Fairley Nielsson for permission to use photographs of St James Cemetery from **www.stjamescemetery.co.uk**, Jane Roberts of **pasttopresentgenealogy.co.uk** for kindly providing details of Esther Hallas in Chapter 5. To **Ancestry.com**, **Deceasedonline** and Canterbury Archaeological Trust, for supplying images, and to staff at the Kent History and Library Centre for help accessing local records. To Margaret Lawrence for copies of her images from East Peckham churchyard, to Anthony Lee for use of the image of St John's Church, and the Ipswich Society for the image of the Jewish cemetery. To Jim Butterworth of Milford-on-Sea Historical Record Society for helping me track down the chronosticon gravestone at Milford Church, and Nick Dexter for substantial time spent at TNA photographing records. To Peter Cracknell for details of the gravestones at Chartham Mental Hospital, Janette Silverman for advice about Jewish burials and gravestones, Heather Nowlan for helping troubleshoot discrepancies in the TNA catalogue, Mark Powell of the British Lichen Society for advice on lichen, Janet Few and Jane Sheehan for supplying copies of images and information, and to Jayne Shrimpton for advice on dating. To Joanne Penn for reading my final text before submission and Mia Bennett for brainstorming my initial book plan all those years ago!

To Jonathan Risby for help and advice as always, and with love and thanks for many shared memories of graveyards in the past. To Reuben and Eli for patience and diversion!

A particularly heartfelt thank you to Helen Osborn, whose insightful suggestions, and moral support, were invaluable at a very difficult time, and kept me going.

And finally, to Andrew Linklater of Canterbury Archaeological Trust, whose many hours of help, discussion, companionship, and advice over the last four years, have helped form this book into so much more than a genealogical guide.

April 2021

ABBREVIATIONS

Some of the more commonly used abbreviations and archival websites that may be of use are listed here for ease of reference. For main website listings for burial and related records see pages 200–217.

CRO	County Record Office
GENUKI	Genealogy UK and Ireland
GRO	General Register Office
LDS	Church of Jesus Christ Latter Day Saints
OS	Ordnance Survey
TNA	The National Archives, Kew

Archives and Libraries

British Library	www.bl.uk
General Register Office (GRO)	www.gro.gov.uk
The National Archives (TNA)	www.nationalarchives.gov.uk
National Archives' Catalogue	https://discovery.nationalarchives.gov.uk
National Library of Wales	www.llgc.org.uk

Organizations and Institutes

Federation of Family History Societies (FFHS)	www.ffhs.org.uk
Institute of Heraldic and Genealogical Studies (IHGS)	www.ihgs.ac.uk
The Society of Genealogists, (SOG)	www.sog.org.uk

INTRODUCTION

This book has been a long time in the writing, for many reasons, and at many stages I wondered if should turn back! But I didn't; I kept going and I hope you enjoy the result. The history of our burial places is a fascinating one. While this book provides advice for researchers who are seeking burial places for specific individuals (often their ancestors), it is perhaps the study of our burial places in their wider context, and how they evolved, that is of greater interest, reflecting, as it does, the changing nature of burial practices and the evolution of human society.

The history of our early parish churchyards is especially fascinating, yet it is also challenging, since there is so little documentary evidence relating to their origins, and so few churchyards have been fully excavated. I hope, in the pages that follow, to provide food for thought, as well as facts. I hope to open the eyes of name-collectors to what lies beneath the ground, and divert the attention of ground-huggers to the amazing amount of information there is to be learned about those people buried in our cemeteries and graveyards.

Before you read further, a word about the terms burial ground, cemetery, graveyard and churchyard. There is a great overlap between them, both in the way they are used today, and how they have been used historically: it is almost impossible to separate them and define them precisely in a way with which everyone will agree. They have been used, and applied, differently by various groups of people to describe various types of burial locations over the years, but some have particular connotations. Below are my thoughts, and interpretations of the various terms, and how they have evolved. Not everyone will agree, but, like most historians, I put this, and many of my other thoughts on the evolution of early churchyards out here for discussion!

A burial ground can be a generic term to cover any place set aside for burial at any period. However, in the eighteenth and nineteenth century, this term was frequently applied to places which specialized in the burial of Nonconformists. It was also often used for burial grounds attached to institutions, and as an alternative word for the new Burial Board Cemeteries introduced in the 1850s.

The word cemetery is most often associated by the general public with the large municipal cemeteries found in towns and cities today. It is also used retrospectively by historians and archaeologists to indicate a place of burial, or interment, for people of any faith or belief, and in any time period. It simply indicates a place designated as a burial site, but not associated with a church. When referring to the Roman and Anglo-Saxon periods, a cemetery includes a place where both cremated remains (cremations) and burials (inhumations) are contained. The Anglo-Saxon word for cemetery was *licburg*, deriving from words meaning 'corpse' and 'settlement'.

Graveyard is a fairly generic term, often also used for a churchyard, and to denote smaller burial areas attached to workhouses, jails and other institutions.

The definition of 'churchyard' is much more specific than any of the other terms. It denotes the area of land surrounding a church, but not all churchyards contain burials.

Other words you may come across include necropolis, which is typically used to refer to large city burial grounds found among ancient, non-Christian civilizations, and the romantic term 'God's Acre' which was popularized for a relatively short while by the poet Henry Wadsworth Longfellow.

Celia Heritage, 2021

Chapter 1

A BRIEF HISTORY OF DEATH AND BURIAL

On a cold, grey winter's afternoon in the early 1990s, I stood in Woodgrange Park Cemetery, East Ham, London, looking desperately for the gravestone of my great-grandparents John Christian Beck and his wife Clara. It was due to be destroyed in preparation for new burials in this part of the cemetery. I could not find it.

Together with my Dad's cousin, Lillian Thomas, and her husband Eric, I'd spent over an hour searching unsuccessfully, despite having the exact plot and square number. I'd also been given a description of the stone by the staff member on duty, who had looked in his register to find this. The gravestone consisted of a large cross on a three-tiered plinth with runners leading to a marble book. He showed us to the right section of the cemetery, but there was no burial plan available to guide us to the exact burial place. The cemetery was a total mess; from the derelict chapel at its entrance, to the portacabin office with its pile of burial registers lying on the damp floor, through to the unkempt and ruinous state of much of the cemetery grounds. Large sections were totally overgrown with brambles and other vegetation, making it hard to see, let alone access, many of the memorials. As I searched, I picked up a long stick to clear away some brambles, only to find that what I had in my hand was not a stick – but an arm bone! Such was the state of Woodgrange Park Cemetery in the early 1990s.

Failure to find the gravestone meant its inevitable destruction – a piece of my heritage and a valuable record lost forever. It was also the memorial chosen with love and care by my family to mark the resting place of John and Clara and four of their children. I wanted to save this piece of my unique personal family history.

In despair I closed my eyes, concentrated hard and willed my great-grandparents to respond if they wanted me to find them. Otherwise, we had to head home. Feeling no positive vibes in return, I turned to go and started along the path. All of a sudden, I glimpsed what looked like the corner of a marble book poking out of a large clump of brambles. It was them!

The large stone cross had long ago fallen away from the three-tiered plinth and lay to one side; the runners connecting the plinth to the marble book had long since been crushed and scattered – but the marble book still lay at the foot of the grave, six feet from the plinth which had been sited at the head. We all have eureka moments in our family history research – and this was most certainly one of mine.

This story provokes several important questions. What is it that makes us seek our ancestors' burial places and why are they important to us? Why did I feel strongly enough to make the journey to London and spend an hour or more fighting my way through thick brambles to locate the headstone and then find a way to move it to a place of safety? After all, my relatives' bones still lie at Woodgrange – it was only the gravestone I preserved. And, of course, why do we feel the need to erect a gravestone or memorial to those we have lost? There are many different reasons why, yet some people feel no connection to or interest in their family's past – and some have no interest in the past at all. Some regard it as simply irrelevant. But for many of us, the past is key to explaining how we got here; it gives us a sense of belonging and a link to those who have gone before. It is also a form of paying our respects, and this way of thinking has formed part of the culture of many societies over the centuries.

In the case of my great-grandparents' stone, it was put to one side by cemetery staff and I hired a man and van to go to London to collect it and bring it home to Kent. Every time I move house it's a bit of an issue, but it has travelled with me to two further houses since and I wonder which of my nephew and nieces I will leave it to in my will, and whether they will find it an honour or a burden. Or will I, at some point, let it go and move on without it, leaving it behind for future owners of my house to puzzle, curse or exclaim over?

Where and how our ancestors were buried was determined by when and where they lived; by the social and religious trends, beliefs and practices of the day; and by a family's affluence and particular wishes. All of these have a bearing on how easy it is for you, the researcher, to locate their burial or gravestone. Cemeteries and graveyards are not simply the places where we go to look for our ancestors. Studying the history of each will also tell us something of the history of the locality, the people who lived there, and the burial places available to them at any one time. It can also provide an insight into religious beliefs and the attitudes of society to death.

There is a massive crossover between family and local history. You can build pedigrees (genealogies) without knowing anything about the places in which your ancestors lived. Local historians can ignore the complex family histories which often form part of the history of a town or village. But, by so doing, each loses the chance of gaining a greater understanding of their subject. While this book is primarily about cemeteries and graveyards, with the emphasis on England and Wales, it is important to understand attitudes to death and burial over time, not just in our own immediate culture, but in other societies too. Studies of funeral practices also illustrate attitudes towards death but, sadly, such a study was outside the scope of this book. The works of people such as James Stevens Curl, Julian Litten, Brian Parsons, Julie Rugg and Lou Taylor make excellent further reading on this subject (see Bibliography).

While cremation and inhumation are the most frequent treatments of bodies after death, some cultures practised 'double', 'secondary' or 'multiple burial', whereby the body underwent a series of transitionary stages before final burial or disposal of the remains was achieved. The first stage was usually excarnation, the de-fleshing of the body, either by natural means, such as leaving the body outside to decompose naturally and be picked over by wild animals, or by letting it decay naturally within a designated internal location. Once only the bones remained, they were placed in their final resting place. This was often in the ground, but sometimes they were ceremonially displayed or generally dispersed; this would vary according to the culture. They might also be periodically revisited and honoured as part of rituals intended to pay respect to the deceased family member and forge links with an ancestral past. The Malagasy tribes of south-east Africa practised double burial and believed that the soul of the deceased could only enter the 'Land of the Dead' when the corpse was completely decomposed. The families took good care of the bodies during this decomposition process, performing music and dances around them, wrapping them in new shrouds and sprinkling them with perfume every five to seven years. Although double burials are no longer practised in Malagasy, many modern-day Malagasy folk still practise the ceremony of the 'turning of the bones'. These celebrations are a sign of respect for their ancestors and also a time for family members to reunite. The ancestral bones are taken out of their crypts and rewrapped in new silk, amid dancing and music.

Other cultures which have practised double burials include early Jews in the Roman Empire, who embraced a two-part burial process, with the corpses being placed on a niche, bench or other temporary location. Once decomposition was completed the bones were collected by relatives and placed in an ossuary or in the family tomb.[1] As we shall see, excarnation was also found among British tribes of the early to middle Iron Age.

Archaeology provides an insight into our ancestors' burial practices, albeit an imperfect one. By its nature the evidence is very incomplete, with only a relatively small percentage of burials having been discovered, let alone properly recorded. However, it does help us understand the evolution which led to the development of cemeteries and graveyards, and illustrates how mankind has practised ritual or ceremonial burials for tens of thousands of years. It also highlights the importance death and burial held for our historic and pre-historic forebears.

A ritual or ceremonial burial is one where care has been taken over the way in which the body has been laid to rest. There is evidence of this as early as the Upper Palaeolithic period (10,000 years ago) in Europe when, due to the fact that much of the continent was covered in ice at the time, families typically dwelt close to large cave entrances and buried their dead in the deeper cave systems beyond. Although few complete skeletons have been found, those burials which have been discovered often contain simple grave goods, such as scallop shells and stone tools or crude jewellery. These were perhaps tokens for the dead to take with them into the afterlife, or sentimental trinkets to aid the grieving of those left behind. Either way, such burials, however piecemeal, show that the local community was burying its dead with care, and reflect a constant theme in burial history. Looking at how pre-historic burial practices evolved (which we will now do) may seem irrelevant to some of you reading this book. However, understanding the evolution of burial practice is important when comprehending the origins of the parish churchyard, which was a natural progression of all that came before. There are also recurrent themes in burial practices which carried over into the period in which our ancestors were buried in churchyards. It's important to have an understanding of Christianity and its early origins in England and Wales too. Once we have all these, we can really begin to appreciate how our parish churchyards originated and how burial practices, as we know them, evolved. It perhaps puts things into perspective to remember that the people who were being buried in the prehistoric times described below were just as much our ancestors as those whose names we can potentially read in burial registers from the mid-sixteenth century onwards, and who form part of our family trees.

During the Mesolithic period (10,000–6,000 years ago) archaeological finds (mostly from modern mainland Europe) indicate a transition from single burials to burials clustered in small groups to form cemetery-style collections. Sadly, evidence of burials of this period from the modern British Isles is scant. However, a significant collection of human remains was recovered from Aveline's Hole at Burrington Combe in the Mendip Hills, Somerset. Numerous skeletons were found, including a possibly cremated individual. Some had accompanying grave goods.[2] Other collective burials and possible cremations have also been identified in more recent years, clearly showing that although humans at this time were hunter-gatherers, following animal migration to survive, they returned repeatedly to the same places to bury their dead.

Climatic shifts towards the end of the Mesolithic period resulted in major cultural changes which affected the way our prehistoric ancestors lived, and indirectly how they dealt with their dead. This was the time of the first farmers and the beginning of the Neolithic period (6,000–4,500 years ago). During this period there is plentiful evidence that our ancestors were living in permanent fixed settlements away from the previous, traditional cave sites. There is also strong evidence for a much more well-defined and methodically ritualistic way of dealing with the dead. This period is renowned for the construction of such sites as Stonehenge and Avebury, and the erection of a multitude of standing stones and timber and earthen 'henges' across the British Isles (these also being ritual sites themselves). It is also synonymous with the construction of long barrows. It must be presumed that long barrows housed the more prominent members of society, due to the relatively low numbers found compared to the overall presumed population. Consisting of an elongated earthen mound thrown over a stone-lined chamber, or series of interconnecting chambers, it is believed these were perceived as permanent receptacles for the deceased's remains. It is possible that access was afforded to family members, where the skeletal remains of their ancestors could be relocated in the side chambers as a further mark of reverence. The majority of burials known from this period are referred to as 'crouched', or 'crouch burials', due to the body being placed on its side in a compressed, or foetal position. It is thought that burying the body in this position may have represented the deceased returning to the womb. However, it must be remembered that cremation was also prevalent during this period.

In the later Neolithic period (4,200–3,800 years ago), a new burial feature appeared in the landscape. Known retrospectively as 'round barrows', these are circular mounds of earth thrown over the site of a

Bronze Age round barrows on the ridge of Bronkham Hill, Dorset (Jim Champion, 2006, reproduced under licence: https://commons.wikimedia.org/wiki/Commons:GNU_Free_ Documentation_License,_version_1.2)

primary central burial, or burials, utilizing the upcast soil from digging an encircling ditch. These are again believed to relate to more prominent members of a community, judging by the relatively low numbers found in comparison to the total presumed population at the time. Other burials, as well as cremated remains, possibly of later family members, were also placed in the top of the mound over time, showing a continued veneration of the site by the local community. The shape and form of the barrows were almost certainly deliberately prominent, to act as a point of focus, and as a reminder of those buried there. Remembering the dead is one of the most important reasons for the existence of graveyards and cemeteries, and this link to an earlier practice should not be overlooked. In many other cultures, tombs and chambers were thought to actually house the deceased's spirit, perhaps temporarily before transition to a better state. It is very feasible that barrows were constructed with a similar belief in mind. Similarly, early gravestones in churchyards were placed to encourage remembrance of departed souls and, as we will see in Chapter 5, the design of some gravestones has been known to reflect the shape of a house.

Long barrows, stone-lined burial chambers and also cists (lined burial chambers sealed with a lid) continued to be utilized for assumed high-status burials, with the majority of long barrows being created between 5,800 and 3,400 years ago. The construction of unchambered earthen barrows continued on a more intermittent basis until about 800 AD, although the vast majority of the Neolithic population possessed no such monument. Instead, they would have been buried in simple earth-cut graves. Even so, like their contemporaries in the barrow, some would have had modest pottery vessels, stone tools or simply fashioned jewellery items buried with them.

As we have seen, barrows clearly represent a ritual focus in the landscape, and the importance of this is reflected by the fact that later cultures are known to have utilized them for their own burials, often extending the ritual association of the site by many hundreds of years. The use of such burial monuments continued throughout the Neolithic period and during most of the Bronze Age (3,800–2,800 years ago), with ever more elaborate collections of round barrows forming barrow cemeteries. As with the earlier periods described above, a majority of the population would have been buried in simple earth-cut graves in crouch positions, though during this period formal clusters of graves forming defined cemeteries were becoming more common. Isolated graves in open countryside were also a frequent occurrence. Small groups of cremations, both with or without funerary pots (urns), were also common at this time.

During the early to middle Iron Age (2,800–2,500 years ago), there was a major break with the above-mentioned burial traditions, which had seen a mixture of inhumation with a small percentage of cremations. Instead, for the common man, excarnation was practised, raising the dead upon timber platforms to decompose, with no final burial being achieved. The semi-decomposed body reverted into articulated parts, which were disposed of unceremoniously in pits, ditches and hollows, with no formal grave being provided. At the same time, it is known that the higher end of society was still being laid in traditional graves, some beneath barrows, and frequently with elaborate grave goods such as bronze mirrors, swords, spears and, on rare occasions, even their chariot and horses, as at Pocklington, East Yorkshire.

By the late Iron Age (2,500–2,000 years ago), the influence of Rome was making its mark on native society ahead of the inclusion of the British Isles in the Roman Empire. This included the strong return of cremation as a method of disposal, with numerous small collections of 'urn-fields'. These were enclosed cemeteries containing cremations placed in funerary pots, many of which were highly decorated and included a simple selection of grave goods, such as brooches. This also heralded the end of excarnation, though the practice probably gradually decreased rather than ending abruptly. Karen Pollock, in her thesis, '*The Evolution and Role of Burial Practice in Wales,*' particularly shows that burial practices in Wales incorporated previous indigenous rites and traditions, including excarnation, which continued into the Roman period.

The Roman settlement of England and Wales was particularly influential on burial rituals and disposing of the dead. The Romans had themselves been influenced by the Greeks and the Etruscans, who were in turn influenced by other cultures. Since Christianity was established during the time of the Roman settlement, its burial and funeral rites came to incorporate ideas and beliefs from all around the known world and many of these have carried down to the modern day.

At the time of the initial Roman settlement in England (43 AD), cremation was normal practice among Roman communities, and this particularly encouraged its use among native communities in the vicinity of Roman towns and military garrisons. Cremation was also more popular in coastal regions close to the Continent where the Romans had first settled. From the second century, influenced by changing preferences in Italy, there was a move away from cremation towards inhumation. This was partly due to the increasing popularity of Christianity, which favoured inhumation, and whose followers grew notably in number during the reign of Constantine, the first Christian Emperor (306–337 AD).

The Roman cemetery at Dorchester-upon-Thames clearly shows the transition from cremation to inhumation, with cremations being found until the late second century, followed by a period of concurrent cremations and inhumations for about 100 years and then, from the late third century, inhumations only.[3]

This new trend towards inhumation instead of cremation was slower to take hold in rural areas. Even in the third century, there was still a mixture of native and Roman burial practices, with cremations, cave burials, and barrow burials all still taking place. Roman cemeteries were frequently placed near to prehistoric burial sites, perhaps to encourage burials there, or due to a lingering recognition of the sacredness of these ancient places. Roman law also decreed that burials should not take place within a settlement, but outside its walls. Apart from the fact that burials could cause hygiene problems if set close to human habitation, the Romans also believed that the spirits of the dead could interfere with the mental health and clear thinking of the living; another reason for siting them away from human habitation.

Excavation of the Roman cemetery at Wotton, Gloucestershire, showed a range of burial customs being practised at the site. By the third to fourth century AD, there appears to have been an increasingly organized approach to the placing of burials within the cemetery. Burials seem to have taken place in clusters, suggesting burial in family groups, and graves also seem to have been reopened to admit second burials – possibly later family members. This more organized approach continued, so that by the late Roman period in Britain there was a growing tendency for cemeteries to be actively managed in terms of the position of the burials, with many corpses being laid in an east to west direction.[4] From this period there is also even stronger evidence that burials were organized in family plots and laid up in formal rows. This practice could be suggestive of actual physical identifying of burials using markers. Not all Romano-British burials took place in cemeteries. In both Roman Wales and England, burials have also notably been found on the periphery of settlements, close to defences.

The eclectic nature of disposing of the dead carried on long after the withdrawal of the Romans from Britain in the fifth century. In Anglo-Saxon times, inhumation was generally favoured by those following Christianity, and a mixture of cremation and inhumation by the remainder of the population. As always, the nature of burial is greatly affected by the wealth or status of the deceased. Just as the barrows of our prehistoric ancestors reflected the pre-eminence of the people buried

Earth-cut grave to a high-status Anglo-Saxon female burial with multiple accompaniments including three glass vessels and iron weaving baton (by feet); also a walrus ivory purse ring (left hand), decorative necklace with gold pendant. Buckland, Dover, Kent. Scale 1m. (Canterbury Archeological Trust)

there, excavations of burials from the Anglo-Saxon period have revealed so-called 'bed burials'. Judging by the grave goods placed with the body, these appear to relate to high-status females, with the deceased being placed on a bed-like structure (indicated only by the survival of its iron fittings) with boulders placed by the side or under the head. The great majority of Anglo-Saxon burials excavated, however, have been in simple earth graves in cemeteries of varying sizes, although approximately half of these have also been found with some sort of accompaniment.

In Anglo-Saxon times, there was a large overlap between Paganism and Christianity, but it was the gradual establishment of a physical (Christian) church with the parish as its unit of local ecclesiastical administration, that built a foundation from which the Christian Church rose to pre-eminence in England and Wales, from the late eighth century onwards. As a result, the parish churchyard evolved, and we will look at this in Chapter 2. In order to fully understand the evolution of the churchyard we must, however, have a rudimentary understanding of the history of Christianity in Britain.

The coming of Christianity

It is a common misconception that Christianity only came to Britain in 597 AD, with the arrival of Augustine; yet there is strong evidence that it was already well established in the third century AD, as the result of trade with the Continent and religious tolerance throughout Roman Britain. It was strong enough to weather the withdrawal of the Romans from Britain in the early fifth century. It survived the ensuing Teutonic invasions, and took its place in Anglo-Saxon Britain, albeit losing strength in the face of the popularity of pagan beliefs brought by the settling tribes. Its strongest footholds at this time were in western areas such as Wales, Cornwall and western Scotland.

Christianity experienced a resurgence from the very late sixth century. This was firstly as a result of missionaries sent out to preach by the Celtic Christian Church based in Iona under St Columba, and secondly thanks to the arrival of the aforementioned Augustine (later St Augustine). A Benedictine monk, sent to convert the pagan Anglo-Saxons by Pope Gregory the Great, Augustine landed in Kent. This may or may not have been a coincidence, but it was fortuitous, since the wife of Ethelberht, the king of Kent, was a Christian, and Ethelberht himself was later converted. The tradition of Christianity brought by Augustine differed from that of the Celtic missionaries based in Iona. These differences mainly related to certain doctrinal niceties, notably the way in which the date of Easter was calculated. Both the Celtic and Roman Churches were keen to convert the remaining pagan population of Britain, but this could not be achieved if they continued to compete with each other. A supreme united Christian Church was required in order to do this. In 664 a momentous church synod, presided over by important church dignitaries from both Churches, was held at Whitby. The synod ruled that the Roman tradition, brought by Augustine, should take precedence. This Roman Church formed the basis of the Christian (Catholic) Church in England and Wales from this time up to the Reformation in the mid-sixteenth century. It is important to remember that up to 1534, when Henry VIII broke with Rome, the Church was Catholic and religious doctrines promulgated by the Pope in Rome would have affected what our ancestors believed about death and the afterlife.

The afterlife and remembering the dead

Belief in life after death has played, and still plays, a major role in the great majority of cultures and communities. Historically, Jews, Christians and Muslims, as well as the ancient Greeks and pagan Romans, all believed that the soul of the deceased was judged, and then passed through various different stages, before moving to a satisfactory state of eternal life. The role of family members in assisting with this transition to the afterlife, typically through remembrance (prayers), and sometimes by physical treatment of the deceased's remains, has historically been key, and continues to be important for many faiths today. Remembrance was also encouraged by the erection of memorials and, as we have already seen, in many cultures burial grounds, mounds and monuments were placed in prominent positions in the landscape so they could not fail to be seen. This could be by a road or on a hillside, or they might be constructed of such a size they were noticeable from afar. There is no doubt that ritual acts of remembrance also helped family members come to terms with their own loss when a loved one died. Mourning and remembering ceremonies also helped to preserve familial bonds of love and respect after death.

In the eleventh century Christian world, there was an ever-growing preoccupation with the journey of the soul after death, especially the need for it to be purified of all sin before being accepted into heaven. This transitory period was referred to as purgatory. From the late-eleventh century, purgatory was increasingly depicted as an actual place. With this came an increasing emphasis on speeding the journey of the soul through purgatory as quickly as possible. The length of time spent there depended on the sinfulness of the deceased's soul to begin with, but praying for the soul (particularly by the saying or singing of masses) was

This doom painting at St Peter and St Paul's Church in Chaldon, Surrey, clearly depicts the possible fate of the soul on the Day of Judgement. (Author's collection)

regarded as one of the most effective ways of reducing this time. Singing masses for the dead was one of the chief roles of monasteries until the thirteenth century, when it became popular for high-status families to found chantry chapels within parish churches, or as independent chapels on family estates. The founder not only paid for the chapel, but also for a priest to say regular masses for the founder and his family after their deaths. Time in purgatory could also be reduced by monetary payments and donations to the church.

For those who could afford it, burial within the church itself and as close to the chancel (the holiest part of the church) as possible was a must; this would help speed the soul on its way to heaven. The more prominent positions in the church were not just those closest to the holy altar, but also those that would be seen by the greatest number of worshippers, thus encouraging them to pray for the souls of the departed.

In early sixteenth-century Europe, a series of religious movements developed that opposed many of the doctrinal beliefs of the Pope and the Catholic Church. These culminated in what is referred to by historians as 'the Reformation', and the rise of Protestant Christianity. In 1534, the King of England, Henry VIII (motivated by his desire to obtain the annulment of his marriage, which had been refused by the Pope), severed all ties with the Catholic Church and the Pope. He established a new Protestant Church in England and Wales, with the monarch as its head, at the same time extending English law into Wales, so that it effectively became part of the kingdom of England. With the exception of the short reign of Queen Mary I (1553–1558), England and Wales have officially been Protestant countries from that day on, with the Church of England as the established Church. Protestant doctrine placed an emphasis on the importance of personal belief and faith in God and the Bible, as opposed to the belief that the deceased's soul was judged by his or her behaviour during life. There was no room for purgatory within the doctrines of this new church. Over the course of the next half century the official liturgy of church services and the burial service changed several times to reflect this. Henry VIII dissolved all religious houses and during the reign of his son, Edward VI, all chantries were abolished following an Act of Parliament in 1547. These two events officially ended the act of saying prayers for the souls of the deceased, which had been so closely associated with the Catholic Church. There was also a ban on the pre-Reformation practice of redemption of sin through monetary payments to speed the soul on its journey to heaven.

While our ancestors' beliefs would not necessarily have changed overnight in accordance with the new legislation, these changes can readily be discerned in the changing format of our ancestors' wills. Church courts were the authorities in charge of granting probate, so the language of probate records was under regular scrutiny by the Church itself. Pre-Reformation wills regularly contain references to masses to be sung for the deceased, monies to be set aside for the year's mind (annual memorial service) or payments for candles to be kept burning at the altar of the deceased's favoured saint in the parish church. Such references are rarely found post-Reformation, since they were against the official teaching of the new Church of England. Intramural burial practices also evolved: no longer was the chancel solely the burying place of the clergy, as it had been pre-Reformation; it gradually became acceptable for members of secular society to be buried there too, providing, of course, they had the means to pay.

For the less well-off, burial took place in the churchyard. Parish churchyards were sacred ground, dedicated to God in a special ceremony of consecration. Until the Reformation, the Church believed that burial in consecrated ground was necessary to ensure salvation. The only people who could legally be excluded from burial in this way were those who had committed suicide, been executed for murder, or those subject to an extant excommunication order at the time of death. The rest of our ancestors had the right to burial in the churchyard, as long as they had been baptized within the established Church, although some incumbents did bend the rules to allow burials when they should technically have not. From the seventeenth century there were an increasing number of Nonconformist churches – Protestant groups whose leaders disagreed with many of the doctrines or methodologies of the Church of England. Many of their members did not wish to be buried in consecrated ground, which was so closely associated with the established Church, and this led to a growing demand for burial places other than the parish churchyard. Over the centuries, lack of sufficient burial space for a burgeoning population presented a far bigger challenge, however. Together, both factors led to the establishment of burial grounds and cemeteries outside the control of the Church of England. Increasing concerns about health and sanitation, and problems caused by overcrowded burial grounds, led to a raft of burial legislation in the nineteenth century, which increasingly moved burial places away from city centres. This harked back to the Roman idea of burials being sited away from settlements. It is an interesting fact that neither the parish, nor any other local authority, has ever been legally required to provide burial space for its local population in England or Wales.

Although cremation was once practised by early Christians, for centuries it was frowned upon by the established Church, which promoted the belief that the body of the deceased had to be present for resurrection to take place. It took a long time for cremation to come back into vogue. Its popularity started to grow in the interwar years, partly as a result of burial space continuing to be at a premium, and arguably, partly as a result of the depersonalization of death caused by the deaths of so many during the war.

Attitudes towards death and burial are still evolving today. Prior to the 1950s and the introduction of antibiotics and modern-day surgery, death was an everyday reality. The Victorians embraced it wholeheartedly; so much so that the renowned scholar Professor Curl retrospectively christened it the 'Celebration of Death'. By contrast, the post-war era in the twentieth century led to change of attitude, with the subject never spoken about unless really necessary – a 'Moratorium on Death'! The catalyst for this was possibly the shockingly excessive death toll of the First World War, which within a short space of time wiped away the remnants of that 'Celebration of Death', making it into an unending horror. Then, with the advances of modern medicine, death, by stark contrast, started to become a stranger, something that most people did not have to think about for many years, with the death of someone before his or her eighties often being regarded as 'premature'. Many people today reach their fifties and sixties without ever having experienced the death of a loved one, and people are arguably far less skilled at dealing with death as a result.

In the twenty-first century, our beliefs are often very different from those of our ancestors. It is only relatively recently, with the rise of atheism, that an afterlife is being denied by an increasing proportion of the population. However, many people who belong to no religious group still possess the belief that there is some sort of life after death. A recent survey of 9,000 Britons undertaken by the Institute of Education (University of London) showed that only 31 percent believed in God, but 49 percent did believe in an afterlife of some sort.[5] The number of funerals which take place without any religious content is on the rise, and there is a growing trend for green or natural burials, which may in time reverse the twentieth-century predilection for cremation. These are suggested to be more environmentally friendly, with no embalming chemicals or coffin material to pollute the ground, and no crematory emissions to pollute the atmosphere. In many cases the only grave markers are trees. Conservation burials are another new idea, whereby tracts of lands are used for burials, but also serve as a haven for endangered native species. Furthermore, alternative methods of treating the body after death are now being mooted, including disintegration! While death and violence are regularly beamed into our households via TV and computers, in twenty-first-century Britain we are, arguably, far less used to coping with death on a personal basis than we have ever been before. As I write the final edits for this book in January 2021, I have a feeling that the Covid-19 pandemic may well alter things in many ways.

Pre- and post-death rituals, such as erecting gravestones and placing flowers on graves, continue to be part of the grieving process, and strengthen our ties to our roots. They give us a sense of belonging that most of us need, but which we seem increasingly to have lost in this modern, self-contained, and individualistic world. While many people visiting cemeteries and graveyards today do so to place flowers on the graves of a recent family member, just as many are looking for the resting place of their ancestors, or seeking those they have been researching in the course of other history projects. It is for the last two categories of people that this book is primarily written, but I hope many will also find it helpful when the time comes for them to consider where and how they, their parents, partner or other loved ones are buried. I hope this brief history of burial, and the remainder of the book, will help put things in perspective and lead to a greater understanding of how the rules and regulations surrounding burial in cemeteries and churchyards have evolved. Naturally, I also I hope this book will help you track down any missing ancestral burials.

Finally, many of you who read this book will find yourselves drawn to it simply because you are attracted to churchyards or cemeteries; maybe you are not even sure why. Perhaps you have no religion, but find yourself at peace there? You are not a family or local historian. You simply hone into the solitude, the fresh air, or perhaps a lingering ethereal sense of the past. Perhaps you just love exploring the grounds and reading the names on the stones? While you are there, you may well be inspired to find out more about the people who lie beneath the soil and what life was like for them. This book will provide a starting point for you, and you may also gain a new perspective on life today as you explore the lives of those who went before.

Chapter 2

THE PARISH CHURCHYARD

To understand the parish churchyard, it is essential to have an understanding of the origins of both the parish and the parish church. Parishes evolved from earlier established minsters, which were religious communities of monks or secular clergy, largely founded in the seventh century and which had a pastoral role in the local community. Following the Great Synod of Whitby in 664 AD, which, as we have seen, gave pre-eminence to the Roman Church, minsters evolved further, becoming centres of ecclesiastical administration as well as pastoral care. Minster churches were also established, enabling the teaching of Christianity among the local population. They were some of our very earliest churches, as were those founded by local lords of the manor. The history of the manorial system is complex, but it was the successor to the Roman system of land management based around villa estates. Although the Romans had withdrawn from England and Wales by the early fifth century, their system of land management continued in many places, evolving firstly into the Anglo-Saxon, and then the Norman-style manorial system. This was led by a new class of landed gentry, the 'Lords of the Manor', who were in charge of one or more areas of land known as manors. While manors varied greatly in size and the lords varied greatly in wealth and power, this system of local administration and land management was a key part of life in medieval England and Wales. The manorial system not only came to form the focus of the medieval agrarian economy, but also the basis of a hierarchical society in which the lord was the protector of the people who lived on his manor, in return for their service and fealty. At a time when the Christian Church had relatively little power itself, it actively encouraged these local lords to provide religious example and instruction to the immediate population through the founding of small private chapels within their manorial estates.

Very little is known about the origins and early history of parish churchyards, since there is virtually no documentary evidence regarding them. Much of what has been surmised about early churchyards is based on various papal promulgations concerning burial practice and brief references to them in English law codes of the tenth and eleventh century.[1] It is often the archaeology that speaks more loudly. Even this frequently raises as many questions as it answers, while another factor that hinders the corpus of evidence is that relatively few churchyards have been excavated.

While we cannot be certain what the original intended purpose of each churchyard was, it is almost certain that there is no one answer that applies to all. However, the view is generally held that the very earliest were not originally intended to be places of burial. The chapels built by the lords of the manor were to become many of our earliest parish churches, initially providing a spiritual 'house' for worship, but with the burial of the dead continuing in traditional locations, frequently away from, but within sight of, the community. By the late ninth century it was increasingly common for the land surrounding these chapels to be consecrated (sanctified) with the intention of using it for burials and this was the norm by the tenth century. The lord's family and his personal priest would typically have been interred within the chapel, with the ordinary inhabitants of the manor buried in the churchyard.

In many cases, a churchyard was delineated out of surrounding fields sometime after the church itself was built. However, in many rural areas there is strong archaeological evidence that some churches were constructed within an enclosure previously marked out from the surrounding landscape. Even where a parish church is of great age (Saxon or early Norman), the churchyard may pre-date it. Evidence suggests that the early Christians often set up crosses where churches were to be built and it may be the case that an area of land, larger than was necessary to build the actual church, was set aside prior to this. It may even have been intended to accommodate building gear and the carts and waggons attending the building site. In many cases this excess ground may have simply evolved to become the church's 'yard'. During the ninth century there is strong evidence that in some towns, designated plots were allocated in advance to incorporate both church and churchyard within the burgeoning urban street plans. Whatever the truth, a churchyard served to enhance and emphasize the sanctity of the church itself and set it apart from the surrounding landscape.

One of the earliest pieces of documentary evidence directly relating to churchyards comes in 1229, when William de Bleys, Bishop of Worcester,

A particularly good example of a churchyard cross at St Martin's Church, Cwmyoy, Monmouthshire. Other less intact survivors may be less obvious. (Author's collection)

specified that all churchyards in the diocese should be properly enclosed.[2] Where such physical segregation was not already in place, the churchyard was likely set apart from the surrounding land by means of semi-permanent features such as ditches, or later by hedgerows, fencing or walls.

The size of a churchyard would have been determined by various factors. In the case of a church built under the patronage of a local lord, this may well have been determined by the amount of land he wished to set aside. Another factor would have been the number of worshippers the church was expected to serve. The method of marking it out probably varied according to date and local practices. Just like the church, sanctification of the churchyard was achieved by means of a special ceremony of consecration, although at what stage it was consecrated no doubt depended on the individual evolution of each church and local diocesan practice. In many Kent parishes, there is evidence that churchyard boundaries may have frequently been marked using stone markers incised with a cross, and it may well have been these that were blessed during the consecration ceremony (see Appendix I). While there are a few other examples of these across the country, in other places wooden crosses may more typically have been used. Further research in diocesan archives may one day uncover further evidence relating to early churchyard consecration (see Appendix I).

As we saw in Chapter 1, organized burials in designated plots of land were a feature of Roman Britain, and this continued during the pagan Anglo-Saxon period, albeit in a less organized manner. Many people presume that all Christian burials took place within a churchyard, but this was certainly not always so. The concept of using the churchyard for burial seems to have been introduced to England during the time of Archbishop Cuthbert of Canterbury (AD 740–760) with the idea being first encouraged in the wider Roman Empire by Pope Gregory I (AD 590–604).[3] Since most churches were close to human habitation, this was contrary to earlier Roman beliefs that burial sites should be away from towns and cities.

Christianity was steadily gaining in popularity from the seventh century, becoming the predominant religion in England in the late eighth century. The idea of churchyard burial slowly took hold, becoming the norm in the

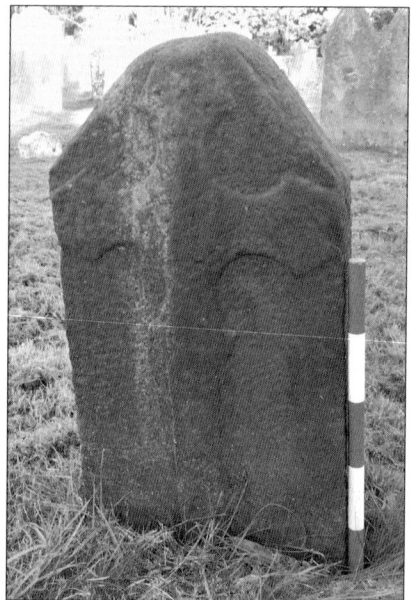

Incised cross markers in Kent churchyards at Goodnestone (left) and Ryarsh (right) may have been ancient churchyard boundary markers. (Linklater and Heritage collection).

ninth century. It is interesting to note that archaeological evidence from Kent shows burials still taking place outside churchyards, in what would today be retrospectively referred to as Anglo-Saxon cemeteries, as late as 800 AD.[4] Religious houses were also used as burial places for those of higher status until the Dissolution of the Monasteries (AD 1536–41).

Although there was no doubt a financial incentive for the Church to encourage burials in the churchyard, since they could charge for the privilege, another key reason was that it would help stimulate prayers for the souls of the deceased. It can be said with some confidence that individual graves were marked in some way in the early days of churchyard burial, either using wooden markers, stones placed on the ground, or by simply leaving a raised mound of earth over the burial spot. This would have encouraged remembrance of individual souls and served a practical purpose, helping prevent premature reburial of grave sites. This idea is supported by archaeological evidence, which reveals the regularity of churchyard burial positions at this date. However, this was not a phenomenon that continued, and from the later medieval period the placement of burials seems to have become less organized, perhaps suggesting that any means of marking earlier graves had fallen out of use, or was less effective with the growing number of people being buried. Churchyard excavations typically show frequent intercutting of graves from this later medieval period and, while the use of permanent gravestones slowly took hold from the mid-seventeenth century, few burial plans were ever made. Many modern churchyard burial rows are superimposed across a historic sequence of unplanned intercutting burials.

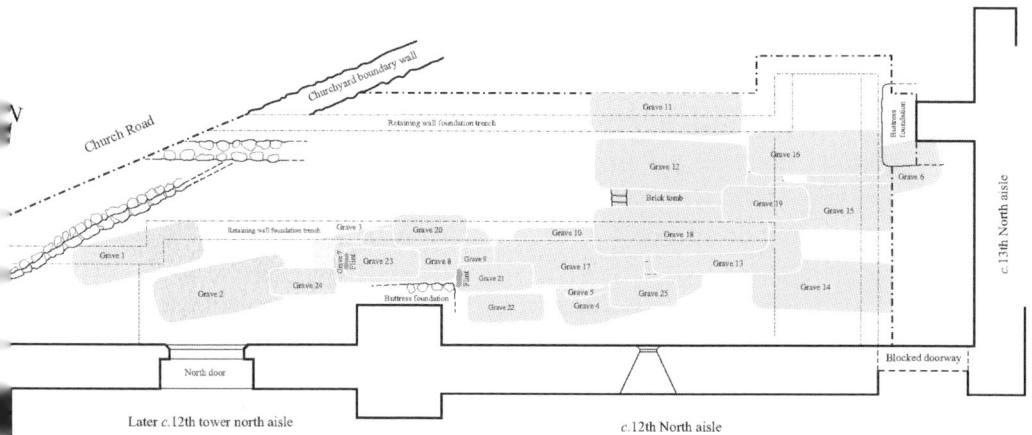

This archeological plan of burials at St Nicholas' Church, New Romney, Kent, shows the erratic nature of grave sites from the thirteenth to sixteenth century. (Canterbury Archaeological Trust, Andrew Linklater)

Burial in the church

Woe betide the family historian who fails to realize their ancestors were not the humble souls they imagined, and neglects to venture inside the church in their quest to find their resting place! While this chapter primarily deals with the churchyard, neither family nor local historians should overlook the primary feature of every ancient churchyard – the church itself. For centuries, the church was the most sought-after burial location, housing the bones of many of our higher-status forebears. Burials within a church are often referred to as 'intramural' burials, the word coming from Latin meaning 'within walls'. Although such burials were originally restricted to martyrs and notable priests, an increasing number of the nobility, and later, landed gentry were buried within the body of the church post-Reformation. Some had splendid tombs, others had simple ledger stones marking the burial site, while some had wall memorials close to their resting place. Prime burial spots were next to the high altar in the chancel, the holiest part of the church, but also close to altars inside chapels. Once room close to the altar was taken, memorials might be placed on the external wall of the church, directly behind the altar. Any site where the grave or memorial was easily noticed was valued, not just because it would encourage prayers for the deceased, but also because it often appealed to the family's sense of pride. Vanity and social status continued beyond the grave!

A person's true wealth and social status may not always be readily ascertained, especially if the researcher's information is based solely on parish registers. It is normal to assume that that the majority of our ancestors were of humble means, but an open mind should be kept as to an ancestor's wealth or status, unless evidence is found either way. The thorough family historian will research all available sources for any trace of their ancestor, not making assumptions about how well-off they were. Sources such as guild and probate records, and parish vestry minutes (to name but a few), may bring unexpected information about a forebear who was previously believed to have been of more humble rank. Burial registers rarely note whether a burial was intramural or in the churchyard. Sometimes the only clue that a burial is intramural will be a reference in an ancestor's will where he records a wish to be buried in the church, although these references are rarely found after the late medieval period. Alternatively, there may be reference to it on a church memorial, perhaps located via monumental inscriptions (see Chapter 6).

Intramural burials either took place straight into the earth (once the floor had been taken up), in brick-lined graves, or in specially constructed burial vaults, with coffins either resting on the ground or on shelves. Crypts were also often used as places of burial, especially in city churches. A crypt is simply a room underneath the church and was not necessarily built as a burial place. A vault was usually designated for the use of one particular family, and was sealed after each interment, while a crypt typically housed unrelated parishioners and was not sealed. You will also see the term 'catacombs'; these were underground chambers specifically designed for burials and usually consist of a series of chambers running off from one another. The terms are used interchangeably by some writers less familiar with the niceties of each.

Many intramural burials are no longer marked by any memorial, but in some cases (depending on the nature of the church floor), these unmarked graves can be determined by changes in the floor levels where tiles and stone slabs have dipped slightly, causing localized depressions across the floor. As easily accessible burial space in churches filled up, burials took place wherever possible and sometimes this involved moving furniture (pews and benches), or other church fixtures and fittings. Ironically, many such memorials have since been hidden again by the placement of new fixed furniture, seating, or organs on top of them, or been covered by later raised church floors. Many would have been removed, or even destroyed, during building works, sometimes with no record of the removal having been made. It is a frustrating experience to search for a memorial that is known to have been in a church, and to find no trace of it. Do not presume that all surviving memorials are in their

This painting by Samuel Prout (1783–1852) clearly shows the scale of disruption necessary when burial took place inside the church. (Author's collection)

original positions. Many have been moved to new sites within the church during building work, or to make way for the tomb of a later, more influential family. Memorials are sometimes uncovered again during later alterations to the church. These days they are usually left in place and covered over again once a record has been made, although historically this has not always happened.

Many counties were well served by antiquarians and others, whose love and enthusiasm for church history led them to record memorials long since hidden or destroyed. Restoration of Benenden Church in Kent between 1861 and 1862 involved covering up many of the memorials in the floor of the north and south aisles. Luckily, these were recorded in the parish register by the Revd William John Edge, who also noted their exact locations. The Revd Edge

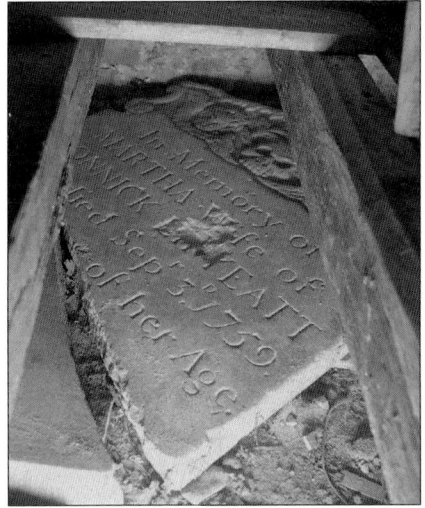

The broken headstone for Martha, the wife of Bonnick Lipyeatt, who died Sept 3rd 1759 (pictured), together with its accompanying footstone, were discovered under the nineteenth-century church floor during building work at St John's Church, Swalecliffe, Kent. Since headstones are churchyard memorials, why it was placed here is uncertain. (Andrew Linklater)

was one of several vicars who recorded details of their churches prior to the ubiquitous church restorations of the late Victorian era. They provide a very welcome record of what was there before.

Secular uses of church and churchyard

Our parish churchyards did not just delineate the sanctity of the area surrounding the church and provide a place for burial: over time they also served many secular needs and could be hives of industry and activity. When new church bells were forged, they might be cast in the churchyard if not in the church itself, as they were cumbersome to transport once cast. Evidence of this was seen at Eastling Church in Kent, where there was clearly once a bell-casting pit in the base of the tower.[5] Sheep and cattle were also grazed in many churchyards and this practice continues in some parishes today, although opinions differ as to how appropriate it is.

Churchyards are not just places of burial and have traditionally also served many secular purposes including the grazing of animals, which helped control vegetation in the churchyard. (Sheep in the Savoy Churchyard, Isabella Holmes, The London Burial Grounds, *1896).*

Prior to the late thirteenth century, churchyards were often the site of local markets and fairs. Despite the sanctity of Sunday as a day for devotion and rest, many medieval markets were held on that day, taking advantage of the influx of churchgoers who could combine trading opportunities with attendance at church. Markets and fairs were lucrative businesses, not just in terms of income from stall hire and sales, but also from toll charges, which could be imposed on adjacent roads. In order to regulate markets, the Crown required a Royal Charter to be granted for each, although in practice this did not always happen. However, since the churchyard came under ecclesiastical jurisdiction, there was no such requirement for markets held in churchyards. As an essential part of village life in England and Wales, markets and fairs brought a considerable income to the church and also provided the opportunity to sell church ale.

By the late thirteenth century, the Church had changed its stance and in 1285, the Statute of Winchester ruled that 'from henceforth neither fairs nor markets be kept in churchyards, for the Honour of the Holy Church'. Markets such as the meat market held in the churchyard of All Saints in Northampton had already been moved out of the churchyard in 1235 but, despite this ruling, they were hard to suppress.

Parish churches also served as useful meeting places, notably for regular meetings of the parish 'Vestry'. The Vestry (which took its name from its original meeting place in the church vestry or vestment room) consisted of local parishioners. From the late sixteenth century through to the late nineteenth century, it had charge of the secular administration of the parish. This included organization of poor relief, maintenance of the highways and upkeep of local law and order. In some churches, poor relief was handed out to parishioners in the churchyard, perhaps making use of dole tables or utilizing handy chest tombs (see also Chapter 5).

The church porch was frequently used for secular processes, being set apart from the main body of the church. This is why many porches have benches along either side. Here our ancestors may have attended processes relating to the local manorial or probate courts. There is certainly evidence to suggest that some probate courts were partially peripatetic, with officials visiting rural areas periodically to hear oaths. It is sometimes suggested that churches had portable altars, on which the necessary oaths could be sworn during the proving of a will. However, an easier approach would surely have been for oaths to have been sworn on a copy of the Bible. In some cases, parish schools are known to have taken place inside the church, in the porch if numbers were small, but also in chantry chapels, aisles or parvis chambers.

Burial sites in the churchyard and elsewhere

Just as the positioning of burials within the church was important, certain locations in the churchyard have been favoured. Aligning of Roman cemeteries and graves in relation to pre-existing topographical features, including roads, is well known, but this phenomenon can also be found among early churchyards, many of which were aligned with pre-existing boundaries. Excavations of Anglo-Saxon churchyards have shown evidence to suggest that burials were sometimes laid out in clusters which seem to take their bearing from natural foci, such as a tree or prehistoric standing stone. Christopher Daniell, in his book *Death and Burial in Medieval England,* notes the phenomenon of so-called 'eaves-drip burials', where infant burials are sited under the eaves of the church. There is a suggestion, with a growing corpus of evidence, that at this period neonates and children aged one year and under were not considered part of society, and were not eligible for baptism until they had reached this age. If they died before their first birthday, their grave was located close to the base of the church wall, under the eaves of the church. It has been suggested that the water running from the roof of the church would provide a posthumous baptism, though this has a strong element of folklore attached.[6]

This idea of segregating burials of the unbaptized, or those excluded by society in other ways, continued throughout churchyard burial history until relatively modern times, with some setting aside specific portions of the churchyard for those who died unbaptized (usually children or stillborn babies), and also suicides. Until 1823, those who had taken their own life had no right to be buried in consecrated ground, although some incumbents made exceptions. Suicide was seen as a rejection of God – he gave life and no one had the right to take it away – and it was also a criminal offence until 1961. I discuss this in greater detail in my book *Tracing Your Ancestors Through Death Records*. Things changed in 1823, from which point suicides could be legally buried in the churchyard, but initially without religious ceremony and at night. In 1882, the rules were relaxed, and they could be buried like anyone else.

Specific areas of the churchyard might also be traditionally used to lay to rest anyone whose burial was paid for by the parish. Until 1808, coastal parishes often buried those who drowned at sea, on the shore close to where the bodies were washed up. From that year, however, new legislation meant they had to be buried in consecrated ground and at parish expense.

At some churches, you may note that the ground level on the south side is far higher than that on the other sides of the churchyard. While this may simply be the natural lie of the land, it often occurs as a result of the far greater number of burials there. Burial to the south of the church appears always to have been most popular, although the original reasoning as to why has been lost in the mists of time. It has been suggested that, as most churches were entered via the south side, a greater number of people would pass by the graves on their way into church, and thus remember the dead in their prayers. Another plausible idea is that the south side is typically sunnier and more pleasant, but there may be a link to lingering beliefs connected with the veneration of the sun. Whatever the reasons, the north side of the churchyard was traditionally regarded as the least favoured. When Archbishop Tenison presented a burial ground to the parish of Lambeth in the early 1700s, he suggested that it would be necessary to charge double fees for interment on the south side of the churchyard to reduce the number of requests for burials there.[7] The north side was typically where poorer interments took place, including those paid for by the parish. In nearly every churchyard, as space on the south side diminished, the north side increasingly came into use. There are exceptions, however, and Walter Johnson notes in his book, *Byways in British Archeology*, that in many town churches the older burials are more evenly distributed around the churchyard, possibly because these churches sit more centrally in the churchyard plot, and some, rather unusually, possess a north entrance.

Exhumation, reinterments and reuse of burial sites

Walking around any pre-Reformation parish churchyard, it is hard to imagine just how many people were buried there. Without a doubt, there is no churchyard of such age that has not been buried many times over, with previous grave sites being recycled. A modest estimate in a rural parish churchyard, which has been used for Christian worship since the Norman Conquest (roughly 1,000 years), would be between five and twelve burials a year, which gives a figure in the region of 5–12,000 burials. More heavily populated parish churchyards would, of course, easily hold a far greater number of burials. Within towns, the number of burials per churchyard would be similar despite the higher population, due to the greater number of churches.

The earliest burial registers only begin in 1538, yet many churchyards still in use today will contain burials from centuries before this, which lie unrecorded. Very few churchyards have a plan of who is buried where, and the percentage of graves which actually have headstones is comparatively small. Present-day churchyard burials often cause disarticulated bone to be unearthed from historic burials.

Many parish churchyards now also have areas designated for the burying of cremated remains and these are usually on the site of earlier burials. In some cases, remains may have been disinterred and reburied elsewhere following building work in a certain area of the churchyard, or the closure

Image showing typical intercutting medieval graves from the parish cemetery of St Gregory's Priory, Northgate, Canterbury. (Canterbury Archaeological Trust)

and clearance of a parish church burial vault. Occasionally whole sections of a churchyard, or cemetery, may be cleared for building or other purposes (see Chapter 7).

Churches without graveyards

Not every church had its own graveyard. Some churches were initially built as chapels of ease to serve larger parishes, especially where it was not easy for the local population to travel to the parish church. The majority were not granted burial rights, these being reserved for the parish or 'mother' church, which benefited from the revenue that burials brought. Burial rights were often granted later, typically if the chapelry became a parish in its own right, with a burial ground then being established in land surrounding the chapel or at a suitable site elsewhere in the vicinity. A good example is the tiny chapel at Longsleddale, Cumbria (formerly Westmorland), which was established in 1670. Originally within the extremely large parish of Kendal, it was re-built and given parochial status, together with a burial ground, in 1712. The present church dates from 1863.

Many urban nineteenth-century churches were built without churchyards. Building land in towns was often difficult to find and it was generally assumed the dead of the parish would be buried in the local cemetery. As we saw in Chapter 1, the Church had no legal responsibility to provide burial space. Few Nonconformist or Roman Catholic churches had graveyards until the late 1800s, and we should remember that all our pre-Reformation parish churches were originally Catholic.

St Martin-in-the-Fields, Westminster, London (formerly Middlesex)

St Martin-in-the-Fields is a good example of a parish church where the churchyard has metamorphosed many times. Today the churchyard is all but built over, while the crypt and 'catacombs' were emptied of their contents many years ago. As with many London and urban churches, its changeable burial history can make it difficult for the researcher to assess who was buried exactly where, and whether the remains and any memorial are still in situ. Over the centuries, this highly populous parish struggled to cope with the burial of its parishioners, and there have been many different burial sites associated with the church because of this.

As a teenager, fascinated by my family history, a distant cousin informed me that one of our mutual relatives, Edmund Dickinson, a physician to King James II, was interred in the crypt in St Martin's in 1707. In the late 1980s, my Mum and I paid a visit to the church hoping to gain access to the crypt to see if there was a memorial. We were disappointed to be told by the verger that while there were many memorials in the crypt, it was not currently accessible.

Nowadays the crypt is easily accessible, since it forms the St Martin-in-the-Fields 'Café in the Crypt'. It displays an interesting selection of surviving memorials relating to some of those who once rested there.

Anecdotal evidence, such as that I received from my cousin, always needs double-checking as it can be inaccurate. These days, I would not make a spontaneous trip to a church to look for a memorial without first carrying out some methodical research work, especially for a London church where it is likely the burial ground will long since have disappeared. As already described in this chapter, burials and memorials in both church and churchyard are frequently subject to destruction or removal, as a result of building works and later burials. Churchyards can also be obliterated wholesale, especially in urban areas, with large-scale removal of memorials and disinterment of corpses (see Chapter 7). Even if you have hard evidence (such as a burial register) to show that your ancestor was buried in a particular churchyard, churches often had several different burial sites associated with them and it may not be immediately clear where your ancestor actually lies. From the mid-nineteenth century, most urban burials would have taken place in cemeteries (see Chapter 4).

For rural churches, their churchyard history is usually straightforward – a churchyard attached immediately to the church itself, potentially followed by a Burial Board Cemetery adjacent to it, or elsewhere in the parish. Urban churchyard history is typically much more complicated, especially in larger cities, and if you truly wish to determine the actual burial site of a particular person, or understand the wider burial history of the church, in-depth research may be required. While it will often prove impossible to pinpoint the precise burial spot, digging deeper into both online and offline sources can prove fruitful. It is worthwhile considering the following searches.

Using St Martin's and the quest to seek the burial place of Edmund Dickinson as an example, the following searches would be suggested.

1. **Check the burial register.** It makes sense to verify whether or not the person in question is really buried at a particular church before you set out to try and identify where he or she might lie. Depending on how the church organized its burial registers, it may, or may not, indicate whether the burials were taking place in the original burial ground surrounding the church, or a later one elsewhere. Occasionally, entries may note if the body was buried inside the church, but in many cases this will not be recorded. Where this is noted, you may see trends within the register entries which suggest that the church authorities were keener to grant permission to bury in the church during certain periods. This might reflect a more lenient incumbent, or the fact that the church was in need of extra funds (the cost of intramural burials being far higher). To determine coverage dates of surviving parish registers, use the online catalogues for the relevant record office or check the genealogy wiki at **www.familysearch.org/wiki** and also *Phillimore's Atlas and Index and Atlas of Parish Registers* (see Chapter 6).

2. **Research the church history.** Starting with parish registers means you may locate the burial record you want, but without an understanding of the church burial history, you may presume it took place in the churchyard when it did not. Much may be gleaned by reading a general history of the church itself. Key points are when it was built, demolished, rebuilt or extended. Rebuilding and alterations will potentially affect the original burial space and may have resulted in removal of burials and memorials, or may have provided new burial areas. A researcher can usually work out the most likely location of a burial by being armed with such information.

3. **Internet searches.** Many church histories are now online, either as part of websites run by local history enthusiasts or historical societies, or as digitized books. You may quickly find an online history of the church which details its various burial grounds, but make sure the websites you use are well sourced. Check the source notes on any website; if there are none, the information needs verification. Many websites contain copy and paste information taken from other websites, so be wary of this. If you are seeing the same information along with the same wording and phrases on more than one site, try and find the original source and determine where it first came from. Adding the search term 'PDF' to your

internet searches is a useful tip for locating more scholarly and, generally speaking, better-researched articles. PDFs are used by many repositories and institutions, as well as PhD students writing theses, as they are an easy method of uploading word documents to the web. They make a rich reference source for the more serious researcher, often bringing previously unresearched or lesser-known subject matter, ideas and information to the public eye. Other potential sources, especially if the church has been the subject of extensive redevelopment work, are post-excavation archaeological reports. British History online, run by the Institute of Historical Research and the History of Parliament Trust (**www.british-history.ac.uk**) is an excellent source of historical information, and many of its texts come from contemporary publications.

4. **Published church histories.** Older publications may not be online, but can be identified using online book sellers' websites, such as **www.abebooks.co.uk**, or via public libraries or archives. Be cautious about information in local church guides; this is not always accurate. Many guides have a tendency to present information that is based on anecdotal evidence or folklore as fact, and relatively few quote sources.

5. **Parish records (other than parish registers).** Where they survive, these will be kept in the County Record Office. If your internet searches do not automatically point you in the direction of the relevant archive, use **https://discovery.nationalarchives.gov. uk/find-an-archive** to locate the relevant repository, or conduct an internet search using 'name of XX parish/borough AND "Record Office"'. Churchwardens' accounts often list payments made for burials, and may give the name of the person buried. In some cases, they also record the position of the burial in the churchyard, or the depth of the grave. For example, there are surviving churchwardens' accounts for St Martin's which date from 1525. Interestingly, they make reference to the ordering of new tiles for repairing the church floor after burial, which highlights the disruption caused when a new burial went in. Account books kept by the Overseers of the Poor may mention payments for burials, or shrouds for the poor. Vestry minutes may contain important contemporary details about the church and proposed changes, including those affecting burial grounds and churchyards.

6. **Churchyard surveys.** These have often been carried out by historical societies or enthusiastic individuals, primarily detailing the gravestones. Some may be online as part of a one place study, while paper surveys may be found within the church or deposited at the record office. Again, search the record office catalogue and use a general internet search to locate these. The older the churchyard survey the better, as the greater number of stones would have been legible when it was made (see Chapter 6 for further information).

7. **Newspaper articles.** Local newspapers often provide church news, including any major building works or restorations. Use **www.britishnewspaper.co.uk** (also available via a **www.findmypast.co.uk** subscription).

Using these various angles of approach, I built up a comprehensive understanding of the rather complicated burial history for St Martin's, as well as determining Edmund's burial site.

I located a very useful website called The London Burial Grounds (**www.burial.magic-nation.co.uk**). Much of the information appeared to come directly from a well-known book of the same name published in 1896 by Mrs Basil (Isabella) Holmes (see Chapter 3). It was unclear who ran the website, so I emailed the owner who turned out to be the author David Orme, who has particular interest in burial grounds. Although the site is no longer updated, it has a good deal of information about London burial grounds in general, based not just on Mrs Holmes' work, but also David's own observations.

British History Online revealed an extract from a digitized version of a book called *Old and New London: Volume 3*. Originally published by Cassell, Petter & Galpin, London, 1878, this tells us that 'Vast vaults extend from the portico to the east end of the structure, which are light and dry, and contain great numbers of bodies, deposited within separate apartments, and on the floor of the open space. These vaults, however, have for many years been closed up, interments being no longer permitted.'

Staff at Westminster City Archives (which covers St Martin's) pointed me in the direction of two really useful books on the history of the church. *St Martin in the Fields,* by John McMasters (published 1916) and *St Martin-in-the- Fields,* by Malcom Johnson (published 2005). Many older books are also available online via websites such as **archive.org**.

I also located a useful post-excavation archaeological report following on from the 2007 conversion of the crypt to a café, and a survey of wall monuments from the church originally published by London County Council in 1940 and available online at **www. british-history.ac.uk/survey-london/vol20/pt3**. Some memorials and burials are also listed on the Findagrave website (see Chapter 7).

From my collective research, I learned that the present-day church is at least the third on the site. St Martin's was originally a chapel with a burial ground, within the parish of St Margaret's Westminster. Its existence is first documented during the reign of Henry II (1133 –1189). There have therefore been regular burials on the site since the twelfth century.

The church was rebuilt in around 1542, St Martin's having been created as a new parish, separate from St Margaret's Westminster, in 1536. New parishes were subsequently carved out of St Martin's, namely: St Anne's, Soho in 1657 and St James' Piccadilly in 1684. In the 1660s, a workhouse was built in the grounds of the churchyard.[8]

A new chancel was added to the second church between 1606 and 1609, which would, no doubt, have disturbed burials in the contemporary churchyard, and new intramural burials would have been made in the new chancel. Since there was by now insufficient churchyard burial space, an acre of land was given to the parish for a new burial ground opposite the church next to the National Gallery. From 1606, most burials would have taken place in this new burial ground, but as a result of the building of an extension to the National Gallery, which began in 1866, the churchyard was built over, with the burials removed and reinterred at Brookwood Cemetery, Woking. There is no record of the names of those people removed.

In 1721, the second church was taken down and the present church built between 1722 and 1726. Notices were placed in the newspapers informing relatives that family remains or memorials would be disturbed by the building works, and there was the opportunity to have both removed elsewhere. Those monuments that remained were later stored in the new church, with some being set up in the crypt or later in the vaults. The building of the new church was not always straightforward and during the building of the portico, there was a problem with the foundations caused by water from a nearby stream. To remedy this, several hundred tombstones (which presumably had already been removed as part of the clearance

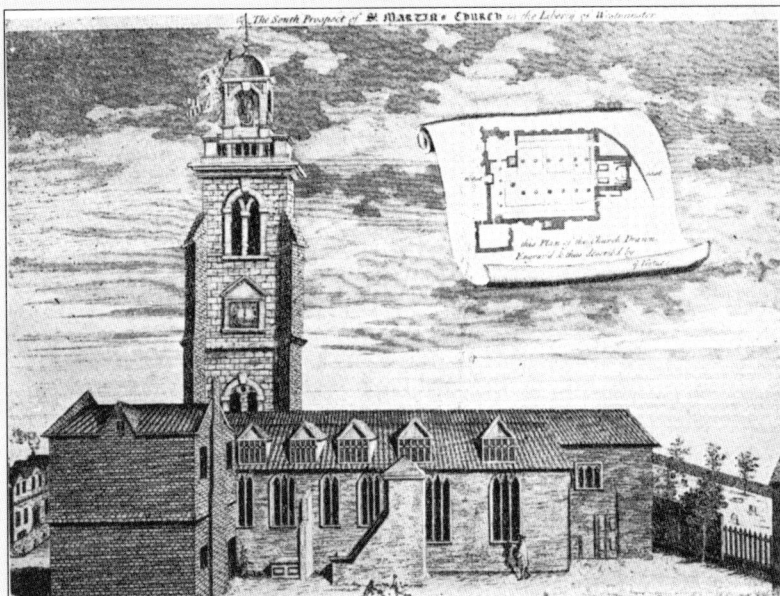

St Martin's-in-the-Fields Church as it would have looked in 1707 when Edmund Dickinson was buried there. (Author's collection).

for the new building) were embedded in mortar in the ground to stabilize the foundations of the tower and portico.

In terms of burial space, the new church had vaults, what was left of the original churchyard, the burial ground across the road near the National Gallery (until 1866), and the crypt.

While vaults are typically used to store encoffined corpses, St Martin's vestry minutes for 1748 show that earth-cut burials were being carried out within the floors of the vaults. These were clearly numerous, since they were starting to affect the foundations of the church. Despite a decision by the vestry to stop this practice, it resumed again within a short space of time, until the vestry passed another order forbidding it in 1773. The increasing pressure on burial space, caused by the ever-growing population, led to a new burial ground being opened for St Martin's parishioners in 1802. This was three miles away in Pratt Street, Camden Town, and became known as Camden Town Cemetery. Many of the burials there related to the poorer classes and this operated as a burial ground until 1856. It became a landscaped public garden in 1889. Many gravestones were moved to the side of the gardens, although many of those buried there would never have had a gravestone. A further burial ground was also opened in the early 1800s at Drury Lane.

Major changes took place at St Martin's between 1827 and 1830, when a large part of the original churchyard, including many vaults, was subsumed into the building of Duncannon Street and related buildings, north of the Strand. To compensate for the loss of burial space, a series of vaults (often referred to as the catacombs) was created, adding to those vaults already there. An Act of Parliament stated that as few burials should be disturbed as possible, and that those that were disturbed should be recorded before removal. A specially printed book was used in which family members could indicate whether they intended to claim the body or bodies of their relatives for reinterment elsewhere (at another burial ground), whether they wanted them removed to the new cemetery in Camden Town, or whether they wished them to be reinstated at St Martin's in one of the new vaults. Those remains which were intact and not claimed by relatives were reinterred at the Camden Town Cemetery and the disarticulated bones of other unclaimed people were put into the three end vaults in the south-east corner of the churchyard by Duncannon Street and Adelaide Street and bricked up.

This evocative description of the new vaults created as a result of the building of Duncannon Street is taken from the *Sunday Times* of 12 June 1831:

'*The new vaults under St Martin's burying ground are the most capacious structure of the sort in London. They were opened on Tuesday, at the consecration of the new burial ground. They consist of a series of vaults, running out of one another in various directions; they are lofty, and when lighted up, as on Tuesday, really presented something of a comfortable appearance. Some of the vaults having been quite filled with the coffins taken out of the old burying grounds, have been blocked up at both ends, – in fact, hermetically sealed, a plan which is to be adopted with the other vaults in succession, when the cold tenants shall be sufficiently numerous. They are of tolerable height; about ten feet to the turn of the arch, twenty in width, and nearly forty in length; capable of holding, we should suppose, one thousand coffins each. They are white-washed around, and at top, and the flagging at the bottom keeps them dry beneath the foot. All the leaden coffins, removed from the burial ground, are placed in one vault. On the end of one conspicuously placed beneath a grating, through which the light descends, was inscribed the name of Lady Hannah Gordon. There are arcades or corridors leading to the vaults,*

which branch off right and left, along which are ranges of head-stones,
recording the names of individuals whose bones, removed from their
old resting place, repose beneath. These have a handsome appearance,
lying as they do, at either side, close to the wall, and looking somewhat
like an artificial balustrade, flanking the wall in the centre. Crowds of
ladies perambulated the vaults for some time, and the whole had more
the appearance of a fashionable promenade than a grim repository of
decomposing mortality.'

Parliamentary legislation of the mid-nineteenth century put an end
to new vault burials in St Martin's because of the associated health
hazards (see Chapter 4). The vestry minutes note that by 1856, the
stench from some of the vaults underneath the vestry was becoming
an increasing nuisance, and some of these were emptied, with the
coffins being transferred to the new catacombs. The vaults were
tidied up periodically (notably in 1817 and 1841) to try to alleviate the
problem, but this did not help much. There were over 3,000 coffins in
the crypt alone, which gives an idea of the scale of intermural burials,
and it was decided to clear the vaults directly under the church. The
churchwardens placed notices in the newspapers asking relatives to
remove family members by 1 February 1859, after which point any
remaining were interred at the Camden Town Cemetery or bricked
up in three vaults in the south-eastern corner of the crypt under
Adelaide and Duncannon Street, where they remained until 1938
when they were cleared. The northern part of the churchyard was
paved over in 1887 with the burials below (presumably) undisturbed.

Where was Edmund buried?

Since Edmund Dickinson died in 1707, logic told me he must have
either been buried in the burial ground which now lies underneath
the National Gallery, or within the church itself. This would not have
been the present church but its predecessor. A biographical source
(*Chalmer's Biography*, pub. 1812) states that he did have a memorial,
but it is not recorded in any of the listings which survive, and I
could not see it when I more recently visited the Café in the Crypt. If
Edmund did indeed have had a memorial it does not appear to have
survived.

St Martin-in-the-Fields burial registers are held at Westminster
Archives, but at the time of my research were also online, alongside
the Bishops' Transcripts and a variety of other registers. Perusal of

the burial register immediately told me that Edmund was interred in the church, since this was actually noted in the register. A further burial book contained more information, in the form of heavily abbreviated notes relating to each burial. Each typically included the cost of the burial pall and any other extras paid for. In Edmund's case these included candles to be lit and prayers to be said for six months after his death. Since this was long after the Reformation, this would have just been prayers rather than masses (see Chapter 1). There is a reference to the mason (presumably to erect his memorial) and we learn that a '2d pall' was used for his funeral. Presumably this was one of the more expensive palls offered, given the fact Edmund was a man of some means. The cause of death is simply given as 'Aged'.

Exploring the parish churchyard: what to look for

External wall memorials
Don't just peruse the headstones in the churchyard itself, but also look for memorials on the external walls of the church, especially at the chancel end.

Early churchyard crosses
Sometimes mistaken for gravestones, these upstanding narrow stones may be on a stepped base. Some may remain only as fragments or the shaft of the cross. Churchyard crosses were erected to commemorate the dead in general, but could also be preaching crosses placed prior to the church being built. They are difficult to date (the earliest are thought to belong to the sixth century), and there is uncertainty about their exact original purpose. It is likely that no one answer applies to them all. David Hey, in his *Oxford Companion to Local History,* suggests they might have marked the resting place of saints. However, this is unlikely since the majority of saints would have been given a more substantial burial place inside the church, where pilgrims would have entered and made their offering to the saint, usually in cash, or goods. They could perhaps have marked the site of an event associated with a particular saint.[9] While few of these crosses survive in the south of England, there are numerous examples in the rest of England and Wales, such as those at Bakewell in Derbyshire. Recent archaeological study showed that these had

been moved from their original position and this must also be true of many similar crosses elsewhere, perhaps moved to make way for later memorials or due to building work.

Dole tables

Usually positioned close to the principal entrance (usually the south) of a church, these large, raised stone slabs, frequently possessing stone sides, were erected in the churchyard and utilized by church officials for distributing funds and food (dole) to the parish poor. Not every churchyard possessed such a permanent feature, and portable dole tables are also recorded. Commonly mistaken for chest tombs, the presence, or lack, of an inscription can help determine one from the other. Prior to the Reformation, as part of their atonement for sins committed, wealthy parishioners sometimes specified that their tomb should be used as a dole table. They were also convenient for business transactions, such as the collection of tithe payments.

What appears at first to be a chest tomb at St Martin's Church, Cheriton, Kent, may actually be a dole table, used for handing out alms to those in need. (Author's collection)

Priest houses

In medieval times, many priests were itinerant. Some churches had a room within the church where the priest would stay overnight (sometimes referred to as a parvis chamber), while in some parishes a priest house was built in the churchyard.

Discarded or recycled gravestones
Look out for memorials which have been moved to the side of the churchyard, stacked against a church wall, set into the path or reused as building material in the church fabric itself during later church alterations. Pay attention to any piles of rubble lying around the churchyard – these have been known to contain important fragments or even whole gravestones which have just been thrown aside. Some gravestones may also have been removed inside or placed in the porch, if deemed worthy of preservation.

Charnel houses or ossuaries
Grave spaces were not bought in perpetuity, but were common property to be reused at a later date, and the exposing of bones from previous burials was perfectly normal. Some churchyards had a charnel pit into which disturbed bones were placed, while others simply reinterred the bones in the newly dug grave. However, some churches stored the bones in charnel houses, or used part of an existing building for this purpose. This was either on a long-term basis or until sufficient bones were collected to merit digging a new grave to house them. A good example is the chapel which sits in the graveyard at Carew Cheriton near Tenby, where the bones were stored in an underground room. Sometimes bones were stored in vaults or crypts in the church itself. Although most of these were cleared of their bones many years ago, those at Rothwell, Northamptonshire, and Hythe, Kent still contain the bones and both are local tourist attractions. At Hythe, the ossuary was originally designed as a passaged walkway for the ceremonial parade of clergy (an ambulatory), following the eastward extension of the church in the thirteenth century. During building work in churchyards today, disturbed disarticulated bone may be placed into specially dug charnel pits at the discretion of the vicar, churchwarden, Parochial Church Council (PCC), or under condition of a faculty (special licence).

Dedications in windows and elsewhere
Look out for dedications to deceased parishioners, not just on headstones, but also in church windows, on churchyard benches and even on the churchyard sundial if there is one. Some families would pay for a new prayer book or Bible in memory of a loved one and very occasionally some of these may still be in the church and on display.

Churchyard surveys
If you are looking for a particular headstone, check inside the church to see if there is a copy of a churchyard survey, which details the gravestones. Many memorial inscriptions are also indexed and online, or available in the record office. Doing your homework first can make your visit to the church much more fruitful (see Chapter 6).

The growth of parish burial grounds and burial boards

By the nineteenth century burial space in churchyards was at a premium and many urban churchyards were bursting at the seams with human remains. With insufficient room for further burials, new grave spaces were frequently recycled prematurely, and these churchyards presented a danger to public health. This problem was not confined to the UK. Burial within towns had been prohibited in France in 1804, amid a growing Europe-wide movement for out-of-town burials. In England and Wales, an Act of Parliament of 1852 forbade the cutting of any new graves in London churchyards, and gave all parishes in the metropolis the right to close existing burial grounds and establish new ones away from the parish church if there was the need. These were to be controlled by local burial boards, formed of ratepayers elected by parish vestries and answerable to the Home Office (later Local Government Boards). The following year, the same powers were extended to the rest of England and Wales. This was the first of many statutes passed in the mid-nineteenth and early twentieth century (often referred to collectively as the Burial Acts) which sought to ensure a sanitary and respectable system of burial for everyone. From 1894, the powers of the burial boards could be transferred to district councils in urban areas and to parish councils in rural areas, meaning these authorities would have overall charge of the burial grounds concerned (see also Chapter 4).

When seeking someone's burial place, it is important to be aware of local burial board cemeteries in a parish, so that these are searched where necessary. The cemetery might be adjacent to the parish churchyard or a mile or so away, depending on where land was available for sale at the time the new burial ground was established. If the family were Nonconformists, they might also be buried in a Nonconformist burial ground, while there are a variety of other ex-parochial graveyards to be considered (see Chapter 3).

Abandoned churchyards

Sometimes you will come across an unexpected graveyard in a town or city, or even in a rural area. There may be no immediate ostensible explanation for these abandoned graveyards, but some were once attached to churches which have been destroyed or even relocated. Good examples are Holy Trinity, (also known as Christ Church) in King's Square, York, where a few surviving gravestones remain in the street where the church once stood (the medieval church was restored in the 1860s but demolished in 1937) and Chapel Hill, Ebony, near Appledore in Kent. The latter is the original site of Ebony Church, which was re-sited in 1850 about half a mile away at Reading Street. The original churchyard can still be seen at the top of the hill, although much overgrown (see also Chapter 3).

The churchyard today

These days, anyone who dies in a parish, or who has lived in that parish, has the right to burial in the parish churchyard, as long as the churchyard has not been officially declared 'closed'. This right of burial also extends to anyone who was on the church's electoral roll but did not actually live in the parish; this is a list of lay church members entitled to vote in the annual parochial church meeting. Others may also be buried in the churchyard, at the incumbent's discretion.

Right to burial does not come with the choice of grave location. This is again at the discretion of the incumbent, unless the family has been granted a faculty (special licence) by the diocese to reserve a particular grave spot. This might typically be next to a previously interred family member. In order to erect a memorial over a grave, approval is required from the diocese, usually via the incumbent or through application on behalf of the deceased's family via the undertaker or stonemason. There are strict guidelines regarding design, inscription and material laid down by the diocese. These will take into consideration the traditional character of the church and churchyard to ensure the memorial is in keeping. The nature of churchyard memorials is, therefore, often different to many gravestones erected in the nineteenth- or twentieth-century cemetery. A family that wishes to erect a memorial that falls outside the diocesan regulations must apply for a faculty. The matter will come before the Diocesan Advisory Committee. This consists of experts in various fields, including engineers, architects, conservationists and archaeologists, although, for the great majority of installations, they would not all need to be consulted. A decision will be made as to whether the memorial is acceptable for placement in the churchyard.

Closed churchyards

A churchyard that is officially closed is one where the authority in charge, usually the PCC, has handed control of the churchyard over to the local town or borough council. The phenomenon of the 'closed' churchyard is caused by two factors; firstly, where there is dwindling burial space, and the number of recent burials is making it difficult to find sufficient new ground that has not been reused in the recent past, and secondly, by the increasing number of memorials erected over graves since the twentieth century. This means graves cannot be recycled as easily after a suitable interval of time has passed. The Local Authorities' Cemeteries Order 1977 (which applied to all burial authorities including churches) stated that the right to erect a memorial could be granted by the burial authority for a period of up to 100 years, the exception being the Commonwealth War Graves Commission, which can still grant burial rights without time limit. This has, in practice, meant that headstones (unless deemed unsafe or moved in advance of building works) cannot usually be removed until 100 years has passed and even then many PCCs would not wish to remove them.

Some PCCs simply find they can no longer manage the costs of maintaining the churchyard and are only too happy to hand its management over to someone else. By contrast, many rural churchyards are never deemed to be full. While thousands of burials will have taken place, there is often sufficient space and time in between burials for the churchyard to cope with the trickle of burials that occur today; the majority of families opt for cremation or a cemetery interment.

Once a churchyard is closed, it then comes under the authority of the district council rather the than the PCC for maintenance purposes. In London, some closed churchyards have been converted to open spaces for recreation. The Metropolitan Gardens Association (MPGA) is a long-established charity which has been heavily involved in preserving many disused burial grounds as open spaces in the metropolis (see Chapter 3). A good example is St Dunstan's Churchyard, Stepney, which closed in 1854. The majority of its memorials were removed in the 1880s, after which the MPGA converted it into a public garden, which opened in 1887.

Recording a churchyard and surveying a graveyard

Our churchyards are often unique and special places, and not just because of the thousands of people who lie buried there. Graveyard monuments are a precious part of our heritage, not just in terms of family history, but also as part of our monumental art heritage. Gravestones, burials, and

---

Church of England Burial Grounds Survey

This is a new Church of England initiative called The Burial Grounds of England Survey. Working with Historic England, the University of York, Caring for Gods Acre, and a company called Atlantic Geomatics, the idea is to develop a system for producing digital plans for each Church of England churchyard or burial ground, utilizing modern technology. The surveys will record not just the gravestones, their design and who they commemorate, but also anything else which lies within the churchyard, including any buildings. Its ecology will also be recorded, and this will all form part of a church's so-called 'Heritage Record', which will also link images of gravestones with transcriptions of the relevant entries from the burial registers. The first of the digital maps, which are for the churches of Kirkburton, All Hallows and Shelley, Emmanuel, near Huddersfield, Yorkshire, are now online (see **www.churchofengland.org/resources/churchcare/churchcare-campaigns-and-project**).

---

the way in which the churchyard was laid out, and evolved with time, help illustrate changing attitudes towards death and burial practice over the centuries. Many ancient churchyards have never been cultivated or subjected to fertilisers or weed killers and also provide a unique habitat for often endangered local flora and fauna.

In the past, many churchyard surveys have been carried out to record the memorial inscriptions on the gravestones. Some are more detailed than others, some include sketches, and in recent times these have evolved into surveys which include photographs and GPS locations for each stone. Every survey, no matter how big or small, intricate or basic, is valuable, as it maps the churchyard at a particular time in its history. Some of you reading this book may be thinking of carrying out your own survey of a local churchyard. There are many different ways of approaching a churchyard survey and many different levels of survey. Appendix II aims to help and encourage you to carry out your own survey, thinking about the points to be considered.

Chapter 3

EX-PAROCHIAL GRAVEYARDS

While the majority of people were buried in the parish churchyards described in Chapter 2 or the cemeteries described in Chapter 4, there were numerous other types of burial grounds, graveyards and cemeteries. Some were profit-making enterprises run by individuals, and some were associated with churches and chapels belonging to religious denominations outside the Church of England. Others belonged to institutions such as hospitals, asylums and prisons, or were established to bury and commemorate the armed forces. There are also many examples of 'unique' burial grounds created in exceptional circumstances or for specific groups of people.

Just like their parish counterparts, study of these burial grounds will tell us more about the history of the area as well as the people buried there. Many of the burial sites described in this chapter can easily be overlooked in the bustle of our everyday lives, even if headstones still stand. Many people will walk by, totally oblivious to the fact that people are buried nearby.

Nonconformist church burial grounds
From the mid-seventeenth century, and increasingly from the eighteenth century, a significant number of our ancestors shunned the Church of England and became members of Nonconformist Churches. The history of Nonconformity is complex, but these were dissenting religious groups which challenged the doctrinal niceties of the Church of England. Many evolved into independent Churches, notably the Society of Friends (Quakers), Presbyterians, Baptists, Congregationalists, and Methodists, which built their own churches, often referred to as chapels. There were also many smaller groups which were relatively short-lived. Although Catholics and Jews are sometimes included when using the terms

Dissenters and Nonconformists, strictly speaking the terms relate only to Protestant dissenting groups.

Since the monarch was head of the Church of England, non-attendance at the local parish church, or membership of a Nonconformist Church, bespoke potential disloyalty to the Crown. Nonconformists, as well as Catholics and Jews, were seen as a potential threat to public order and were persecuted by the government, to varying degrees, for centuries. The Act of Toleration (1869) was a big step forwards in granting freedom of worship to Protestant dissenting groups (although Dissenters were still restricted in other respects), and the great majority of Nonconformist chapels post-date this. However, up to the late 1800s, relatively few chapels had burial grounds, perhaps due to the reluctance of the Church of England to relinquish precious burial fees. Until the nineteenth century, the majority of Nonconformists were buried in the parish churchyard and burial had to be accompanied by a Church of England service. From 1880, new legislation allowed burials to take place without such a service, if the vicar was informed at least forty-eight hours in advance. Where available, Nonconformists often chose burial in private cemeteries in unconsecrated ground, and some cemeteries specialized in attracting these clients (see below and Chapter 4).

Just like parish churches, intramural burials took place within Nonconformist chapels, and brought a welcome source of revenue, while the actual churchyard would be sited according to the availability of land, sometimes adjacent to the chapel, but often a short distance away. Similar to their parochial counterparts, many urban Nonconformist chapels were subject to 'over-burial'. The most notorious example was the Enon Baptist Chapel in London, which opened in 1822 in St Clements Lane. From here, the Revd William House ran a squalid trade, offering cheap burial space in the basement of the chapel, and accepting far more burials than there was space for. In order to accommodate the demand, recent burials were disposed of by a variety of nefarious means, and grave slots recycled almost immediately. Revd House continued this practice until his death in 1842, burying an estimated 12,000 bodies in this small burial chamber. Those bodies remaining under the chapel were later re-interred in Norwood Cemetery thanks to the efforts of George Walker, one of the great campaigners for burial reform.

While some families were staunch members of a particular Church for successive generations, others were less consistent in their loyalties. You may never suspect that a particular generation of your family worshipped at a Nonconformist chapel. This could, in turn, mean you fail to locate an ancestor's burial in a Nonconformist churchyard or within the church itself. Such was the transient nature of some Nonconformist chapels; it can be hard to pinpoint which were in existence when and where. A useful finding aid is the *John Evans List of Dissenting Congregations and Ministers, 1715–1729*. This lists Baptist, Independent and Presbyterian congregations in England and Wales extant between these dates. The Welsh Chapels database (**www.welshchapels.org/chapels-database**) is a growing project aiming to detail all Nonconformist churches in Wales, notably those for which there are no surviving registers. Reading about the place where your family lived using websites such as the Family Search Wiki (see Chapter 6) or **www.genuki.org.uk**, as well as in general histories, will help you form a picture of which churches and chapels were to be found in a particular place. GENUKI (**www.genuki.org.uk**) is a free virtual reference library of genealogical information aimed at research in the UK and Ireland, and while the quantity and quality of data varies from county to county, it is generally an excellent source of information. You are also likely to find information about other burial grounds discussed in this chapter.

Many Nonconformist chapels have been taken down, or converted into housing. In some cases, an associated burial ground may remain, but equally it could have been cleared (with the human remains exhumed and relocated), or turned into recreational land or gardens. Ynysgau Cemetery in Merthyr Tydfil was attached to the Ynysgau Independent Chapel and had gravestones dating back to the 1770s when it was demolished in 1967 as part of town improvements. Those buried at Ynysgau Chapel were exhumed and re-interred in Cefn Cemetery. There are no surviving registers for this chapel and, while records were made of those tombstones which stood when the chapel was demolished, only a small percentage of these were legible. Without any knowledge of the local area, it would be easy to overlook the existence of this Nonconformist burial ground, and there will be many similar examples across the country.[1]

The Society of Friends (Quakers) was founded in the mid-seventeenth century, and their earliest burial grounds date from the late seventeenth century, pre-dating those associated with other Nonconformist churches by many years. The burial ground at Pales, Llandegley, is one of these, dating back to the 1670s, and is still open for burials today. The Quaker belief that all land belongs to God, and consecration is unnecessary to make it sacred, encouraged some early members to opt for burial in their own gardens or orchards. Early burial grounds were often established on land donated by church members. Some began as unofficial burial sites with a few burials initially being allowed by the landowner, with the site later becoming established as a recognized burial ground. Brigflatts in Yorkshire is one example. Here, the farmer allowed a handful of Quaker burials in his field, before transferring ownership of the ground over to the Friends for a nominal sum.

Early Quaker burial grounds were devoid of any gravestones or memorials, these being regarded as a form of vanity. Many Friends also believed that the grander memorials, so often encountered in the parish churchyard, served to emphasize the domination of the wealthy upper classes in society, which was perpetuated after death. Over time, these views softened, and from the mid-nineteenth century, simple memorials of regular size and shape were deemed acceptable for Friends' burials. If you have an interest in the history of the Society of Friends, the Quaker Family History Society has an informative website at **https://www.qfhs. co.uk/index.html**.

While conventional Christian churchyards followed a tradition of burying the dead facing east to west, the few excavations of Quaker burial grounds (notably Kingston upon Thames and North Shields) suggest that the Friends would bury in orderly rows, as best suited the layout of the burial ground. Traditionally, graves were dug in orderly succession, as demand occurred, rather than in plots reserved in advance for family members. Over time reserved family burial plots did become more commonplace, where there was sufficient space.

Since early graves had no headstones, grave mounds would have been heavily relied upon to indicate the presence of earlier burials. Although this was not a foolproof system, the importance attached to it is perhaps shown in an order of the London Society of Friends in 1693, which stated that no graves were to be levelled in the burial ground 'without order of the Meeting'. As in parish churchyards, archaeological evidence has shown that charnel pits were used to receive the disturbed bones of previous occupants during grave-digging, these sometimes being located at the foot of the new grave. In 1850, the Yearly Meeting of the Kingston upon Thames Friends ruled that grave markers should be used in order to identify earlier burial places, revoking an order of 1717 that had forbidden them. It specifically stressed that their erection was primarily to protect earlier burials, and not to glorify the dead. Comparison of the Kingston burial registers, which run from 1711 to 1829, with the number of bodies excavated, shows that at least forty-one people were missing from the burial registers.[2] This is a phenomenon that must surely apply across all burial grounds of any denomination.

CASE STUDY

Mrs Basil (Isabella) Holmes, (1861–1949)

One of the most referenced books in terms of London churchyards is *The London Burial Grounds. Notes On Their History From The Earliest Times to the Present Day*. This was written by Mrs Basil Holmes and published in 1896. It is a wonderful first-hand account of London's burial grounds as they were in the 1880s and 1890s.

'Mrs Basil Holmes' was actually Isabella Holmes (born Isabella Gladstone). She married Basil Holmes, secretary of the Metropolitan Public Gardens Association (MPGA) in 1887. In the introduction to her book, she writes that her interest in London burial grounds was stimulated by looking at an early map of London by John Rocque. She noticed that many of the burial grounds and churchyards marked on it were no longer in existence, and undertook extensive research into those that did survive, and the locations of those already lost. She carried out much on-foot exploration of the various sites, and her account very nicely illustrates the wide range of burial grounds that existed in the metropolis at this time.

Isabella Holmes, author of The London Burial Grounds, *which provides a precious record of the numerous graveyards in London in the late nineteenth century, many of which were soon to be lost. (Jake Holmes)*

Her research was initially published in a report to the MPGA in 1881. Founded in 1882, the MPGA aimed to preserve open spaces for the use and enjoyment of the general public in the metropolitan area. These included disused churchyards and burial grounds, as well as gardens and open spaces of various different types.

In 1894 Isabella agreed to help London County Council's Parks Committee compile a list of burial grounds in London, detailing their size, ownership and current condition. Her research included a report, accompanied by sixty twenty-five inch-to-the-mile Ordnance Survey maps, which she colour coded. The colours represented burial grounds still in use, those which had been converted into public recreation grounds and those which were disused. Isabella found a total of 362 burial grounds, forty-one of which were still active between 1894 and 1895. Ninety were disused but, by then, formed public gardens or playgrounds.

Isabella's work is very precious, as it provides an invaluable eyewitness account of the state of London burial grounds at this time, as well as anecdotal evidence relating to the disappearance of many more. She emphasizes that this was a time when much building work was taking place and land prices were at a premium. While the Disused Burial Grounds Act of 1884 aimed to prevent development of burial sites without prior permission, one adverse side-effect was instances where builders did find human remains but hushed up their existence so that building work was not interrupted. Her findings are still used by historians and archaeologists today, and are an eye-opener in terms of just how many small burial grounds of different sorts were in existence in London at this time. Most of these have now disappeared without trace.

The London Burial Grounds is available for free via the Internet Archive (archive.org) or through Project Gutenberg (**www.gutenberg. org**).

Foreign church burial grounds

Churches serving foreign Protestant congregations were built in some towns and cities following migration from the Continent, often associated with religious intolerance. Flemish and Walloon refugees were granted special permission to erect churches in England and Wales long before 1642, which was when English and Welsh Nonconformists were allowed to build their own churches. Many towns and cities in the south-east of England, such as London, Norwich, Canterbury, Sandwich, Colchester, Southampton, Norwich, Ipswich, Exeter and Plymouth, to name but a few, became ex-pat centres for these religious migrants. In the eighteenth century, refugees also arrived from what was to become Germany.

Very few of these churches had their own burial grounds, with the majority of their congregations being buried in the parish churchyard. The exception was in London where examples include the Flemish burial ground in St Olave's, Southwark, which adjoined a chapel in Carter Lane (now mostly under the site of London Bridge Station), and Mount Nod burial ground, which was attached to the Huguenot Chapel in Wandsworth. It operated from 1687–1854 and the burial ground survives today, although it is kept locked. St George's German Lutheran Church in Aldgate was founded in 1762 by Dietrich Beckman, a sugar boiler, and had a burial ground in its courtyard, which was in operation until 1854.[3]

Roman Catholic graveyards

Following the establishment of the Church of England in 1534, Catholics were harshly persecuted, or, at best, subject to myriad restrictive laws by the government. Until 1844, they could not be buried anywhere except in the parish churchyard, and you may see the annotation 'Papist' next to their entry in the registers. From 1852, they were officially allowed their own burial grounds, although a small number had been established in the years leading up to this. Relatively few Catholic churches have their own burial grounds, and your Catholic ancestors will usually be buried in the parish churchyard or, from the nineteenth century, in privately-run or municipal cemeteries. Some cemeteries were particularly associated with Catholic burials and this can often be ascertained from background reading.

Jewish cemeteries

Few early Jewish synagogues had associated cemeteries and members were typically buried in the parish churchyard, and occasionally in private gardens. Many Jewish cemeteries were established on an ad hoc basis to serve growing Jewish communities as demand required, subject to suitable donations of land, and are therefore located away from the synagogue. In London, the earliest Jewish cemetery is Old Mile End Cemetery, established in 1657, with a new burial ground being opened along the road in the 1720s. If there was no Jewish cemetery nearby, families would often pay for transportation of a loved one some considerable distance, while many Jews made use of local non-denominational cemeteries as they were established.

It is a common misconception that Jewish burials only take place with one burial per grave space. Multiple burials are allowed, providing that 'six hands breadth' of earth is placed between them. Jews strongly believe burials should lie undisturbed in perpetuity, and this is why many Jewish cemeteries in towns and cities survive, often surrounded by incongruous modern buildings. Many are locked, and access can be difficult, or they can be hard to locate, such as the one in Canterbury, Kent, which is tucked away out of sight behind residential housing. In Ipswich, Suffolk, the Jewish cemetery was originally attached to the Rope Walk Synagogue, which was demolished in 1877. The boundary walls of the cemetery are now Grade II listed, but the evolution of the

The Jewish cemetery at Ipswich, Suffolk, in its incongruous setting surrounded by houses and yards on one side and a car park on the other. (The Ipswich Society)

surrounding urban landscape means it now stands alone in the middle of car park and accompanying car wash.

A good study of the progression of a Jewish cemetery is the cemetery at Lambhay Hill in Plymouth. This was first used for burials in the 1740s, following a donation of land by a local Jew, Sarah Sherrenbeck. The land originally formed part of Mrs Sherrenbeck's garden, and burials there began as an act of kindness, followed by a formal granting of the land to the Jewish community at a later date. Further land was added in 1758 and 1811, as the community grew. Interestingly, in this last addition of land, the plot in question was transferred into the names of three people, one of whom was not Jewish. This was a safeguard due to lack of clarity in contemporary law as to whether or not Jews were legally entitled to hold land. A new burial ground (Gifford Place Jewish Cemetery) was established in 1868 and is still in use, but burials in Lambhay continued until the early nineteenth century. Surveys of the gravestones in Lambhay were made by Revd Dr M. Berlin and more recently in the 1990s by Rabbi Bernard Susser, whose fascinating article on the Lambhay cemetery can be found at **www.jewishgen.org/ jcr-uk/susser/plymouthcemeteryintro.htm**. There are some interesting parallels between Jewish cemeteries and Christian churchyards. Unfavoured individuals, such as ex-communicates, apostates and those who had married outside the faith, were frequently buried in a specific, less-favoured section of the cemetery, or towards the side. Similarly, in some cemeteries, small children were buried along the boundaries of the cemetery, possibly reflecting a similar way of thinking to the 'eaves-drip', burials found in some Christian churchyards (see Chapter 2). Suicides, although officially forbidden burial in the Jewish cemeteries, were sometimes allowed at the discretion of the rabbi, on the grounds that the deceased was mentally ill.

Isabella Holmes provides a useful insight to Jewish cemeteries in the London boroughs at the time she was writing in the late nineteenth century:

'Within the Metropolitan area there are at present nine Jewish graveyards; there are others more lately acquired, and all still in use, at Willesden, West Ham, Edmonton, Plashet, and Golders Green, Hendon. The disused grounds which belong to the United Synagogue are those in Brady Street, Bethnal Green, E., Hoxton Street, N., Alderney Road, Mile End, E., and Grove Street, Hackney, E., and I cannot, unfortunately, call them well kept, but the neatest is the one in Alderney Road. In all of them the tombstones are upright, rather above the average size, and with inscriptions upon them which are almost invariably in Hebrew. The one in Hoxton is very small. It was originally formed for the use of the Hamborough Synagogue, Fenchurch Street, and was first used about the year 1700. All these grounds are old, part of the one in Alderney Road dates from about 1700, while the Brady Street Cemetery was formed in 1795.

Lastly, there are the cemeteries of the Spanish and Portuguese Jews – one, closed for burials, behind the Beth Holim Hospital in Mile End Road, and one, nearly five acres in extent and still in use, just beyond the People's Palace. These are neatly kept, the former, or at any rate a part of it, being actually turned into a sort of garden for the patients in the hospital, with trees in it, paths and seats. The latter is bare of trees or shrubs, but is divided into plots, with paths between. In both of them the tombstones, unlike those in the other Jewish grounds, are flat, either slabs on the ground or low altar tombs; and in the large ground there are many children's graves, marked by much smaller altar tombs dotted amongst the large ones, which are very unique and interesting. The Hebrew inscription at the entrance tells us that this is "The House of the Living," – "Beth Hayim." The *cemetery was acquired in 1657, and contains the remains of the ancestors of Lord Beaconsfield, the Eardley family, Sampson Gideon, the Samudas, D'Aguilars, Ricardos, Lopes, and many others who trace their descent from Sephardi Jews.'*

For information on Jewish gravestones and burial records see chapters 5 and 6.

Private cemeteries and burial grounds prior to the 1830s

While large privately-run and municipal cemeteries were predominantly a feature of the post-1830 burial scene, there were also burial grounds with no connection to either the Church of England or any Nonconformist chapel in existence before this.

Bethlam Burial Ground, or 'New Churchyard', was an early municipal cemetery established in the City of London in 1569, close to Liverpool Street, and was London's first significant ex-parochial burial ground.

It was recently the subject of archaeological excavations prior to development in connection with the Crossrail project. Despite its name, it was not specifically a burial ground for Bethlam Mental Hospital. While the land did originally belong to the hospital, in the mid-sixteenth century it was sold to the Corporation of the City of London, and a non-parochial burial ground established to help meet the increasing demand for burial space in the City, notably in times of epidemic. The alternative name, 'New Churchyard', was a misnomer, for it was not associated with any church. The colloquialism no doubt evolved to distinguish it from its older parochial city counterparts. Although earmarked for use during times of epidemic, it was heavily used throughout its history, notably by parishes with limited churchyard burial space. Although no burial fees were charged, there was a charge for grave digging (capped at six pence per burial) and the deceased's parish church would have charged a fee. When the ground closed in 1739, an estimated 25,000 people had been buried there.[4] Since it was independent of the Church of England, it was favoured by Nonconformists, as was its better-known counterpart, Bunhill Fields Cemetery, a mile or so away in City Road. The early origins of Bunhill Fields are not clear cut. It is certain that the Corporation of the City of London acquired land here in 1665 for use as a plague burial ground, but writers are divided as to whether any such burials actually took place: the balance of evidence suggests they did.[5] What is certain is that soon after this, the land was leased to a Mr Tindal who established it as a permanent burial ground. Its popularity with Nonconformists was encouraged by the burial of well-known Nonconformist figures such as

John Bunyan and Daniel Defoe. The cemetery was closed in 1853 and is now a public garden maintained by the City of London Corporation. It became a Grade I-listed park in 2011 and, while many gravestones still stand, most are railed off and can only be viewed at a distance.

Outside London, The Rosary in Norwich was founded as a private cemetery with shareholders in 1819. Although founded by a Presbyterian minister, the Revd Thomas Drummond, it was officially open for the burial of all faiths or denominations, but since the land was unconsecrated it attracted many Nonconformists. By contrast, Chorlton Row Cemetery in Manchester (founded 1820) and the Liverpool Necropolis (1825) were founded by Dissenters specifically for Dissenters. These were very much business enterprises, formed as joint stock companies and intended to make a profit. This was prescient of what was to become the norm in the 1830s and 1840s: the cemetery as a commercial enterprise (see Chapter 4).

There were also many smaller burial grounds established by individuals looking for a way of making easy money. The key target area was London, with its ever-growing population and rapidly decreasing burial space. Typically their charges were lower than the parish burial fees, in order to attract more customers. In some instances they did so well that they became notorious for 'over-burying'; reusing grave spaces before earlier burials had been left for an appropriate length of time. (See also Chapter 4.) Isabella Holmes records the following sites in London in the late nineteenth century:

'In Central London there were Spa Fields, Clerkenwell; Thomas' burial-ground, Golden Lane; the New City Bunhill Fields, or the City of London burial-ground, Golden Lane. In North London there was the New or Little Bunhill Fields, Church Street, Islington. In East London there were Sheen's burial-ground, Whitechapel; Victoria Park Cemetery, Bethnal Green; the East London Cemetery or Beaumont's ground, Mile End; Globe Fields burial-ground, Mile End Old Town; the North-east London Cemetery, or Cambridge Heath burial-ground, or Peel Grove burial-ground, or Keldy's Ground, Bethnal Green; Gibraltar Walk burial-ground, Bethnal Green; Ebenezer Chapel ground, Ratcliff Highway. And in South London (12) Butler's burial-ground, Horselydown, or St. John's; the New Bunhill Fields, or Hoole and Martin's ground, Deverell Street, New Kent Road; and a ground in Ewer Street, Southwark.'

Cemeteries and burial grounds for the armed forces

Soldiers who died while garrisoned at barracks might be buried in the local parish church, or in the barracks' church if there was one, but if you are seeking the burial of army or navy personnel you should also consider military and naval cemeteries. The respective Royal Hospitals at Greenwich and Chelsea (retirement and nursing homes for naval and military servicemen) had their own burial grounds, where many pensioners, and also some members of staff, were laid to rest. The original Royal Chelsea Hospital Burial Ground opened in 1691 within the grounds of the hospital and over 10,000 people had been buried there when it closed in 1855. Since 1894 the hospital has had a burial plot at Brookwood Cemetery in Surrey. Due to limited funds, and the cost of maintaining the gravestones, most were removed from the Brookwood plot in 1954, while very few gravestones remain in the original burial ground. A new plot has now been established at Brookwood near the Canadian military section.

The Royal Hospital at Greenwich operated from the 1690s to 1869 on what is now the site of Devonport House.[6] It provided long-term accommodation and medical treatment for Royal Navy veterans and an estimated 20,000 retired seamen and marines were buried between 1749 and 1856.[6] A new burial site at Westcombe, East Greenwich, opened in 1857, and this is now a park known as the East Greenwich Pleasaunce. Isabella Holmes notes that the original burial ground was 'to the west side of the Royal Naval School. It is enclosed and full of tombstones. …This space is well kept, containing some fine trees and only a few monuments. The gate from the school playground is generally open. Then there is the Hospital Cemetery in West Combe, nearly six acres in size, and first used in 1857.'

Other Royal Navy cemeteries include the Ministry of Defence (MOD) cemetery at Portland, Dorset, used for the burial of servicemen and officers stationed at the island until 1995, and the cemetery at Devonport near Plymouth, which buried sailors from the adjacent Royal Naval Hospital between 1824 and 1897.There are also the Haslar and Clayhall Royal Navy cemeteries in Gosport, Hampshire, and the naval cemetery at Shotley Gate, Suffolk, which was the site of the Royal Naval Training Establishment, HMS *Ganges*.

For burials of armed forces during the world wars, the Commonwealth War Graves Commission Cemeteries are primary burial sites, although many people killed in active service were buried in their local churchyard or cemetery.

The Commonwealth War Graves Commission (CWGC), formerly the Imperial War Commission, was founded by Royal Charter in 1917. It was the initiative of Sir Fabian Ware, who noticed there was no official mechanism for marking or recording the graves of those killed in the

This shot of Commonwealth War Graves Commission headstones at Brookwood Military Cemetery, Surrey, clearly illustrates their uniform design and arrangement. (Author's collection)

First World War: he set about rectifying this. While the great majority of CWGC cemeteries are sited overseas, close to battle locations, there are a few in England. The largest is the Brookwood Military Cemetery, which forms part of the Brookwood Cemetery in Woking and covers approximately thirty-seven acres. CWGC cemeteries are known for their simple, formal layout, with neat rows of uniform gravestones.

There are also a number of military cemeteries owned by the Ministry of Defence (MOD). Although they are the property of the MOD, you may find some CWGC war graves within them. These cemeteries are usually sited in towns which have a long association with army barracks. One of the largest is at Aldershot in Hampshire which has been the site of numerous regimental and corps depots over the years. This cemetery includes burials from both world wars and many other conflicts, notably the Falklands War. There are also graves relating to family members of armed personnel, and some civilians who had careers associated with the army. On a smaller scale there are cemeteries such as Shorncliffe Cemetery at Cheriton near Folkestone, Kent. This contains 471 First World War burials of many different nationalities, including several Chinese who were part of the Chinese Labour Corps in the First World War. Some of those buried include victims of air raids on Shorncliff.

The German Military Cemetery at Cannock Chase, Staffordshire, is the resting place of many German nationals – both servicemen and civilian internees of both world wars – who died in the United Kingdom. Originally buried in various non-CWGC cemeteries they were reinterred in one national cemetery at Cannock in 1959, following agreement with the German government.

Institutional graveyards

Some institutions, notably prisons, hospitals, workhouses and asylums, had their own burial grounds. From the mid-nineteenth century such institutions were legally responsible for the burial of anyone who died in their care. This might involve directly arranging the burial or liaising with the family if they wished to arrange it themselves. While there was no obligation for an institution to establish its own burial ground, sometimes this proved a more convenient option than organizing burials in the local churchyard or cemetery, and some had their own burial grounds prior to the mid-nineteenth century. Institutional burial grounds were typically, but not always, on site.

Prison burial grounds

In many cases, the bodies of prisoners who died while serving sentences would have been claimed by family or friends and buried in the parish or other local churchyard. However, many prisons did have their own burial ground within the prison walls where some of those who died in prison or who were executed there were buried. Where their graves were marked, this was often only by means of initials. From 1922 prison authorities were instructed not to identify the name of those executed using 'names, initials, or any other marks' because this perpetuated the memory of the crime, caused unnecessary pain to relatives, and roused a morbid interest in the criminals. As a result, many earlier grave markers were erased. Those executed for murder might have been buried elsewhere in the prison grounds rather than in the burial ground itself since, up to 1832, they were legally denied burial in consecrated ground. From 1752, their bodies might have gone to be anatomized. (See page 60). While many prison burials are not recorded, there are some records at TNA (see Chapter 6).

Archaeological evidence sometimes reveals the burial of prisoners in unmarked sections of the prison grounds. Prior to redevelopment at Oxford Castle in 2002 (the castle having served as the county prison for centuries), sixty-two burials were found in the backfill of the moat of the Norman motte. Nearly all were young men and buried in 'plain undecorated wooden coffins'. It is highly likely that they relate to executed criminals and prisoners who died there between the sixteenth and early nineteenth century, with the majority probably dying in the late seventeenth–early eighteenth century.[7] Leeds Castle in Kent was never the site of a prison, but work for a new pathway in 1996 revealed an unexpected surprise: the skeletons of eight men. Excavation, in conjunction with documentary research, indicates that these burials may well relate to Dutch prisoners who were housed at the castle during the Anglo-Dutch wars in the seventeenth century.[8]

Workhouse burial grounds

A few of the Union workhouses established following the 1834 New Poor Law, and some of their predecessors, had their own burial grounds, but many inmates who died during their stay would alternatively have been buried in the local cemetery or parish churchyard. There are also a few examples of burial grounds associated with almshouses, notably in London, such as the Goldsmith's Almshouses in Shoreditch and College Yard at St Saviour's Almshouses, Southwark.

In workhouse burial grounds, graves were typically unmarked. Some workhouses later became hospitals or asylums, so if you are trying to track down the site of an old workhouse burial ground, this should be borne in mind. Isabella Holmes provides useful information on the location and state of some of London's workhouse burial grounds in the late nineteenth century:

> 'The workhouse graveyard, belonging to St. Clement Danes, was in Portugal Street. The workhouse itself was re-adapted and re-opened as King's College Hospital, but the burial-ground was used until its condition was so loathsome, and the burning of coffins and mutilation of bodies was of such every-day occurrence, that it must have been one of the very worst of such places in London. It is now the garden or courtyard and approach, between the hospital and Portugal Street.'

Outside of the capital, workhouses that had their own burial ground included those at Bath, Somerset (opened 1838) and Gressenhall, Norfolk (opened 1785). An entry in the *Bath Chronicle* of 29 July 1847 recorded that at 'half-past three o'clock, the Bishop proceeded to the Union Workhouse and consecrated a piece of ground for the interment of such poor persons as may die within the house. Thus, the inconvenience of removing the bodies to different parishes will in future be obviated.' This graveyard lay to the south-east of the workhouse chapel and some 1,100 people were buried there before a new burial ground was opened in 1858 which in turn saw some 3,100 people laid to rest. This closed in 1899, after which inmates were buried in burial board cemeteries.[9] At Gressenhall, inmates were buried on site as early as 1797. By 1900 the burial ground was largely full, an attempt to open a new burial ground having been blocked by the Local Government Board. After this, the bodies of paupers were sent back to their own parishes for burial in the churchyard, with a few exceptions, believed mainly to have been stillborns.[10]

Hospital and asylum burial grounds

The Royal Hospitals at Greenwich and Chelsea have been mentioned, but burial grounds were also to be found within non-military hospitals and asylums. Few short-stay hospitals had burial grounds compared to those which treated long-term patients, but there were some. The London Hospital (originally the London Infirmary and now The Royal London Hospital), was founded in 1740. Originally located in Moorfields, it moved to Whitechapel Road and admitted its first patients there in 1757. Funded by subscribers, it dealt with patients recommended by them, but also 'Accident and Emergency' cases. There was also a school of anatomy at the hospital between 1785 and 1852, and the hospital had its own burial ground, which was officially in use from 1840 to 1854. However, archaeological excavations undertaken in 2006 indicate that burials were actually taking place in another part of the grounds as early as the 1820s, and these burials appear to have included three groups of people: those who had died during surgery, those whose bodies were subject to autopsy, and those whose bodies had been anatomically dissected. The 1832 Anatomy Act allowed the bodies of those who died in an institution and whose bodies were unclaimed by family or friends to be taken for dissection. Prior to this, dissection was only legally allowed on the bodies of executed murderers. Although the deficit in supply was alleviated by 'bodysnatching', the remains found by archaeologists suggest that deceased hospital patients were actually being dissected prior to the 1832 Act.[11] It is estimated that as many as 500 related to people buried in this earlier burial ground.[12] Isabella Holmes provides interesting anecdotal evidence that burials were taking place here later than the documented 1854:

'The "unclaimed corpses" from the London Hospital found their last resting-place very near home. In 1849 the whole of the southern part of the enclosure, quite an acre and a half, was the burial-ground, and here, although it was closed by order in Council in 1854, it appears that burials took place until about 1860, one of the present porters remembering his father acting as gravedigger. The medical school, the chaplain's house, and the nurse's home have all been built upon it, and it is sincerely to be hoped that no further encroachments will be permitted. The remaining part is the nurses' and students' garden and tennis-court, where they are in the habit of capering about in their short times off duty, and where it sometimes happens that the grass gives way beneath them – an ordinary occurrence when the subsoil is inhabited by coffins!'

Newcastle Infirmary, Northumberland, was founded in 1751 and closed in 1906. Initially providing ninety beds for the poor of Newcastle, its capacity doubled in the nineteenth century and it had an active burial ground up to 1845. This was excavated in 1996, revealing at least 600 burials had taken place within its history. Once again, evidence suggests that many had been dissected prior to the 1832 Anatomy Act.

The number of people living in mental asylums rose dramatically from the mid-nineteenth century, as new schools of thought promoted the idea that those with mental health problems should be cared for in institutions, rather than in the community. The Lunacy Act and the County Asylums Act of 1845 led to the compulsory establishment of County Lunatic Asylums, and the establishment of a Lunacy Commission to help set up and regulate them. Initially catering primarily for the poorer end of society, a further Act in 1890 gave asylums a wider remit and increasingly led to the admission of wealthier patients. By the end of the century there were some 120 new asylums in England and Wales, housing over 100,000 people.[13]

Figures for county asylums show that by 1860 the average number of residents in a county asylum was upwards of 450, with some housing more than 1,000 patients.[14] Rich or poor, patients were often outcasts from society; sometimes part of families whose members did not want further responsibility for them, or paupers with psychological disorders, sent as part of the workhouse system. Many inmates never left, and the asylum managers were presented with a significant challenge to fulfil their obligation to take care of the burial of anyone who died while a patient. Establishing their own burial ground on site was often easier and more cost effective than arranging burial in the local churchyard or cemetery. Provision for establishing on-site burial grounds was included in several of the various lunacy acts passed during this century.

The Middlesex County Lunatic Asylum at Hanwell was the largest asylum in England when it opened in 1831. It initially utilized the burial ground of nearby St Mary's Church, but such was the need for burial space that it soon set aside land within its own grounds for a burial area. Many others followed suit, although in some cases asylums reserved advance plots in local cemeteries or churchyards. Over time, just like churchyards and cemeteries, some asylum burial grounds became overfull and were regarded as health hazards due to their close proximity to dwellings. Despite this, some rural asylums continued burying until relatively recently. It was not just the patients who were buried in these burial grounds; members of staff, or their families, might also be laid to rest there.

Some asylum burial grounds have now been built upon, such as at Hanwell, where the human remains were removed before being reinterred in one part of the old cemetery which was rededicated as a Garden of Remembrance.

Epidemic burial grounds: 'Plague Pits'

Epidemics are regular visitors throughout history. The most notable are the plagues of 1348–1349, 1360–1361, and 1665–1666. That of 1348–1349 (often known as the Black Death) is estimated to have wiped out between forty and sixty percent of the English and Welsh population. In the nineteenth century cholera was a major problem, causing several outbreaks of epidemic level, notably in 1831–1832 and 1848–1849, while other diseases, such as typhoid and smallpox, also caused major problems. During times of epidemic, great strain was placed on the burial infrastructure, and usual funeral practices often had to be discarded or adapted. In some cases, contingency burial sites were opened away from normal burial grounds. Examples are the cholera burial grounds opened in Upton-upon-Severn, Worcestershire, and York in 1832 and Cefn Golau in Blaenau Gwent, in use from 1832 to 1855. During the London plague of 1665–1666, there is no doubt that large burial pits (often colloquially referred to as 'plague pits') were dug within many churchyards to cope with the stream of dead parishioners. Vanessa Harding, in her excellent article on the subject, hypothesizes: 'It seems likely that most, perhaps all, of the larger suburban parishes of London ended by burying their plague dead in mass graves, but that the smaller city-centre parishes did not need to do so.'[15]

Evidence from archaeological excavations during the Crossrail project showed that Bethlam burial ground (see above) was also used in the London plague epidemic of 1665. A mass grave was found, and DNA analysis provides evidence that those buried were victims of the plague. It is interesting to note that the majority of the burials, although very closely packed, were laid in neat rows and were in coffins. Over the centuries these had decayed causing dispersal of the remains and, while forty-two individual skeletons were identified, archaeologists believe that up to 100 people were buried in the grave.[16]

By this time, the burial ground had been open for ninety-six years and this put too great a strain on its capacity. The civic authorities therefore acquired a new burial ground in Finsbury Fields to ease the situation; this was to become Bunhill Fields (see pages 54–55).

Reliable information relating to epidemic burial sites is often scant and apocryphal. Daniel Defoe's, book *Journal of a Plague Year* has become a much-quoted source for the sites of London 'plague pits'. In it, the narrator, known as H.F., is a saddler living in Whitechapel. He relates details of the events of the London plague, including burial sites and numbers. Defoe was only a few years old when the London plague was raging, so these were not his own memories, yet he is widely quoted as if he were an eyewitness! There is a suggestion that his information may have been based on memories of his uncle, Henry Foe, who was a saddler living in Whitechapel. Although some of what he writes is almost certainly true, we cannot be certain everything he relates is accurate.

In between major outbreaks of disease, there would have been smaller, more localized outbreaks. These could also have put pressure on local burial systems and led to the creation of extraordinary burial sites, dug as a contingency measure and used only once. However, we must not automatically make the assumption that the discovery of a burial site incorporating numerous burials is an epidemic burial site. In some parishes, pest houses were used to house those with highly infectious diseases, such as smallpox, tuberculosis, cholera and typhus. Some of these had burial grounds attached to or associated with them, such as that for St Martin-in-the-Fields, which served not only St Martin's, but also a number of other parishes. Isabella Holmes shows how burial grounds might be adapted to serve the immediate needs of the time, and how easily those burial sites might later be lost:

'Shoreditch, St Paul's, Covent Garden, and St Giles (in Short's Gardens) have also disappeared; so also has the one allotted to the use of St James' Workhouse in Poland Street, which was a part of the old pest-field, although a remnant of the pest-field exists still as the workhouse garden. The original Whitechapel Workhouse was built in 1768 on a burial-ground, and then a plot of land immediately to the north was set aside for a poor

ground and consecrated in 1796. This in turn became the playground of the Davenant Schools, one of which (facing St Mary's Street) was built in it. A recent addition to the other school has also encroached on the burial-ground. In 1832, 196 cholera cases were interred in an adjoining piece of ground, which was probably what is now used as a stoneyard and is full of carts.'

As in every aspect of life, there are exceptions and anomalies to be found among burial grounds. These include many tiny, often long-forgotten, burial grounds created to suit very specific circumstances, although the facts of why they were created can become blurred and open to debate with time. For example, a burial ground outside the Fitzherbert Gate of Dover Castle is believed to have been established to bury nineteen men from the Oxfordshire Regiment, who died of smallpox while garrisoned at the castle. However, there are differing accounts as to why it was created.

John Bavington Jones, in his *Annals of Dover* (published in 1916), wrote that,

> *'From 1796, for about 20 years a great many regiments were crowded into Dover Castle, and in the year 1800 a graveyard was consecrated for the burial of soldiers outside the Castle walls near the top of the Northfall Meadow. That graveyard still exists and there used to be a good many small headstones there indicating that the soldiers there buried belonged chiefly to Militia Regiments from Oxfordshire, Shropshire, Cornwall, Yorkshire, Sussex, and Wales. Some, it was mentioned, died in the Castle of smallpox, which led to the supposition that this burial ground had been specially used at the time of an epidemic, but the evidence seems to indicate that it was generally used for the Castle Garrison interments'.*[17]

Jones may be partially right, in that it was not just men of the Oxfordshire Regiment buried there, but if the graveyard was an overspill for the garrison soldiers, then it begs the question as to why was it so small. The memorials were removed to Shorncliffe Cemetery, Cheriton, in the 1990s. There is now almost nothing to show the location of the site, although the human remains are in situ. There are, no doubt, other similar cases across England and Wales.

Locating defunct burial grounds

The burial grounds described in this chapter are the most likely to lie disused. As we have seen, many institutional burial grounds had very few or no gravestones, while in other cases these will have been removed. This means that in many cases all obvious trace of the burial ground may have disappeared. The land may have been built over, may form part of a local park or garden, or have simply been left to be reabsorbed by the surrounding countryside. The above-mentioned 1884 Disused Burial Grounds Act introduced strict laws to protect closed burial grounds from being built on. Building only legally happens under strictly controlled measures, which include the removal and re-interment of those buried there. That is one reason why defunct burial grounds are prime candidates for becoming parks and gardens.

Tracking down the site of disused burial grounds can be immense fun, whether you are doing so to locate your ancestor's burial place, or as part of a local history study. There are many finding aids to help you both on and off-line, notably a wide range of historic Ordnance Survey (OS) maps (nineteenth century onwards) and the ever-useful Google Earth, which can help you visualize what the site looks like today. Local history publications (including websites, blogs and books in paper form or reproduced as e-books) often provide quick and easy information regarding the sites of old burial grounds based on the research of other people, but do verify the information you find using original sources and look for any discrepancies or inconsistencies in what has been written. If you are searching for an institutional burial ground, general internet searches and studies of record office catalogues can quickly determine whether or not there was, for example, a hospital or asylum in the area. Larger institutions will be marked on larger-scale OS maps (six and twenty-five inch-to-the-mile) and the burial ground will often also be marked.

OS maps come in different scales. One-inch maps provide a good overview of an area in general, but you will need six-inch or twenty-five-inch maps for sufficient detail to mark burial grounds. The latter started to be published from the 1850s onwards and while all towns had been mapped at this scale by the 1880s, rural areas are not always covered. Six-inch maps will typically be found from the 1840s.

You will find historic OS maps in local libraries and archives and The National Archives at Kew, but many can be viewed online or bought as reasonably priced reproductions. The National Library of Scotland website is one of the best places to browse maps, offering a great variety of historic OS maps for England and Wales for no charge (**https://maps.nls.uk/index.html**). The National Library of Wales also has a good selection of online OS maps, again for free (**https://www.library.wales/collections/learn-more/maps**). Alan Godfrey Maps (**www.alangodfreymaps.co.uk**) and Cassini Maps (**www.cassinimaps. co.uk**) are useful ports of call for paper reprints, as is **www.old-maps. co.uk**. Tithe records may also record ex-parochial burial grounds, if they were located on land historically subject to tithes (an ancient ecclesiastical tax). If this was the case, they should be listed in the tithe schedule in the column that records land usage and the relevant plot of land will be located by identifying the relevant plot number on the map. Some maps are more detailed than others and the burial ground may even be labelled as such on the map. Tithe records typically range in date from 1836–1846 and provide large-scale mapping which pre-dates the first larger-scale OS maps.

The free computer program, Google Earth, which provides a 3D representation of our planet based primarily on satellite imagery, makes a boon companion to your research. Used in tandem with map research, it can not only help you detect the burial ground site as it is today, but also, for many locations, offers a timeline of historic imagery which can show you how the site has changed over the years. It is also very useful for helping pinpoint current buildings close to the disused burial ground, which will give you a bearing to use when you visit the site in person. In some cases (depending on the conditions when the imagery was taken) you can identify the neat rows of burials using the aerial view feature.

CASE STUDY

Chartham Mental Hospital, Kent (1875–1993)
Also known as St Augustine's Hospital, and once a workhouse, this mental asylum just outside Canterbury opened in 1875. It had a burial ground from the start and burials took place from 1875 through to 1972. There are three burial registers, now held at the Kent History and Library Centre (references MH/T3/Kz 2-4). During the First World War, the asylum housed patients from other parts of the country, where hospitals had been commissioned by the government for military casualties.

Inspection of the burial registers and other records throws light on the organization of the burial ground and its expansion over the years, as well as providing useful information about those buried there. The first burial register runs from 1875–1917 (Kz 2) and consists of a pre-printed book, which provides consecutively numbered register entries in chronological order, an accompanying grave number, name, sex, age, and details of who performed the ceremony. There is also a column entitled 'Remarks', and another recording to which poor law union the burial should be charged. The latter clearly reflects the early period in the hospital's history, where the great majority of the inmates were paupers, rather than private patients. This column is left blank from part-way through the second register (Kz 3) and does not feature at all in the last register which covers 1925–1972 (Kz 4).

The original area set aside for the burial ground in 1875 allowed for some 900 burials, each with an allocated advance plot number. Emma Jane Brown, aged thirty-three, was the first person to be buried, on 9 November 1875, and her details were duly entered into the register with an allocation of Entry No.1 and Grave No.1. The entry numbers and grave numbers should have run consecutively, but for a mistake when burying the fourth person, William Cock, aged sixty-eight, on 10 July 1876. Grave No.1 was accidentally reopened, and so William Cock lies in the same grave as Emma Jane Brown, and the grave numbers from thereon run one behind the entry numbers! Apart from this blip, the grave numbers run sequentially after this, suggesting that plots were allocated in consecutive order as people died, up to Entry No.881 (Grave No.1880) which is for Charlotte Waller, aged sixty, on 30 October 1897.

At this point it appears a new section for burials must have been started within the burial ground, for the grave numbers begin again at No.1 and follow on sequentially, but interspersed with numbers from the previous sequence, suggesting that some burials were still taking place in the old part of the burial ground. Burials were no longer being allocated strictly consecutively as people died. From the 1890s, many entries have no accompanying grave number and there are numerous alterations to grave numbers too, making it hard to determine just what was going on in terms of the allocation of burial plots. However, it is believed there were over 200 further burial spaces in this second section of the burial ground.

A third burial area was in use by December 1909, and the allocation of grave numbers appears much more erratic by this time, with the quality of the record-keeping deteriorating. There is at least one instance of the same person featuring twice in the register.

The two later burial registers overlap, covering 1917–1972 and 1925–1972 respectively (Kz 3 and Kz 4), and use new grave numbering systems. Logic dictates that each must relate to two specific parts of the burial ground which were in use concurrently at these periods, although in the limited time for research (due to archival closures as a result of the coronavirus pandemic), there was insufficient time to establish which. While the two earlier registers were indexed semi-alphabetically by first initial of surname, there was no index for the third register (Kz 4.)

All three burial areas were adjacent to each other and close to the asylum's mortuary chapel. Totalling up the number of burials recorded in the registers indicates that over 6,000 burials took place in the burial ground as a whole throughout its history. The last person buried there was Amy Flora West, aged seventy-nine, on 11 October 1972.

It was not just inmates, but also members of staff who were buried there, and these are often noted in the remarks column, such as that for Alexander Macpherson who was buried on 24 October 1887, aged fifty-five. His entry records that 'The deceased was the Asylum Gardener & is buried nearly opposite to the Cemetery Chapel door'. Other comments made in the remarks column often include the deceased's faith (where it was not Church of England), or the fact that friends paid for or provided the coffin. Later register entries record the number of friends who attended each funeral.

As was typical of institutional burials, the majority of graves were not marked by headstones, but it is known that some certainly were. In 2006, asylum specialist Peter Cracknell visited the site and discovered nine surviving headstones. These were clearly not in their original locations, and were largely broken, appearing to have been piled close to the boundary wall, near to the mortuary chapel. Some related to asylum inmates, but over half related to members of staff or their families, such as Norman Henry Sibley, clerk and steward of the asylum, whose stone shows he was born at Whatstandwell, Derbyshire, and Eliza Holt, mother of the resident asylum minister, Neville A. Holt, who died in 1910, aged eighty. There were also gravestones for two nurses, Helen Blanche Mott, who died on 29 December 1901, aged thirty-one, and Mary E.K. Cahalan who died on 3 February 1898, aged twenty-six.

Study of other records held at the Kent History and Library Centre dating to 1968 and relating to alterations to the burial ground was fruitful, particularly relating to the application (and granting) of

The gravestone for Mary E.K. Cahalan, nurse at Chartham Asylum. (Peter Crucknell)

a faculty to remove headstones to the boundary wall of the burial ground (Reference DCb/E/F). This also included the levelling of the burial mounds in the disused section of the burial ground, and the erection of a dividing fence or hedge between the disused section and that which was still in use. The paperwork accompanying the faculty application includes a plan of the burial ground. This shows the locations of the burial ground's two chapels (a general chapel and a mortuary chapel) and, more interestingly, the location of each headstone still standing in the disused area of the burial ground in 1968. The plan also records the deceased's name and date of death, this information most likely being taken from the headstone inscription. Twenty-one headstones were recorded on the plan, including two children (Irene and Eric Holt), and the document also confirms that Alexander MacPherson was indeed buried 'nearly opposite the mortuary chapel door'. However, there was a mistake somewhere – either on the plan, in the burial register or perhaps on his headstone – for his date of death appears to post-date that of his burial! The plan also shows that the area of the burial ground still being used was that furthest away from the mortuary chapel.

The correspondence makes interesting reading. The Diocesan Advisory Committee (see Chapter 2 p 42) initially refused permission for re-siting the headstones, wishing instead to preserve them in situ, so that the original character of the burial ground could be maintained. However, the hospital chaplain, the Revd Martin, countered this with a two-point argument which won the day. 'Headstones when standing in isolation attract the attention of certain types of patients. Indeed, many of them, particularly crosses, have been broken. Blending with the background against the boundary walls they would escape such unwelcome attention'. He continued, 'The headstones in their present positions are the main difficulty in maintaining the grounds in a manner becoming its character. The labour position being very difficult, it was proposed to use a power mower, the use of which at regular intervals would keep the ground in first class condition.'

The Revd Martin and the hospital committee got their way, and a faculty was duly granted and one hopes he and the hospital committee enjoyed looking at their bowling green lawn.

The asylum closed in 1993 and while the general hospital site has been largely redeveloped for housing, it retains some of the original buildings. Apart from the site of the mortuary chapel, which has since been rebuilt as a modern dwelling, the burial grounds have not been built on, but are fenced off and form part of the grounds of this dwelling.

Using historic OS maps via the Kent County Council Heritage Maps app (**https://webapps.kent.gov.uk/KCC.HeritageMaps.Web. Sites.Public/Default.aspx**), in conjunction with Google Earth, produced some very useful results, and helped clarify the exact location of the old burial ground site in relation to the present-day development. In addition, a geophysical survey had been carried out prior to the redevelopment of the workhouse site to determine the extent of the burials and which land could easily be developed.[18] Although the geophysical survey results were useful for determining overall coverage of burials, the images provided by Google Earth's historic timeline were more interesting. Those for 1960, 2007 and 2019 were particularly clear, revealing many neat rows of burials and individual grave sites.

An aerial view of the burial ground of St Augustine's Asylum, Chartham, Kent, from 1960, clearly showing the neat alignment of graves in planned regular rows. (Google Earth Image: Historic Timeline: Kent County Council 2021).

Chapter 4

CEMETERIES AND CREMATORIA – THE NINETEENTH CENTURY ONWARDS

An increasing lack of burial space in towns and cities, and accompanying sanitary issues, were to be key drivers of major burial reform in the nineteenth century. This resulted in a massive shift towards burial outside the churchyard, typically in privately-run, and often very large, commercial cemeteries, or locally administered burial board cemeteries. The twentieth century then witnessed the slow but steady rise of cremation as a more popular alternative to inhumation, and the establishment of crematoria. Cremation had become more popular than burial by the 1990s.

Whether you have decided to visit a cemetery to hunt for a specific grave, or whether you are drawn in simply out of curiosity, there is a lot to observe and learn within the cemetery walls. It benefits both family and local historians to be aware of the different types of cemetery and how they evolved. If you are looking for particular burial, it is also vital to identify all those which were open, and actively burying, at that time, to ensure all cemeteries have been considered in your searches.

There is far more to cemeteries than many people at first realize. A comprehensive appreciation of their history is irretrievably bound up with many different branches of the arts and science, ranging from architecture and landscape design, through to horticulture, medicine and public health. It was the convergence of new schools of thought within these various branches of science and the arts, which came to define the way in which we buried our dead in this period.

The origins of cemeteries in the nineteenth and early twentieth century: lack of burial space and the promotion of the garden or landscape cemetery

The parish churchyard was the most typical resting place for our ancestors up to the nineteenth century. But burial space was running short, especially in urban areas, where the acute rise in the population was causing issues as early as the second half of the seventeenth century. By 1851, deaths in London had risen to 2,360,000 from a figure of just under one million only fifty years earlier.[1]

Lack of burial space was exacerbated by the increasing use of gravestones, together with a growing aversion to the recycling of earlier graves. Regular clearing of burials, with old bones housed in charnel houses and ossuaries, was not enough to stem the tide of the overcrowded dead. Concerns were raised about the detrimental effect on public health, caused by gases emitted from rotting corpses in urban churchyards, and partially decomposed corpses were frequently exposed when new burials took place. This was most problematic in the City of London where churchyards sat cheek by jowl with housing, and were disproportionally tiny compared to population density. Scandals such as that of the Enon Cemetery mentioned in Chapter 3, and periodic outbreaks of cholera from the 1830s, added to public concern.

Another issue was insufficient unconsecrated burial space. Nonconformist burial grounds were relatively few in number. As we have seen, consecrated ground was the remit of the Church of England. Many Nonconformists saw burial in consecrated ground as unacceptable, since it was specifically associated with a Church to which they did not belong, and with whose doctrines many fundamentally disagreed. By the early 1800s, there was a growing call for a rethink regarding the practice of burying in churches and churchyards, in favour of out-of-town burial grounds, unaffiliated to any religious denomination. These could offer a more pleasant environment for burial and, more importantly, alleviate the health risks increasingly associated with burials in churches and urban churchyards. They could also provide burials in both consecrated and unconsecrated ground, a concept which appealed to many. There was commensurate interest not only from those concerned with public health, but also from specialists in many fields: landscape designers, architects, horticulturalists, and also business entrepreneurs. Specialists in all these fields were keen to promote a wide range of ideas; some philanthropic ideas for improving sanitation and public health, some led by a strong desire to promote the arts and science, e.g., architecture and horticulture. Many believed trees helped to absorb dangerous vapours which spread disease through the air, while beautiful planting schemes would also play an important part in the new-style cemeteries, encouraging an air of tranquillity and oneness with nature, and providing a much more pleasant setting for burial and visiting graves. This was in a stark contrast to many urban churchyard burials which took place in cramped, smelly and grimy surroundings. Other ideas were driven by business entrepreneurs, who could see lucrative profits in the burial market.

Such cemeteries would not only provide landscaped grounds with considered planting schemes, but also afford the opportunity to foster the appreciation and development of the fine arts. Architecture could be displayed via sepulchral architecture (memorials) and cemetery buildings such as chapels and mortuaries. Over the years, the idea of carefully landscaped burial grounds, often accompanied by architecturally themed buildings and mausolea, took hold and flourished, followed later by a more formal garden-style of planting.

During the eighteenth century, there had been a trend among landed gentry to build mausolea on their estates. These were stately buildings containing burial chambers for the family dead. They were designed to architecturally impress, and acted as status symbols. In the churchyard, funeral monuments ranging from simple headstones through to grander

This early-Victorian print of Kensal Green Cemetery, London, clearly illustrates the recreational, horticultural and architectural aspects of cemeteries, alongside their funerary purpose, here emphasized by the family in mourning by the grave at the front of the picture. (Author's collection)

chest tombs (and occasional mausolea) typically took a poor second place to the church, which naturally dominated the churchyard. In the proposed new cemeteries, the monuments were to be the primary focus, set against a landscape of horticultural or sylvan elegance, and act as fitting memorials to the dear departed. Many monuments were also to be works of art in their own right.

Cemeteries were not just to be places for burying the dead, but very much places for the living, who would be encouraged to take walks and find peace among the setting. This was not all. Professor Curl, in his book *The Victorian Celebration of Death,* astutely points out that the 'benefits of cemeteries might seem startling, even excessive, but many more advantages were to accrue in the next couple of decades; cemeteries were held to be good for morals, public health, virtue, education, the development of artistic taste, sentiment, kindness, appreciation of sculpture and architecture, instruction in botany and landscape-gardening, and much else'.

Overseas influences

Shortage of urban burial space was not confined to the UK, but was very much an issue on the Continent. In Paris, the notorious Holy Innocents cemetery (adjacent to the church of that name) was closed in 1780 due to overcrowding. In 1876, the human remains were transferred to new catacombs formed out of an old quarry works beneath the Plain of Montrouge, south of Paris. It was in France that the idea of the modern out-of-town cemetery first really took hold. The first was Père Lachaise, which opened east of Paris in 1804.

Père Lachaise was a great influence on Fir Park Cemetery, which opened in Glasgow in 1831. Situated on a hillside overlooking the city, it was already an established arboretum, making it an ideal candidate for the conversion to a landscape-style cemetery. It was, in turn, influential on its counterparts in England and Wales.

Further inspiration was found in colonial Asia, where out-of-town cemeteries had also been established. The English cemeteries at Surat in Gujarat, India, and the South Cemetery in Calcutta, which date to the seventeenth and eighteenth century respectively, provided extensive out-of-town burial areas. One great advantage of these burial sites was there was ample room to build grand, high-status monuments with which to impress society. Death was always such a good opportunity to show off the family wealth! There was also competition between the English and Dutch settlers in Surat, who strove to out-do each other with their funerary monuments. America was also a forerunner in terms of cemetery design. Despite the much sparser population, some American towns suffered overcrowding in burial grounds, and there was much concern about the spread of disease; in this case yellow fever. This led to the establishment of several cemeteries situated away from towns by the late eighteenth and first half of the nineteenth century. These cemeteries were good examples for those pushing forward the new cemetery movement in England and Wales.

Barriers to the cemetery movement and the growth of private cemeteries

Change was not straightforward, and there were several barriers. The Church of England perceived that burial in cemeteries, as opposed to the parish churchyard, would weaken the ties of its parishioners to the church. Another major concern was the substantial loss of revenue from fees for burials and the erection of memorials: these were an important source of income for the incumbent of each parish. After much discussion, this problem was alleviated by a system which arranged for each incumbent to take a share of the burial fee every time one of his parishioners was buried in consecrated ground in a cemetery. He also took a percentage of the fees for any gravestone or memorial erected. This arrangement continued until the Burial Act of 1900. One further challenge was the necessity for an individual Act of Parliament to be passed to establish each cemetery; this being a requirement until 1847. Despite all the challenges, the returns proved well worth the effort.

The hopes and dreams of those calling for burial reform started to be realized from the 1820s, with the opening of cemeteries to serve bursting city populations, notably in the industrial towns of the north, such as Manchester and Liverpool. The great majority of cemeteries established between the 1820s and 1840s were joint stock companies, whereby investors received an annual dividend based on the profits made. Many were inter-denominational and specifically targeted unhappy Nonconformists who sought alternative options to burial courtesy of the established Church. While these early cemeteries often purported to be on the outskirts of town, the fast-growing urban population meant that most were surrounded by housing within a relatively short space of time, and burial space soon began to run out, presenting the same old problem.

Low Hill Cemetery, also known as the Liverpool Necropolis and later as Toxteth Park Cemetery, was a largely Nonconformist cemetery founded in 1825. The weekly magazine *The Mirror of Literature, Amusement, and Instruction* carried out a detailed report on the cemetery in 1830, which nicely sums up the circumstances surrounding its opening.

'The new cemetery, called the "Low Hill General Cemetery" has been established by a number of persons of various religious faith and persuasion with a view of altering the custom that has hitherto prevailed of interring the dead amidst a dense population and also at the same time of giving that decency and retirement to the ceremony and security against depredations, that is so peculiarly gratifying to surviving friends.

The cemetery contains about 24,000 superficial square yards. The form of the enclosure is an oblong square secured by a thick brick wall, thirteen feet high.

The house of the registrar and the chapel, are in Grecian style of architecture, built after a design of Mr. John Foster, jun., of Liverpool. The front of the buildings and the adjoining wall are of cut stone. A border of ten feet wide immediately adjoining the interior side of the wall, and surrounding the whole ground, is set apart for an arcade, or colonnade, roofed with slate and railed in by ornamental iron-work, set upon a stone plinth; this border will be used for tombs and any monumental inscription, table, or work of sculpture, that may be erected, and will be placed against the wall at the head of the respective tombs.

The centre of the ground is appropriated to vaults and graves, laid out in regular order, and numbered according to a plan that may be seen at the registrar's office. Each corpse interred is regularly registered in the books of the institution.

The chapel will be at the service of such persons who may wish to use it; and any religious funeral ceremony may be performed in it by the minister, or other person chosen by the parties who may require its use....

Such part of the ground as is not immediately wanted for graves is planted with ornamental shrubbery, under the direction of Mr. Shepherd, curator of the Botanic Garden.

For the purpose of greater security, a watchman will at all times of the night be upon the ground.

A committee will at all times have a superintending control and will take care that nothing offensive, ludicrous, or in evident bad taste, shall appear among the monumental inscriptions or in any other way....

The Cemetery is the property of a public company; and the expense of the whole was at first stated at £8,000.

The funds of the company may be considered in a prosperous condition; the shares yielded 8½ per cent.

A Cemetery of this description has likewise been formed at Manchester, the shares in which yield 12½ percent. At Cheltenham too, a similar project is mooting, and sooner or later this salutary plan of interment will be adopted by the inhabitants of all large towns.'

Low Hill Cemetery, Liverpool, c.1830. The entrance was dominated by two substantial lodges in the Greek Revival style. Today Grant Gardens is situated on the site of the cemetery. Drawn by T. Allom. Engraved by Robert Wallis. (Author's collection)

Chris Brooks, in his book, *Mortal Remains*, states that its design, by Liverpool's leading architect John Foster, was 'Restrainedly dramatic' and that there 'the awareness of the cemetery's functional relationship to the city in whose architectural display it joined, at once useful and ornamental, embodied, for the first time in England the self-consciousness that marks a new building type. From that point the cemetery [as a building type] began to acquire its own architectural identity. But it was an identity that was not to become fixed to any one model'. Low Hill was closed in the 1890s due to health risks and is now the site of Grant Gardens. The walls and lodges were taken down in 1913.[2]

A rival cemetery, St James', opened in 1829. Like Low Hill it was a joint stock cemetery, but it was affiliated to the Church of England. Also designed by John Foster, it was very different in style and in many ways more impressive. Foster used the opportunities provided by the contrasting height and depth of the old quarry to great effect with a series of dramatic inclined roads, flanked by catacombs cut from the surrounding rock, down which funeral processions could progress into the cemetery.

These early joint stock cemeteries were soon realizing impressive dividends. If not always quite as high as those quoted by *The Mirror of Literature*, they proved that independent burial grounds set in impressive grounds, and aimed at members of the established Church, or mixed

View of St James' Cemetery, Liverpool, looking north, by Thomas Mann Baynes and Rest Fenner, dated 1829. Note the catacombs to the right of the picture utilizing the former quarry cliffs. (stjamescemetery.co.uk)

faith denominations, was indeed a winning formula, as the business entrepreneurs had predicted. Deborah Wiggins, in her thesis *The Burial Acts. Cemetery Reform in Great Britain 1815–1914,* quotes a general expected return of five to six percent for the cemetery companies, and they provided a worthwhile investment opportunity for middle class Victorians.[3]

In addition, the new cemeteries were practical, providing a wide selection of burial options, including earth-cut graves, brick-lined graves, vaults and catacombs, and offering plenty of space where fine mausolea could be erected, if expense was no object. Another perceived advantage of the cemetery environment was that the dead would be safer from the ravages of grave robbers. Catacombs and vaults would be far more difficult to penetrate than an ordinary grave site in the earth, and cemeteries were walled and locked at night, often with watchmen to look after them. Having said this, nothing was totally secure, since groundsmen and watchmen could be bribed!

Kensal Green Cemetery and the growth of provincial private cemeteries, London

In 1830 the barrister George Frederick Carden, one of the main forces behind the cemetery movement, formed the General Cemetery Company and applied for a private bill in parliament to open a cemetery at Kensal

Green, in open countryside west of London. No doubt encouraged by an outbreak of cholera in the city, the bill was passed in 1832. Permission had, therefore, been granted for the establishment of the first large-scale cemetery to serve the metropolis.

Kensal Green Cemetery opened in 1833. Formed of fifty-five acres (a further twenty-two were later added), the new cemetery proved very popular and by 1839 the original shares had doubled in value.[4] The cemetery was divided into two different sections: thirty-nine acres allocated for burials in consecrated ground, and fifteen acres for those who wished to be buried in unconsecrated ground. This was an important distinction, and increased its appeal immensely. Its popularity grew further after 1843, when the Duke of Sussex chose to be buried there.

The business success of Kensal Green soon led to the founding of other cemeteries in London, notably West Norwood (1836), Highgate (1839), Abney Park (1840), Nunhead (1840), Brompton (1840) and Tower Hamlets (1841). They were later to become collectively known as the 'Magnificent Seven', this term first being used by historian Hugh Mellor in his book on London cemeteries in 1981. They all provided burials for Londoners in sites well away from residential dwellings. Significantly, apart from Abney Park, each catered for people of all faiths, consecrating some land for Anglicans, but leaving some unconsecrated to suit Nonconformists or those of other religions. Kensal Green also had two chapels, one Church of England and one for Dissenters. This became the norm where space and funds permitted, and was followed by all of the Magnificent Seven, apart from Abney Park. Abney Park was different in more ways than one. Not only did it predominantly cater for Nonconformists, but also, unlike the other six, it was not formed following an Act of Parliament, thus avoiding the requirement for a portion of the burial fees to be paid to the deceased's parochial clergyman.

Early-nineteenth-century city cemeteries, such as Low Hill and St James' in Liverpool, were key to proving how successful cemeteries could be, but it was the foundation of the large London cemeteries in the 1830s and 1840s that encouraged a wave of smaller-scale cemetery foundation in the provinces, such as at Cheltenham, Gloucester, Leeds, Newcastle, Nottingham, York, Exeter, Sheffield and Birmingham. While many of these provincial cemeteries were joint stock companies, some were financed privately by individuals. Abbey Cemetery in Bath was built on land bought by the Rector of Bath on behalf of the Church of England. Others were established by town councils. A good example of the last is Southampton General Cemetery, founded in 1846, designed

Literary influences on the cemetery movement

Newspapers were highly influential in stimulating debate about the need for burial reform in the early nineteenth century, but there was a range of other important literary influences.

John Claudius Loudon (1783–1843) was a botanist and landscape designer and his seminal book, *On the Laying Out, Planting and Managing of Cemeteries and on the Improvement of Churchyards*, published in 1843, was the first on cemetery design and one of the greatest influences on the subject. Highly detailed and well-illustrated, he exhaustively expounded his concept of the landscape, or garden-style, cemetery, which included clear labelling of plants to educate those who visited. He combined this with practical advice on how to achieve all he promoted. Once a cemetery became full, he believed the monuments should be preserved, and the space used for quiet contemplation. Apart from Southampton, he also designed the cemeteries at Histon Road, Cambridge, and Bath Abbey, but his work influenced the design and planting of many more.

George Walker (1807–1884) was a London surgeon and ardent campaigner for burial reform. His 1839 publication, *Gatherings from Grave-Yards, Particularly Those in London*, was pivotal in spreading the word about the risk to public health from burial in overcrowded urban churchyards, and in persuading the government to legislate against this practice. He incorporated keen facts with graphic descriptions of the noxious and dangerous state of metropolitan churchyards to illustrate his point. His work also influenced the social reformer and civil servant Edwin Chadwick, whose own *Report on the Sanitary Condition of the Labouring Population of Great Britain* (1842) proved links between the ill health of the poor, and inadequate sanitation and led to the 1848 Public Health Act. You can read Walker's book via **archive.org** at **https://archive.org/details/b21902963**.

Between 1742 and 1745, the poet Edward Young wrote and published his epic poem, *Night Thoughts*. Written in nine sections, each one representing one night, it constituted Young's thoughts on death, and was one of several works of this time idealising death and the individual. It was republished with a set of illustrations by William Blake in 1797, and is often cited as a contributory factor in the popularity of the landscape cemetery movement. Young's poem can be found at **https://archive.org/stream/nightthoughtson00youniala/nightthoughtson00youniala_djvu.txt**.

by one of the staunchest promoters of the cemetery movement, John Loudon (see above).

After the First World War, other styles of cemeteries emerged, moving away from the landscape design and incorporating more stylistic planting schemes based around formal grid plans, infilled with borders of bedding plants or shrubs, and also lawn cemeteries where lawn was the predominant feature and promised ease of maintenance.

What these private commercial cemeteries did not do was to cater for the poor; they were not good for profits! It was the burial board cemeteries of the mid-nineteenth century which addressed this issue.

Burial board cemeteries: an answer to the burial crisis

The private cemeteries of the 1820s and 1830s went only part-way to resolving the burial crisis. From the 1840s, the government was increasingly concerned with the health issues associated with continued use of burial sites in many parish churchyards and the shortage of alternative burial options. Burial reform took a long time to achieve, and was accompanied by much debate, and a series of parliamentary Acts aimed to tackle the issues. It was an extremely bitty and long-winded process. Numerous nineteenth-century 'burial acts', in tandem with the Cemetery Clauses Act of 1847, the Cemetery Act of 1902 and new legislation relating to public health, finally resolved the burial crisis, as we shall see.

Two of the most significant burial acts were those of 1852 and 1853. These gave parish vestries the power to raise loans against the poor rate to fund new burial grounds. These were to be headed by 'burial boards' consisting of local ratepayers, the boards to be financially accountable to parish ratepayers, and their members to be elected periodically.

The Parish Vestry had dealt with the secular running of the parish since the sixteenth century. Among its many responsibilities, it took care of the poor and had power to levy a poor rate to do so. The tax was levied on everyone, not just members of the Church of England, and was another source of irritation to many, especially Nonconformists. Not only did they resent paying a tax to a Church to which they did not belong, but they also were not eligible for poor relief and, as we have seen, many preferred not to be buried in parish churchyards.

Stipulating that funds for the new burial board cemeteries should come from the poor rate was a clever idea, since the new cemeteries were to be non-denominational and to include both consecrated and unconsecrated ground. Nonconformists would, at last, feel they were getting something back for their money. It also meant that they could (and did) take an active part in the new burial boards. The 1852/3 legislation was permissive. Parishes were under no obligation to set up burial boards; only if they saw the need. There was also the option of joining together with neighbouring parishes to provide a common burial ground, if there was the demand. This helped obviate the situation where there were insufficient parish ratepayers to fund it. The rates for burials were also subsidized from the poor rate, making them much more affordable than the fees charged in the joint stock cemeteries. In addition, the boards were given the power to make their own decisions on a range of matters, including the fees paid to clergy and sextons for carrying out funeral services and burials, and whether grave plots were sold in perpetuity or for a limited time period. Where new burial grounds were not formed, parishes were encouraged to arrange for burials in any available private cemeteries.

The size and format of these new burial board cemeteries varied greatly. They included massive city cemeteries, such as the City of London Cemetery, and the Southern Cemetery in Chorlton, near Manchester, through to medium-sized town cemeteries and tiny rural

DOWLAIS CEMETERY.

Description of Grave, Interment, &c.	CONSECRATED GROUND.				UNCONSECRATED GROUND.				Searcher.
	Charges to be paid to the Board.	Fees payable to the Vicar.	Fees payable to the Clerk & Sexton.	Total Fees payable for Burial in Unconse-crated Ground.	Charges to be paid to the Board.	Offici-ating Minis-ter.	Grave Digger.	Total Fees payable for Burial in Unconse-crated Ground.	
	£ s. d.	£ s. d	£ s. d.	£ s. d.	£ s. d.	£ s. d.	£ s. d.	£ s. d	s. d.
Common Grave for Parishoners	0 5 3	3 6	0 4 6	0 13 3	0 5 3	2 6	3 0	0 10 9	..
If purchased in perpetuity (extra)	1 1 0	..	..	..	1 1 0	..	..	....	..
For re-opening a Common Grave, if within 3 yrs	0 3 0	3 6	0 4 6	0 11 0	0 3 0	2 6	3 0	0 8 6	..
Brick Grave	0 11 0	0 15 0	0 12 6	1 18 6	0 11 0	5 0	5 6	1 1 6	..
If purchased in perpetuity (extra)	2 2 0	..	..	..	2 2 0	..	..	....	..
For re-opening Brick Grave	0 7 6	5 0 0	3 6	0 16 0	0 7 6	5 0 0	2 0	0 14 6	..
For ditto, if purchased	0 2 6	5 0 0	3 6	0 11 0	0 2 6	5 0 0	2 0	0 9 6	..
Vault, 2 corpses abreast	2 19 0	1 5 0	1 5 0	5 9 0	2 19 0	0 18 6	1 5 0	4 16 6	..
If more than 9 feet, per foot extra	0 15 0	..	..	..	0 15 0	..	..	....	..
For re-opening	0 15 0	0 10 6	5 0	1 10 6	0 15 0	0 10 6	5 0	1 10 6	..
Vault, 4 corpses abreast	5 5 0	1 5 6	1 16 0	8 6 6	5 5 0	0 10 6	16 0	7 11 6	..
For re-opening	1 1 0	0 10 6	5 0	1 16 6	1 1 0	0 10 6	5 0	1 16 6	..
If more than 9 feet deep, per foot extra	1 1 0	..	..	..	1 1 0	..	..	....	..
For interments in select situations for a Common or Brick Grave	0 10 6	..	..	..	0 10 6	..	..	....	..
For a Vault	1 1 0	..	..	..	1 1 0	..	..	....	..
For tolling the Bell for an hour or part of an hour	0 0 6	..	..	..	0 0 6	..	..	....	..
Entry of Registry of Vault or Grave in perpetuity	0 2 6	..	..	..	0 2 6	..	..	....	..
Certificate thereof	0 2 6	..	..	..	0 2 6	..	..	....	..
For erecting a Tomb over a Common Grave	1 1 0	..	..	..	1 1 0	..	..	....	..
Ditto in Brick Grave	1 1 0	..	..	..	1 1 0	..	..	....	..
Ditto over any Vault	2 2 0	..	..	..	2 2 0	..	..	....	..
For Railing round any Brick or Common Grave	0 10 6	..	..	..	0 10 6	..	..	....	..
For Railing round any Vault	1 1 0	..	..	..	1 1 0	..	..	....	..
Searchers, &c.									
Searching Register of Burial first year	..	..	..	..	..	..	..	....	1 6
Second year	..	..	..	..	..	..	..	....	0 6
Certificate of Burial	..	..	..	..	..	..	..	....	2 6

This advert placed by the Dowlais Burial Board (Glamorgan) in an edition of the weekly newspaper Y Gwladgarwr, *dated 25 August 1860, provides an insight into the many different charges associated with burial and the erection of memorials, as well as fees for register searches. (National Library of Wales)* cemeteries. They not only provided new burial space, but some were also an important source of publicly funded architectural patronage, notably in larger cities. Many architectural firms specializing in cemeteries emerged as a result of the 1852/53 legislation. Competitions were held for architects to design local cemeteries (just as they had been for the designs of cemeteries such as Kensal Green and Highgate. Chris Brooks' book *Mortal Remains* is an excellent source of information on this topic. He lists many of these firms, specifying the geographical influence of each in terms of the cemeteries they designed.[5]

Burial board cemeteries proved a great success, and effectively solved the problem of lack of burial space in both urban areas and more populous rural parishes. Following the Local Government Act of 1894, they passed into the management of the newly formed local authorities at district, town and parish level, and in 1899, the responsibilities of the London burial boards were passed to the newly formed Metropolitan Borough Councils.

To read more about the individual Burial Acts see pages 97–99 and also John's Clarke's website at **www.john-clarke.co.uk/burial_acts.html**.

The decline of the Victorian cemetery in the twentieth century

While many of the privately-run (non-burial board) Victorian cemeteries were established with the hope that they would mature into beautifully landscaped settings, sadly the cost of maintaining the buildings, grounds and the planting schemes proved too much. Signs of decline began to appear by the 1870s, exacerbated by constantly rising labour prices from the turn of the twentieth century. This meant maintenance costs increasingly outweighed the income brought from burials, so that by the first half of the twentieth century the great majority of these cemeteries were suffering badly from neglect, and were no longer commercially viable. One way to reduce costs was to clear away older monuments.

Many cemetery managers failed to see the benefit in preserving older monuments for their historical interest, or as works of art. New legislation meant it was no longer possible to recycle grave space as frequently, while the burial board cemeteries attracted more business, as they offered much cheaper burial rates. While the grander Victorian cemeteries were hit hardest, as cremation grew more popular, burial board cemeteries were in turn affected, as they lost business to the crematoria. Those cemeteries that continued to flourish, generally speaking, had a crematorium within their grounds.

The Disused Burial Grounds Act of 1884 made it unlawful to erect any buildings upon a disused burial ground, except for the purpose of

Woodgrange Park Cemetery – a case of sheer neglect

Woodgrange Park Cemetery in East London was founded in 1888. As a teenager in 1985, I made a visit. I was not just looking for the grave of my great-grandparents already mentioned in Chapter 1, but also for that of my grandmother Florence Heritage and her young son, Clarence. I was shocked by the state of the cemetery, which was totally overgrown with brambles and nettles in many places. I came out scratched and bleeding, having failed to find the graves. This was sadly typical of Woodgrange Park and other London cemeteries at this time, although Woodgrange is probably one of the worst examples. An Act of Parliament in 1993 exceptionally allowed the owners of Woodgrange to sell some of the cemetery grounds for housing development, this being contrary to the 1884 Disused Burial Grounds Act. Some of the funds received went into a restoration and maintenance fund for the cemetery. Around 14,000 bodies were exhumed and re-interred elsewhere in the cemetery, and a memorial garden created on that spot. Despite the funds from the sale, the cemetery is still in a state of partial neglect, and its chapel was razed to the ground in 2008 after a fire caused costly damage.

Another example of neglect came in 1987, when Westminster Borough Council sold its cemeteries at Mill Hill, East Finchley and Hanwell (all of which were still in use) to a private company for a matter of pence, in order to save money on what it saw as exorbitant maintenance costs. The new owner immediately sold these cemeteries on for a massive profit of £1.25 million and the subsequent owner was not bound by law to maintain them properly. They fell into a state of severe neglect until, in 1987, a Local Government Ombudsman ruled that the council must buy the graves back, and that the original sale was unlawful.[6]

These are just two examples to illustrate some of the threats to cemeteries in the modern age. In some places, local authorities have stepped in to bail out ailing private cemeteries, but in many cases the legislation under which they were established has made this difficult.

enlarging a church, chapel, meeting house, or other place of worship. Many cemeteries have, therefore, been converted to parks and recreation grounds following their closure, such as Victoria Park Cemetery, a short-lived private cemetery in Bethnal Green. Opened in 1845, it closed in 1876 and became Meath Gardens. St James' Cemetery, Liverpool, was converted to public gardens during the late 1960s and early 1970s. The majority of gravestones were removed from their original sites and laid one on top of the other at the Upper Parliament Street end of the cemetery and grassed over to make a sloped embankment. Others were moved to the edge of the cemetery, and some transferred to the nearby cathedral to be used as paving stones at its back entrance.[7]

There are some exceptions to the 1884 Act, such as Mile End Cemetery in Portsmouth, which now forms part of the car ferry terminal. In this case special dispensation was granted by the government to leave the burials in situ, although the contents of the vaults were reinterred elsewhere.

Ironically, it is partly as a result of neglect that many cemeteries have become havens for wildlife, and with careful management this aspect can now be enhanced. In recent years, many Friends' Associations have been formed to help preserve and maintain some cemeteries. The National Federation of Cemetery Friends at **www.cemeteryfriends.com** lists all registered groups, and many offer cemetery tours and information about the cemetery concerned.

The evolution of crematoria

Cremation is today far more popular than burial in the UK. Although cremation was used by Christian communities prior to the fifth century, the Church later deemed it unacceptable, and promoted the belief that the body had to be present for resurrection to take place. By the seventeenth century, however, the idea of cremation was being discussed, both in the UK and on the Continent, as a much more hygienic way of disposing of the dead, and a means of saving burial space.

Ideas regarding the advantages of cremation were particularly well advanced in Italy, and the subject was keenly promoted at a medical conference in Florence in 1869. Following further research by professors Gorini and Brunetti, the latter put his cremation chamber on display at the Vienna Exhibition of 1873, together with a specimen of the ashes it produced. He also published reports of his research and practical work in this field. This was, in turn, noted by Queen Victoria's surgeon, Sir Henry Thompson, who went on to become one of the strongest advocates of cremation in the UK. He argued that not only was it more affordable than burial, but also that it did not spread disease. Thompson founded the Cremation Society in 1874, and a growing lobby for cremation began to evolve, although there was much opposition. In 1879 the society arranged for Professor Gorini to conduct a test cremation on the body of a horse, on land bought by the society at Woking in Surrey. Although the trial was a success in terms of proving that cremation was an effective means of disposal, there was a group of locals opposed to the idea. They appealed to the Home Secretary, who banned any further cremations until the matter had been investigated by Parliament. While cremation was not actually illegal, there was a lack of clarity in the law as to whether or not it could be carried out legally.

In 1882, Captain Hanham of Blandford in Dorset expressly requested a cremation for his wife and mother, and the society once again applied to the Home Secretary for permission to carry out cremations. Permission was again refused, but the captain constructed a crematorium on his own land and cremated his wife and mother himself. He died a year later and was also cremated. Although the government took no action against the family, in January 1884 an eccentric Welshman, Dr William Price, attempted to cremate the body of his infant son. He was put on trial for illegal disposal of a corpse. The trial served to clarify the status of cremation in the UK. The court ruled that cremation was legal, as long as no nuisance was caused to others in the process. The first person to be cremated following this ruling was Jeanette Caroline Pickersgill, who was cremated at the Cremation Society's crematorium in Woking in March 1885. Two further cremations followed that year. In 1902, the government passed the Act for Cremation which came into force on 1 April 1903. This still forms the basis of legislation regarding the running of crematoria in England and Wales today.

The popularity of cremation took a while to build. In 1900, 0.07 percent of bodies were cremated in the UK, but this had only risen to 0.87 percent by 1930, 3.85 percent by 1940 and 7.8 percent by 1945. Cremation numbers steadily increased after the Second World War, as issues with burial space continued. In 1940, there were just fifty-six crematoria in the UK, but this had risen to 148 by 1960, 225 by 1990, and 273 in 2014. Cremation numbers correspondingly rose: 34.7 percent in 1960, 69.58 percent in 1990 and 74.8 percent in 2014, with 78.13 percent of bodies being disposed of in this manner in 2019.[8]

Cremation is cheaper than burial, since there are no costs involved in digging graves, while crematoria also cost less to run, since there are none of the expenses involved in the upkeep of older burial spaces, and plots can be reused within a relatively short space of time. Plaques and memorials associated with the burial of ashes in crematoria are leasehold and for a limited period only, at which point another fee can be levied for a renewal, or a new memorial can be placed, thus bringing in further income for the cemetery owners.

In 1937, the Croydon
Crematorium Company
launched an advertising
campaign to promote its
services. (From Surrey
Mirror by permission
of Surrey Mirror/Reach
Licensing).

CROYDON CREMATORIUM CO.
Ltd.
Phone Head Office: UPLands 5500.
8, PURLEY PARADE, High St., PURLEY.
Also at 118, Brighton-road, Purley, and
518, London-road, Thornton Heath, Croydon
CREMATORIUM FEES £4 4s. 0d.
Cremation now less expensive than earth
burial. No neglected graves. No mainten-
ance for relatives.
Brochure and full particulars on applica-
tion.

Some crematoria have columbaria, which are walls with built-in niches, in which cremated remains can be stored, usually with a small plaque commemorating the deceased. The name originates from the Latin word for dove, since the niches resemble the openings in a dovecote.

A growing trend in the twenty-first century is for the scattering of ashes at locations other than within crematoria grounds. This is often at a particular place favoured by the deceased. In 2019, the Cremation Society reported that the total percentage of ashes removed from crematoria after cremation was 79.74.[9] There are also some private commercial initiatives to establish columbaria outside crematoria where ashes can be stored.

Burial procedures and types of graves

Apart from some general stipulation as to the location of cemeteries, and regulations on grave depths established by the 1847 Cemetery Clauses Act, cemeteries have always had their own by-laws governing the way they operate. Procedures relating to the selling of grave space can therefore vary.

Private or purchased grave
A private or purchased grave is almost always one where the right to burial in a particular plot of land is reserved for one person, or family, exclusively. The grave might be an earth-cut or brick-lined grave, or a vault. Extra fees were levied each time someone was buried, and for the erection of any memorial. There are always exceptions. At Margate Cemetery in Kent, a person could be buried in a private grave without the family purchasing the exclusive burial rights to that space. However, if the rights to the grave were not purchased, then no headstone could be placed. In a case like this, the cemetery could ask the family to buy those rights if the grave was reopened for a later burial. On rare occasions, fixed-term burial rights in specified graves were sold on to an unrelated

person after the term had expired, meaning two or more unrelated people could rest in the grave space. Until 1977, private grave spaces were just that – private: no one else could be buried there, unless the exclusive burial right had been sold with an expiry date. The Local Authorities Cemeteries Order of 1977 limited rights of burial to a maximum of 100 years. In some cemeteries, this is now set at fifty years, and after that point the grave space is eligible for reuse. Commonwealth War Graves are excepted from this ruling and can still be granted in perpetuity.

Common, unpurchased or public graves
These graves catered for families or individuals who could not afford to buy the sole rights to a burial space. Dug to a great depth, to take a large number of burials, contrary to popular belief burial in a common grave did not necessarily indicate a pauper burial. A family still had to pay for the grave space, and the first and deepest burial in a common grave might cost more than later ones, since it involved more digging. In Victorian times, public graves were commonly dug to a maximum depth of 18 feet and then gradually filled upwards, but more recently it has become 12 feet. They contain the graves of many unrelated people. Many cemetery burials took place in common graves and this practice continues today.

Common graves are dug in both consecrated and unconsecrated ground, according to the faith of those to be buried, where this is known. Depending on the cemetery and demand for common grave burials, graves are sometimes not completely backfilled, but temporarily covered with a wooden plank until each is full. While there are not usually any memorials on a common grave, cemetery staff will have a record of the location of each grave and the names of those buried there. Some cemeteries allow you to retrospectively erect a simple marker in memory of a family member buried in a common grave. My great-grandmother, Mary Wilson, was buried in a common grave at Whitton Cemetery in Middlesex in 1926. Having located her resting place, I paid for a simple wooden cross with her name on it to be erected on the site, although this no longer survives. Some cemeteries also offered so-called 'Inscription Graves' as a variation on the theme of a common grave. The only difference was that a headstone could be erected, but it served to commemorate two or more (usually) unrelated people.

The 1977 Local Authorities Cemeteries Order set a minimum of three feet of earth to separate any coffin from ground level, or two feet if the coffin is of perishable material. There has to be at least a six-inch layer of earth separating the new coffin from any other coffin previously buried in the grave. Some cemeteries bury deeper, while some faiths require burials at different depths. For example, Muslim burials must be a minimum of four feet and are all single-depth burials.

Pauper's grave
This is a colloquial term for burials paid for by the local authorities because the family could not afford burial fees, or no family could be located. Today, responsibility for such burials still lies with the local authority, either where the deceased died, or where they usually resided. From 1948, these burials officially became known as Public Assistance Burials.

Memorial styles
Cemeteries have always formed their own policies on the nature of memorials allowed within their walls, and the types and costs of grave spaces offered. When Kensal Green opened in London in 1833, a decision was taken not to place any restrictions upon the style of monuments erected, and many other cemeteries followed this example.

The types of memorials in those cemeteries established in the nineteenth century may vary greatly, ranging from works-of-art by well-known sculptors through to humble headstones representing the ordinary man in the street. From the later twentieth century, many cemeteries have become dominated by row upon row of uniformly shaped black or white headstones, with an increasing trend to include photographs of the deceased. This is partly as a result of families being offered standard packages by funeral directors and stonemasons, and having no knowledge of what other options are possible. Occasionally a bespoke stone will shine out. The most common stones used for cemetery memorials in the twentieth and twenty-first century are marble, nabresina (an Italian limestone) and granite.

Historically, symbolism on cemetery gravestones is similar to that found in parish churchyards, in particular in the crossover period of 1853–1900, when we see the transition from burial in the cemetery, as opposed to burial in the churchyard, becoming the norm However, there is typically greater variety among cemetery memorials and, these days, erection of memorials in parish churchyards is subject to stringent regulations set by the diocese. I look in detail at gravestones and memorials in Chapter 5.

Architectural styles of cemetery buildings
Different architectural styles were in vogue for cemetery buildings at different times, and often reflect contemporary fashions in architecture,

Cemetery chapels not only served the practical purpose of accommodating funeral services, but were also a chance for the architect to enhance the cemetery's architectural style. The chapel at Brompton Cemetery, in west London, is designed in the Neo-Classical style and acts as a central focal point in the cemetery layout. (Author's collection)

although the designs and symbols used for mausolea and tombs often continued long after they had fallen out of favour elsewhere. In-depth study of architectural styles and fashions is beyond the scope of this book, but a book such as *Rice's Architectural Primer* provides a good introductory read (see Bibliography).

Locating your cemetery: which towns does it serve?

Looking at a paper or online copy of an Ordnance Survey Landranger or Explorer Map (**www.ordnancesurvey.co.uk**) will clearly show you the location of the cemetery. (Refer to Chapter 3 for further information on OS maps.) Which town or area it served, or serves, will depend on its origins, and could have changed with time, as new cemeteries sprang up, or new houses were built. If a commercially run cemetery, then there will be no designated 'catchment' area. As profit-making businesses, they did not charge an extra fee for burial of those from outside the local area and, as time passed, and a wider range of private cemeteries were established, many offered incentives and special offers which appealed to different types of clients. Families increasingly buried their loved ones in cemeteries further from home, perhaps choosing one that offered a better price, or a more attractive ambiance or outlook. Undertakers often received commission on burials and cremations, and many had arrangements with certain cemeteries to encourage their clients to select those cemeteries. In the 1930s, Streatham Park in south London paid a higher commission to undertakers than many other cemeteries, and therefore attracted burials from a wider area. It also had a very nice chapel and provided a decent range of burial options, so attracted a large number of burials. Greater choice for our ancestors can make it harder for you to locate a missing burial, as it means the deceased is less likely to have been buried in the cemetery closest to home, or to where he or she died.

Most cemeteries have their own website and you can make this a starting point to find out more about its history. I describe how to identify the particular cemetery where your ancestor is buried in Chapter 6. If the cemetery originated as a burial board cemetery, it will have been established to serve a parish or group of parishes, although some people from outside the area may also been buried there for a variety of reasons. To find out more about the origins of a particular cemetery, use online catalogues and original sources to extend your research. The respective catalogues of The National Archives, which covers England and Wales, and the National Library of Wales are worth searching, notably in connection with the opening and closing of cemeteries, as well as for references to the removal of graves (see also Chapter 7). The National Library of Wales has millions of pages of Welsh newspapers, which are freely available via its website, and make an excellent source when researching cemetery histories. Likewise, the British Newspaper Archive website provides access to digitized local newspapers from around the UK. It not free, but can also be accessed as part of a Findmypast subscription, although the search engine is not as powerful.

Cemetery names can evolve with time and this can cause confusion. West Norwood Cemetery, in the London Borough of Lambeth, is also known as the South Metropolitan Cemetery, while Bolton Cemetery, Lancashire, is also known as Tonge Cemetery. Following jurisdictional changes, it is now classified as Greater Manchester rather than Lancashire. St Marylebone Cemetery became East Finchley Cemetery, while the Islington and St Pancras Cemetery in North London is actually two adjacent cemeteries (see the Case Study on Islington and St Pancras cemeteries on page 95.)

Some cemeteries have received listed status. While this will usually be mentioned in the cemetery guide or website, you can also check the National Register of Historic Parks and Gardens site at https://historicengland.org.uk/listing.

Preparing for your visit and what to look for

Many cemeteries have detailed guides; many are available online and worth reading before you visit. Note the date the cemetery was established and read up about its history and who designed it. If you are looking for the opening date of a crematorium, the Cremation Society has a listing on their website. Look to see if a cemetery has a friends' group, as their website may provide a more detailed history than the official cemetery website. Rather than just digesting what has already been written, do your own thinking and seek out independent research tools in so doing. Go back to that OS map. Now consider not just which towns the cemetery might serve, but also ask yourself where the cemetery sits in the actual landscape. Having studied the modern map, as mentioned above, next use historic OS maps to get an idea of what the local landscape and environment would have been like when it was built. Compare with a modern-day map to see how much the outlook has changed. When it was built, it may have offered fine views across the countryside, or towards a particular town, city or beauty spot, which made it an attractive setting in which to bury people. If it was set on a hillside, it would have made a prominent feature overlooking whichever town lay beneath, and this in itself was a good form of marketing. The modern-day outlook might be quite different. Search The National Archives or local CRO catalogue for any surviving cemetery plans, which may show the original design and layout.

Check opening and closing times before you visit, especially if you are travelling some distance. Unlike churchyards, many cemeteries have set opening hours, which may vary according to the season. If you are seeking a specific grave, it helps to know the plot number in advance. However, even if you know this and have a cemetery plan, it is a good idea to contact the cemetery office before you visit. Staff will often provide a plan with the grave marked on it, and advise on accessibility. If it is an unmarked grave, they may offer to put a temporary marker on the site, given sufficient notice. Some cemeteries are extremely large and the numbering sequences can be confusing. Even with a plan and the plot and section number, it can still be tricky to find the site: in practice numbered rows of graves do not always follow on neatly from each other on the ground. One trick is to note where two rows abut each other and use this as a starting point, following that particular row of graves along until you find the one you are looking for.

When you are walking round the cemetery, keep an enquiring mind, noting any anomalies or points of interest that occur relating to burial locations, or particular surnames that repeat. Perhaps a modern stone, placed among stones of far greater age, relates to a family link between the old and the new? Look carefully at the inscriptions on your ancestors' gravestones, investigating any surnames which are unfamiliar to you and suggest a marriage into the family, or a member of a different branch of the family, who had closer ties with your own branch than you expected. (See Chapters 6 and 7 for information on memorial inscriptions.) Especially when visiting older cemeteries, you may notice that particular areas of the cemetery were being used at certain dates and some were favoured by the wealthy. Those graves with an elevated view or a sheltered location may have been more costly, or perhaps the cemetery favoured a more equal approach to burial, where spaces were filled chronologically?

Many graves lie unmarked by any memorial – not just public graves – and you may note large spaces in between gravestones as a result. Until the start of the twentieth century, the cost of memorials was beyond the means of most people, while others have simply not survived. You may notice a particularly prolific style or design of gravestone, or the frequent use of one particular symbol on several stones. Some symbols were particularly fashionable at different times or favoured by certain families, but it is also the case that people would copy stones they saw in situ because they liked the look of them.

Look too at the cemetery walls, as sometimes memorials will be attached to these and can easily be overlooked if you are concentrating on spotting ground-sited headstones or tombs. Cemetery gates were locked at night time and provided an added measure of security from grave robbers. The passing of the Anatomy Act in 1832 released bodies of paupers for medical dissection and the phenomenon of body snatching gradually died out, making security less of an issue.

When looking at the cemetery plan, don't just focus in on the grave you are looking for, but consider the overall design of the cemetery as well. During your background reading, you may have read about the original layout and what type of planting scheme was used. See how much of this remains in the current shape and planting of the cemetery. Over the years, the paths, drives and choice of planting may have evolved greatly, sometimes as part of new planting policies, but sometimes as a result of gradual evolution, or even neglect. If your visit to the cemetery is impromptu, see how observant you can be: look for patterns in the layouts of the paths and planting areas where relevant. Look at the trees. What types of trees are there? Are they planted in straight rows or clusters and how old do they look? Are some areas of the cemetery left as nature conservation areas? Or perhaps the cemetery is rather run down and nature is doing her own job of returning it to its original state, providing a haven for wildlife and plant species. Don't just look for people's names on the gravestones; look at styles and designs and look out for cemetery buildings too, thinking about the shapes and patterns used in the architecture. In some cases there will be two funeral chapels, one for Anglican and one for Dissenting

---

CASE STUDY

Islington and St Pancras Cemetery: the evolution of two neighbouring cemeteries

Back in the early 2010s, my husband and I were researching his ancestor Adeline Curling (née Woodman) who died on 1 February 1865 in Hoxton, London. A search of **deceasedonline.com** showed she was buried on 5 April 1888 in St Pancras Cemetery and furnished us with the burial plot reference: S12/150. The burial and grave registers showed that Adeline died in the workhouse and was buried in a common grave. Despite the fact we knew there would be no memorial, we decided to pay a visit. Although we were armed with the grave number, we failed to locate any grave space with a similar number, let alone the grave site itself! We had been fooled by the fact that the Islington and St Pancras Cemetery is actually two adjacent but independent cemeteries, each with its own grave plan and numbering system. No doubt many people will have had the same experience, not realizing they were actually searching in the wrong cemetery. Delving into the history of the cemetery is enlightening.

In 1852, the newly established burial board for St Pancras parish bought eighty-eight acres on Finchley Common to form its own cemetery. However, it sold thirty acres to the neighbouring parish of St Mary's, Islington, so it could establish their own burial board cemetery. While the two cemeteries sat side-by-side, they were independently owned and managed by the respective vestries. There was originally a fence running west to east between them and, although this was later removed, a dividing line still marks the course of the boundary. What makes it confusing, is that the two cemeteries were treated as one in terms of design, landscaping and layout. It is now the largest 'cemetery' in London (a further ninety-four acres having been added in 1877) and the two cemeteries are currently managed by the respective London Boroughs of Camden (St Pancras Cemetery) and Islington (Islington Cemetery).

services. They may appear almost identical, but the Anglican chapel will often have a bell cote over the gable end. In some cemeteries, they were combined into one building, with a dividing line demarcating the Anglican and non-Anglican halves, while in other cases the two were linked by a covered passageway, effectively making them one building. You may not be familiar with the names of the different architectural styles, but observation is key and will potentially enhance the enjoyment of your visit, as well as increase your understanding of the history of the cemetery and how it has evolved. One of the delights of visiting cemeteries is that they embrace so many potential topics of interest aside from genealogy and history, including horticulture, nature conservation and architecture.

Designated parish areas in cemeteries

Many larger cemeteries are divided into specific sections, sometimes by faith, but in some there may be areas reserved for people from a particular walk of life, or a specific parish. Ramsgate Cemetery in Kent, for example, had an entire section reserved for the neighbouring village of St Lawrence, which became subsumed into Ramsgate in the 1930s. Some London cemeteries had special arrangements with local parishes, or workhouses and other institutions, to bury their dead. Brookwood cemetery in Woking, Surrey, is a good example. Here, there are designated sections signposted with the names of individual parishes. Established in 1854, Brookwood remains a very active cemetery and is today one of the main places of burial for Surrey and London. It covers 400 acres and, like many large cemeteries, it also has sections for people of different faiths or from particular backgrounds. These include national communities, such as the Latvian and Russian communities, and separate sections for Muslim and Hindu burials. Brookwood is of such a great size that there are an amazing number of plots within it which were reserved for various different social or community groups. It also has a large military cemetery within its grounds. Originally established for the burial of Commonwealth and American soldiers who died in the London area after being sent home wounded from the front, it was later expanded for casualties of the Second World War, including Allied soldiers and German and Italian prisoners of war. It is of special interest to many local and railway historians, as it was linked via the Necropolis railway to London, with bodies being brought for burial by train. Much has already been written about Brookwood and John M. Clarke's book *The Brookwood Necropolis Railway* is a fascinating read. His website has a useful list of churches and parishes known to have used Brookwood Cemetery at **www.john-clarke.co.uk/churches.html**.

Cemeteries today

Today in England and Wales there are many cemeteries dedicated to faiths other than Christianity. Recently, there has been an increasingly popular movement to establish green cemeteries, offering environmentally friendly burials. With our ever-growing population, burial space is an ongoing concern. The Cemetery Research Group, University of York, which aims to expand an understanding of current and past burial culture, has put forward a number of options to alleviate this, including above-ground mausoleums, more intensive use of existing burial space and the continued promotion of cremation.

Many contemporary cemeteries offer an attractive, if rather uniform, floral environment for burial and cremation such as here at Beckenham, Greater London.

Burial laws in the nineteenth and twentieth century

To fully understand the evolution of burial legislation in England and Wales would require a book in itself. There is plenty of further reading on the subject and the writer and historian John Clarke has an excellent web page where you can access the text of each burial act: **www.john-clarke.co.uk/burial_acts.html**. The full text of the Public Health and Burial Acts can be located at **http://www. legislation.gov.uk**.

Below are some of the key features of nineteenth-century legislation affecting cemeteries and burials.

1847 Cemeteries Clauses Act: effectively removed the requirement for an individual private Act of Parliament each time a cemetery was established. As long as that cemetery was deemed to be for the public good, land could be compulsorily purchased for that purpose. Each cemetery had to have adequate drainage and sewerage. It also had to be enclosed by walls or railings at least eight feet in height, no part of which was to be within 200 yards of a dwelling, while no burial in any vault under the cemetery chapels, or within 15ft of its walls, was allowed. Consecrated and unconsecrated land had to be set aside for burials, together with use of a Church of England chapel and one for other denominations or faiths. The cemetery company had to pay a portion of each fee received from burials in consecrated ground to the incumbent of the parish where the deceased had lived, this being in compensation for loss of burial fees. Rights of burial and the right to erect a memorial had to be sold in perpetuity or for a time-limited period. Burial registers had to be kept and searches allowed in these by members of the public. Each company was required to make a numbered plan of appropriate scale to clearly show each burial. The fee for registering an entry of burial in the register of grants was to be no more than 2s 6d, and no more than one shilling if the search was on behalf of a grantee, or one of his assigns. Right of burial was to be considered as part of the personal estate of the grantee and could be assigned as part of a will. Any assignment of the right to burial passed via a will had to be registered in the register book within six months of probate.

1847 The Towns Improvement Clauses Act: laid down rules for burials, stipulating that at least 30in of soil should lie between the upper side of the coffin and the ground surface. This provision related only to coffins buried in graves, and not to those deposited in vaults or catacombs.

1848 Public Health Act: established the General Board of Health (the City of London came under the Metropolitan Commission of Sewers instead). The Board had the power to close churchyards and burial grounds to further burials if deemed injurious to public health, and intramural burial was prohibited.

1852 and 1853 Burial Acts: effectively banned further burials in City of London churchyards (with a few exceptions), as well as the opening of any new burial ground within two miles of London. It established the principle of burial boards and burial board cemeteries. In London, the City's Commissioners of Sewers continued to serve as a burial board for the parishes in the City.

1879 Public Health (Interment) Act: created a new legal framework for cemeteries, which lay outside the burial acts.

1900 Burial Act: the church could no longer receive monument fees in consecrated sections of cemeteries, and would receive burial fees only for services rendered. There was a new presumption that land in the cemetery would be unconsecrated, unless a case was made otherwise. Burial business was transferred from the Home Office to Local Government Boards.

1902 Cremation Act: provided for the formation of crematoria approved by the Local Government Board. It still forms the basis of regulations governing crematoria today.

1977 Local Authorities Cemeteries Order (subsection of part of the 1972 Local Government Act): confirmed points made in much earlier legislation, and the power of burial authorities to take steps, as they thought necessary, to carry out the proper management, regulation and control of a cemetery, within certain guidelines; for example, a sufficient part of the cemetery had to be unconsecrated, and not set apart for the use of particular denominations or religious bodies. The proper keeping of burial records and plans was reiterated.

Chapter 5

GRAVESTONES AND GRAVESITES

I started researching my own family history when I was fifteen. Among the most thrilling moments have been those which involved finding an ancestor's grave and paying a visit. There is great poignancy in standing before the resting place of one of your forebears, whether it is marked by a grand memorial, a simple headstone, or even where it is unmarked by any stone. Later, when I became a professional genealogist, I was privileged to carry out extensive work on family histories for other people. Some of these families became as familiar to me as my own, and I felt a similar connection when visiting their burial places. While not everyone experiences this sense of connection, gravestones are, of course, a great potential source of genealogical information and also provide a glimpse into the world in which our ancestors lived.

While wealth and status are obviously reflected in the grandeur and expense of our ancestors' gravestones (or the lack of them), they also affected what lay below ground, in terms of the type of grave into which they were laid. There were various burial options, and while you will only occasionally be able to determine the type of grave in which your ancestor lies from what you see above ground, it is helpful to understand the options available.

Earth-cut and brick-lined graves

The simplest and cheapest way to bury someone, whether in the church, churchyard or cemetery, was to lay the shrouded body in a simple earth-cut grave, excavated into the underlying soils. Christian burials usually took place with the person's head to the west and their feet to the east, and coffined burial plots naturally had to be made wider than those for shroud-only burials. Enclosing the corpse in a coffin before burial was rare before the mid-sixteenth century, from which time it started to become more normal, but only for the wealthiest of families. Archaeological evidence from Kent suggests that on average about one-third of burials were coffined by the period 1650–1675, the rest being shroud-only burials.[1] Coffins for the population as a whole started to become typical by the end of the eighteenth century.[2]

When several people are recorded on the gravestone, it is usually the case that they are all buried in that particular grave site, but in some cases names might be added to the gravestone despite the fact they were buried elsewhere. The initial burial would have been dug deep enough to allow for future burials to be placed directly above the first, and the depth of the grave would also have influenced its cost. The first person to be interred would rest in his or her coffin, which was placed on the bare earth. The burial depth may be noted in the burial or cemetery register, so it could be referenced when future interments were made. Successive burials would be spaced above the previous one, until the grave space was full. If a double-width family grave was purchased, the coffins could be placed side by side. The same theory applied for any grave, whether earth-cut, or one of the options described below.

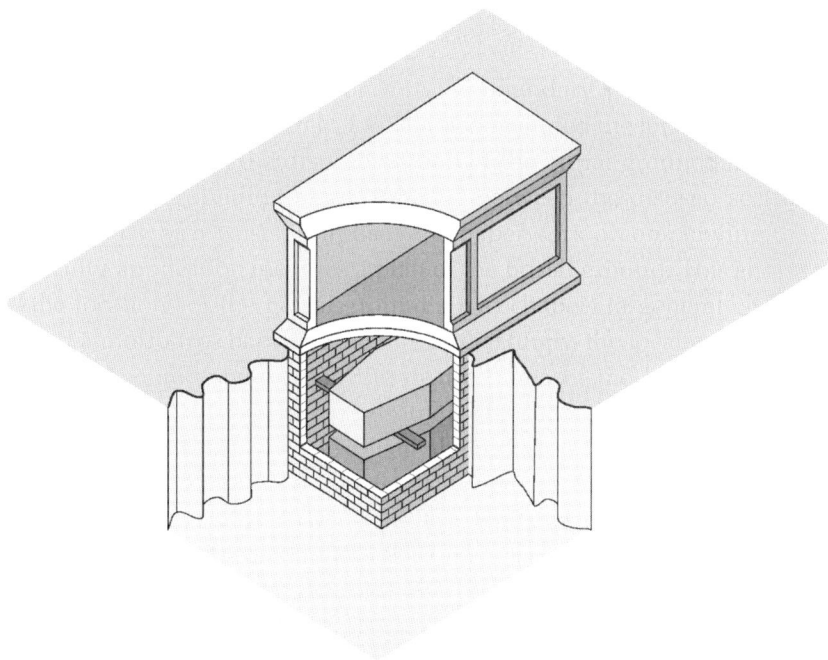

Cut-away illustration of a brick-lined grave surmounted by a chest tomb illustrating the typical placement of coffins below ground separated by stretchers. (Andrew Linklater)

There was a range of more expensive burial options, all of which offered burial in a drier environment than that of the earth-cut grave, and afforded greater protection against grave robbers, something which was regarded as particularly important in the eighteenth and early nineteenth century (see Chapter 4). One was the brick-lined grave, sometimes referred to as a 'shaft grave' or 'walled grave'. These were utilized for burials within the church and in the churchyard. Their breadth was restricted by the maximum width of stone that would cover the burial space without sagging. They are, therefore, typically one coffin wide in dimension, but again could accommodate several coffins depending on how deep the grave was dug. Most were surmounted by an inscribed grave slab or ledger stone and in some cases by a grander memorial, such as a chest tomb.

Vaults, catacombs and mausolea

Burials in catacombs, vaults and mausolea represented the top end of the burial market, and offered burial in a dry environment in a chamber. Vaults will be found in churches, churchyards, burial grounds and cemeteries and vary greatly in capacity. Originally an architectural term to denote an arched roof, in relation to burials a vault indicates a burial chamber covered with an arched (vaulted) ceiling. Constructed from brick or stone, the idea of the vaulted design was to make the ceiling of the burial chamber stronger and the vault more spacious. The term is frequently (but incorrectly) applied in a general manner to brick-lined graves and crypts (see above and below). The construction of a burial vault beneath a church floor was not just expensive because it involved digging up the church floor, but because a faculty was required. This was a licence from the diocese granting permission to alter the church fabric. Due to the lengthy construction process, vaults were often built long before the death of the first occupant. They first came into use in the mid-late sixteenth century, but were increasingly popular from the early seventeenth through to the mid-eighteenth century.[3]

Catacombs are underground passages divided into chambers or loculi, in which coffins were placed, usually on shelves. These are typically found in larger cemeteries, carved out of the natural rock formation. They contain the dead of many different families, although loculi (compartments) in a specified part of the catacombs, could be reserved for one particular family. Mausolea are individual buildings resembling small houses in which the dead of (usually) one family were placed on shelving within. Many had glass roofs or doors so the coffins could be seen by passers-by, and the family surname was often inscribed in a prominent position. Mausolea are typically found in cemeteries, although occasionally you may come across one in a churchyard, or on estates and lands associated with very wealthy families. From the church historian's point of view, they can arguably be seen as successors to side chapels dedicated to the burial and commemoration of one particular family.

Many coffins designed for vaults, catacombs or mausolea had depositum plates (also known as coffin plates) fixed to the coffin, often with a separate plate affixed to any internal shell of the coffin too. These provide details of the deceased, and although they are generally only available to view on the rare occasions when the burial space is opened for building works, you may find details have been published by antiquarians, or as part of archaeological reports. Depositum plates may simply include names and dates of birth and death, but sometimes there is far greater detail, such as that for Mary Lowman at Ash, near Sandwich, Kent, which reads as follows:

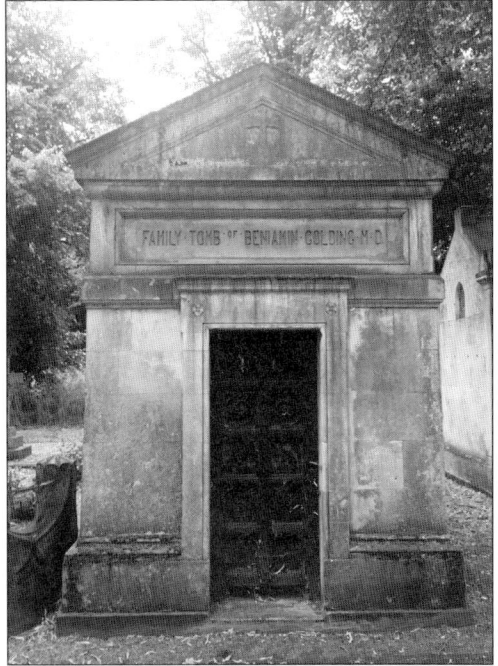

The Grade II-listed mausoleum of Benjamin Golding (1793–1863), founder of Charing Cross Hospital, is at Brompton Cemetery, London. (Author's collection)

> 'Mrs. Mary Lowman Wife to Henry Lowman & Daughter to Gregory Butler in the County of Northumberland. She was Laundress to King William & King George The First & Joynt house & WardeRoab [sic] Keeper at Kensington With her Husband to King William, Queen Ann & King George the First. Died November 29th 1737. In the 84th Year of her Age'[4]

In the past, due reverence has not always been paid when entering vaults and similar sites, and there are examples of depositum plates and other items being removed from vaults. This is evident from the fact that a depositum plate for one vault inhabitant at Ash, Mary Kien, is to be found mounted on the wall of the stairway to the parvis chamber.[4]

Two shots of vaults taken during renovations at Ash, near Sandwich, Kent. The first (left) is an external view of the top of a vault marked W.B., dated 1760, and clearly shows the typical arched roof which gave this type of burial chamber its name. The second (below) is an internal view of the Lowman family vault. (Canterbury Archaeological Trust, Andrew Linklater)

Examination of depositum plates in comparison with accompanying memorials in the church, which claim to record the inhabitants of the vault, sometimes reveals the presence of uncounted coffins or 'interlopers' in the vault. Families did occasionally give permission for a non-family member to be buried in a family vault. Alternatively, if a family died out and space was available, new deposits might be agreed by the incumbent of the church. In some city churches, the incumbent had control of a nominated vault to which he could give, or sell, burial space to anyone he liked. Although vaults were typically associated with one particular family, the right to burial in the vault could also be attached to a particular property, meaning that successive families had the right to burial as ownership of the property changed.

The size of a vault and number of coffins within varied greatly, ranging from those designed to hold twenty or more people, through to small vaults capable of holding just two or three coffins. The width and depth of the vault would dictate how the coffins were placed within it. In a large vault there would have been plenty of room to place coffins side by side, or on ready-made shelves around the edge. Coffins could be placed directly on the floor with later arrivals stacked on top. Although

Depositum plate from the coffin of Charles Lefeore [Lefevre] Garnier, infant son of the Revd Thomas Garnier (Dean of Winchester and Lincoln) and his wife Lady Caroline Gardiner, who was born 23 March 1851 and died 25 August that year, aged five months. Buried St Peter's, Thanet. (Andrew Linklater)

these were often separated by wooden bearers, once one coffin, or one of the bearers, collapsed, this could result in the whole stack of coffins falling over, depositing their contents across the vault floor. A better method was to use shelving, or even simple iron rods or racks placed across the vault, onto which the coffins could be laid. This system was also used for single-width brick-lined graves.

While some vaults were never filled to capacity, some became overcrowded. As coffins disintegrated, the remnants of these, together with the bones which had lain within them, might be cleared away and put into charnel pits or cists (chests) within the vault. This made space for new coffins and can account for the apparent non-existence of coffins known to have been placed in the vault.

A vault might be topped by a grand memorial in the form of a chest or wall tomb commemorating the main occupants of the vault. By contrast, it could simply be topped by a flat slab (sometimes with a lifting ring) or a ledger stone. When inspecting floor memorials in a church, it is sometimes impossible to determine whether you are looking at a brick-lined grave or a vault, as each might be covered by a simple ledger stone. In many cases, while the original stone covering a vault entrance may have been inscribed with the family's name, or a person's initials, this has later been replaced by an unmarked stone, perhaps following damage to the original during reopening. This can make vaults hard to locate. Some vaults are more obvious, being built with vents to let in light, while some appear to have been built with 'peep holes', so that later generations could see how full the vault was. Larger vaults might be accessed via their own set of steps, while some vaults inside churches were accessed via an entrance in the churchyard.

It is tempting to imagine that every significant wall monument or tomb in a church is sited above its associated burial. While this may originally have been the case, a great many wall memorials and tombs have been relocated due to church building work. You should also not believe everything you read on memorials! Some have been known to pretentiously declare that they commemorate the remains of someone who was buried in a 'vault near here', but building works reveal that the so-called vault was actually just a brick-lined grave!

Another familiar term associated with church burials is 'crypt'. A crypt is not a place specifically designated for the deposit of human remains. In its true sense, the term simply indicates an underground chamber belonging to a church. However, many church crypts have historically been used for intramural burials when the church was running short of burial space, or wished to bring in further income. Space inside could be charged at a much higher rate than burial in the churchyard.

The evolution of gravestones

Having considered the underground perspective of our ancestors' graves, the more obvious aspect in both churchyard and cemetery is, of course, the gravestones themselves. Grave markers and memorials have a very long history, but our knowledge is incomplete, since there is no doubt that many have perished with no trace. Inscribed gravestones of various types, but particularly inscribed tablets and slabs, were used in Roman England and Wales but only by higher-status families. The numbers found indicate they were significantly fewer in number compared with elsewhere in the Roman Empire. One example can be found at Lincoln, where a stone originally dedicated to a Roman citizen called Sacer and his family can be seen in the outside wall of the church tower of St Mary-le-Wigford. The memorial was recycled in the eleventh century, when it was reused as a dedication stone for the church, with the original inscription being over-inscribed.[5]

Although the Roman army withdrew from England in AD 410, the use of permanent grave markers for high-status families continued into the Anglo-Saxon period (AD 410–1066). The number of Anglo-Saxon and Anglo-Scandinavian gravestones that have been dug up in churchyards or their vicinity, or uncovered in church fabric, shows that this tradition continued once burials were routinely taking place in the environment of the church and churchyard from the late ninth century. They appear to have taken varying shapes and forms, including coped stones, cross slabs and headstones, often of a discoid shape. Archaeological evidence from the excavation of the church of St Peter-le-Bailey, Oxford, in 2008, suggests that undecorated lidded stone cists were being used for high-status churchyard burials by the eleventh century.[6] In Norman times (1066–1154), styles and forms changed gradually. Notable twelfth-century memorials survive within former monastic burial grounds at Old Sarum, Hampshire, and Strata Florida, Ceredigion (Cardiganshire). Those at Strata Florida consist of several slabs with headstones and three also have footstones. However, these are not in their original location, as once presumed, but were moved from the original monastery site half a mile up the road.[7] Therefore, we cannot be sure that the headstones and footstones originally paired up with the slabs they now accompany. In terms of churchyard burials, a large number of stones were discovered in 1841 during church restorations at Bakewell parish church in Derbyshire. Many were broken but were clearly originally ledger stones, or coped stones with head and footstones attached, suggesting these were typical of the time and place. Frederick Burgess, in his book *English Churchyard Memorials* (published 1963, Lutterworth Press), suggests this indicates the 'remains of an extensive parochial necropolis at Bakewell'. This may well be true, but it also begs the question why this is the only place where so many have been found?

During the thirteenth century, the inclination of the wealthier classes to erect permanent gravestones evolved, and they increasingly sought to commemorate themselves by means of fine upstanding monumental tombs within the church. The rest of the population continued to be buried in the churchyard, primarily in earth-cut graves with no permanent grave markers, but permanent churchyard memorials, including what we would think of as the traditional headstone, gradually started to evolve.

Frederick Burgess lists several examples of fragments of what appear to be discoid-shaped headstones, believed to date to the early part of the period 1200–1550.[8] At least one of these (New Romney) may actually be a cross denoting the boundary of the churchyard (see Appendix I). Many presumed headstones of this period bear no dedication and perhaps we are too hasty in assuming that they are gravestones. Burgess spent many hours visiting churchyards and studying gravestones. His book was first published in 1963, and much of what he writes came from his personal observation of those gravestones that survived in the 1950s and 1960s. So many of these stones no longer stand, we should be immensely grateful that he collected so much information. His sketches and the photographic plates at the back of his book provide a priceless illustration of what many stones would have looked like.

During the later medieval period, there is occasional documentary evidence relating to the gravestones although, frustratingly, it is often not clear cut. For example, in his will dated 1502, John Cook of Bury St Edmunds specifically asked for markers to be placed at his head and feet. He does not specify what they were to be made of, but since burial locations were probably marked in some manner anyway, this would seem to indicate a more permanent marker.[9]

Despite a small number of notable examples, the earliest surviving inscribed headstones in a typical pre-Reformation parish churchyard will very rarely pre-date the seventeenth century, and even stones from the first decades of the seventeenth century are relatively rare. It was then that rise of the traditional churchyard headstone (as opposed to grander chest tombs) really started to get under way. In some churchyards, these survivors are very few or non-existent. Many have been removed as a result of building works, or at the whim of a later family who prized a particular burial site, while many others no longer stand due to natural decay. Two major factors appear to have led to the increasing placement of permanent memorials in churchyards: a growing lack of burial space in the church, and the growth of an increasingly prosperous middle stratum of society (consisting of lesser landed gentry and the rising professional classes) who wished to erect permanent and memorable monuments to themselves. A prominently placed burial spot in the churchyard was much more affordable, and often far more noticeable. There was also far greater potential to erect a larger and more impressive memorial outside, and chest tombs provide some of our earliest known surviving churchyard memorials.

Wealth and status were not the only factors governing the erection of gravestones. The availability of local materials suitable for carving was also key. Stones were much more affordable in areas where suitable stone was readily available, such as the Cotswolds, Yorkshire, Cumbria, and in the south-west with its slate and granite. This was in contrast to the south-east and East Anglia, where there is a predominance of

Cross slabs and house tombs

These terms have been retrospectively allocated by historians to two specific types of high-status medieval gravestone. Cross slabs are decorated coffin lids, the earliest dating from the tenth century. Most, if not all, would originally have been sited inside the church, set over burial sarcophagi in the floor, but very few remain over the original graves. A large proportion are incised with a cross (hence the name), while from the thirteenth century onwards some were carved with symbols representing the deceased's status or occupation. As literacy among those of higher status grew, some were inscribed with the name of the deceased around the edge of the lid; these usually date to the thirteenth and fourteenth century. Many cross slabs were later relocated outside, as changes were made to the interior of the church.

Experts have dated many individual cross slabs according to the style of cross, but this method is not foolproof. Designs could be used retrospectively, or simply because the commissioner liked the design, so precise dating is challenging. The popularity of cross slabs peaked during the twelfth and thirteenth century, falling

Look out for cross slabs against church walls, in porches and inside the church. As with these at St Mary's, Gosforth, Cumbria, very few, if any, remain in their original location. (Author's collection)

Well-preserved 'hogback' tombstone at Gosforth, Cumbria. (Author's collection)

out of fashion at the Reformation, perhaps because the use of the cross was deemed a sign of popery. They are most numerous in the north of England, probably due to the plentiful nature of stone suitable for carving. However, examples can be found throughout the country. Keep an eye open for them in church porches, church floors and walls (either entire or as fragments), hidden away behind cupboards, or even recycled as thresholds to church doors. Much has been written about cross slabs, and the different styles of crosses, symbols and patterns to be found on them. It's an interesting subject and if you would like to read more look at Peter Ryder's book, *The Cross Slab Grave Covers of Cumbria* (Cumbria County Council). In the south and east of England, cross slabs were overtaken in popularity by monumental brasses (see below).

House tombs are predominantly found in Anglo-Scandinavian settled areas and are carved in the form of a house, often with representations of roof tiles. A variant form has retrospectively been dubbed the 'hogback', because it appears to resemble the shape of a pig. These intricately carved stones must have taken hours of work and been extremely expensive to produce. Some excellent examples can be seen in the parish church in Kirkby Stephen, Cumbria. These were discovered during restoration of the chancel in the nineteenth century. It is likely that such high-status memorials would originally have been placed in the east end of the church which was deemed to be the most sacred.

Chest tombs

One of the earliest types of surviving churchyard memorial is the chest tomb, sometimes referred to as a table tomb. As the name indicates, these took the form of a large chest-shaped monument erected over the grave, the body being buried either in the ground, or in a vault beneath the monument, *not* in the cavity created by the chest monument itself. Churchyard chest tombs are similar to their grander cousins found within churches, but few of these external ones would bear recumbent effigies on top. Of those that do, it is not always clear whether these were originally internal monuments later moved into the churchyard from inside the church.

The chest tomb gave masons a field day, as they had several panels on which to display their skill. The design and imagery often more closely reflect the architectural designs in fashion at the time, as the proportions of these monuments meant the skill of an accomplished stonemason was required. They were only commissioned by the wealthier classes, who could afford to bring in someone from outside the local area if necessary. They proved very popular in the seventeenth-century post-Restoration period, when a lavish style of

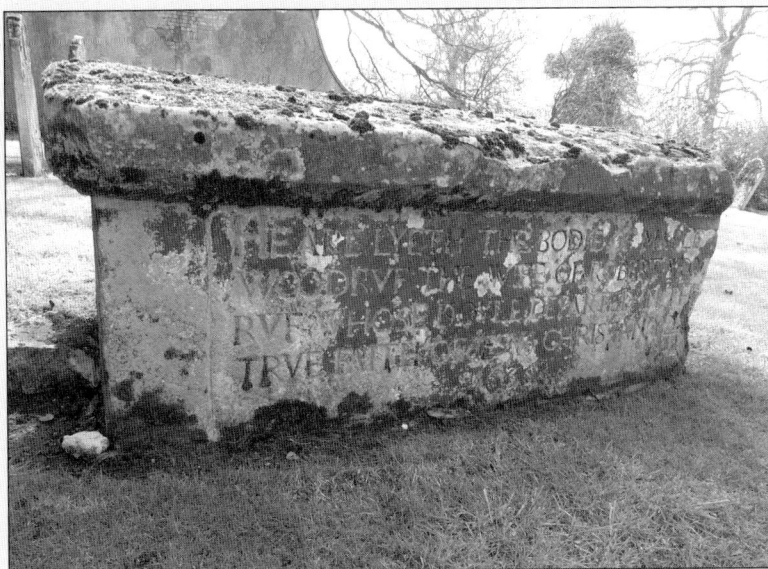

Two contrasting chest tombs. The first is a seventeenth-century example from Achurch, Northamptonshire, for the Woodruff family (note the plain design and thick-set lid) and in comparison (below), a finely decorated tomb to the Twort family from the early 1800s at Horsmonden, Kent. (Author's collection)

art came into vogue following the austerity of the Commonwealth era. Bale tombs were a variation of the chest tomb, frequently found in the Cotswolds. The bale-shaped top to the monuments is believed to represent tied-up bales of wool, reflecting the fact that this was a prime wool-production area.

Be careful if you try to date a chest tomb using a date of death inscribed on it: ensure you have examined all the dates on all the panels. Some may have initially been left blank, so that later family members could be added. In some cases, one tomb will commemorate family members who have died centuries apart.

While chest tombs were particularly popular in the seventeenth century, there are several surviving examples that pre-date this, notably the fourteenth-century tomb at St Katherine's Church, Loversall, Yorkshire, and several fifteenth-century tombs at Bishops Cannings in Wiltshire and Norton, near Sheffield. Pre-seventeenth-century chest tombs typically have very thick lids. The earliest known chest tomb is that for Richard Perceval at Weston in Gordano, Somerset, which is said to date to 1202, although its provenance is uncertain.

Chest tombs fell out of favour in churchyards from the late nineteenth century, possibly due to the amount of space they required, at a time when the increasing number of memorials meant that space was at a premium.

chalk and clay. In these areas, stones had to be transported in at great cost and only the very wealthy could afford it. In areas where suitable stone was not available, memorials were frequently raised using wood or iron, notably in Essex, Hertfordshire, Shropshire, Sussex, and parts of Kent. Some Kentish gravestones were made from the local ragstone, but since it is an extremely hard and inconsistent stone to cut, the design of such memorials had to be very simple. The Weald of East Sussex and Kent was a prime location for iron making, and iron memorials are to be found far more frequently in these areas, both inside the church and in the churchyard. Wadhurst Church in Sussex is a good example. Here, there are over thirty iron ledger-style memorials within the church, which date from the early seventeenth through to the late eighteenth century, while there is a cast iron memorial slab dating to the fourteenth century in nearby Burwash Church. In some areas, wooden memorials often consisted of 'grave boards', also known as 'dead boards', 'leaping-boards' or 'grave rails.' These were long planks of wood stretching from the head to the foot of the grave. At Harlow in Essex, there are examples of both iron grave boards and wooden cross-shaped memorials.

The British Geological Society website has an excellent 'Geology of Britain Viewer' app at **www.bgs.ac.uk/map-viewers/geology-of-britain-**

Where easily carved local stone was in short supply, other materials were often favoured for memorials, such as this iron grave board memorial at St Mary's Church, Harlow, Essex. (Author's collection)

viewer/ where you can select any place in the UK to determine its natural geology, and discover the types of natural stone available in each area.

Sadly, the durability of wooden memorials is short, while many iron ones were no doubt later carted away to be melted down for metal. Yet the durability of stone memorials is limited too. Sandstone, although easy to carve, is very soft and weathers more quickly than other stone types. Even slate, which is durable and often maintains its incised inscriptions for years, is prone to fracturing and may laminate along its bedding plain once exposed to successive years of cold and frost.

Regional differences were more pronounced up to the late eighteenth century, when the building of a network of canals reduced transport costs and started to make the stone market more accessible. This accessibility increased dramatically with the advent of the railways in the nineteenth century, which meant stone could be brought in from elsewhere, including abroad, at affordable prices.

Gravestones were not just memorials to the deceased, but became fashion statements. The wealthiest families might have vaults and mausolea, or be buried within the church itself, but affluence was also keenly displayed in the churchyard. This is reflected in the design and decoration of the monuments, and their placement within the churchyard. A memorial on the external church wall behind the altar was a prime location, while there are many cases where later memorials have been selfishly placed so that they encroach upon earlier gravestones in a prized spot.

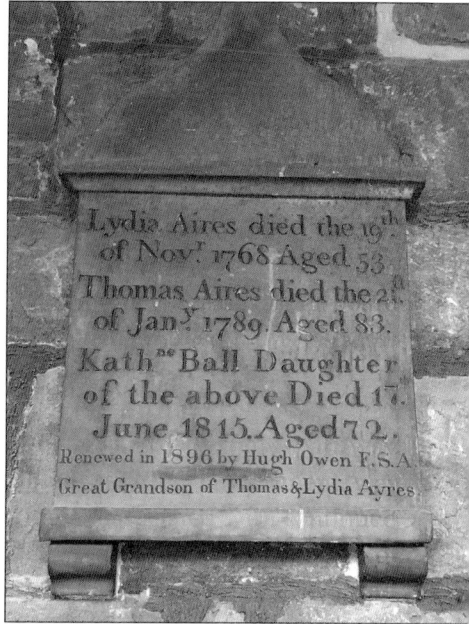

Look out for memorials on the external walls of a church, often close to the altar. This one is from Chester Cathedral (and has subsequently been renewed), but many are found on humble parish churches too.

Memorials in brass

In the Midlands, south and east of England, monumental brasses were a feature of the intra-mural burial scene from the thirteenth century. Known contemporaneously as 'latten' (the name of the copper alloy of which they were made), they were originally set into ledger stones.

Their popularity lasted through to the seventeenth century, although some later examples are found. Many brasses were made on the Continent, and this may well account for their higher distribution in the southern counties of England. Often engraved with the person's name and accompanying figure, from the fifteenth century a number depict the deceased in his or her shroud, giving us an idea of burial garb of the time.

Although this type of memorial is usually found inside churches, there are a very few cases where brasses are found as part of external

There are many examples of early brasses in churches which clearly display the deceased wrapped in a shroud, and from these we can get an idea of the types of shrouds and how they were tied. This one is at Leigh in Kent. (Andrew Linklater)

monuments, such as at High Halden in Kent where the remnants of one can be seen on a chest tomb. This may be where an internal monument has been relocated outside following the reordering of monuments inside the church. Occasionally stones bearing the indent of a former brass may be found discarded in the churchyard, possibly as a result of ancient church clearances.

Etiquette of brass rubbings

From the 1970s to 1990s, brass rubbing was a popular hobby, but there was also a substantial amount of commercial misuse of brass rubbings, and the making unlicensed copies for profit. Sadly, much damage was done to many brasses as a result. Brass rubbings are now discouraged, and you should always ask prior permission from the vicar if you wish to make one. If permission is granted, take your rubbings in the following manner:

- Check the condition of the brass. Brasses should not be rubbed if the pitch that acts as a bond between the brass and the stone floor has perished, creating a space between the brass and the floor. You can tell if this is the case by tapping the brass in various places. If there is a hollow sound, then the pitch has perished. If you rub a brass in this condition, the pressure applied may cause the brass plate to bend and crack.
- Clean with a soft brush to remove any grit, but do not rub abrasively. Do not tread or kneel on the brass.
- Use acid-free paper, taping it down over the top of brass.
- Use one of the various non-acidic wax compounds available to make the rubbing.

There is further information about taking brass rubbings online via the Monumental Brass Society Website at **www.mbs-brasses.co.uk/ brass_rubbing.htm**

The craft of the stonemason

Those people buried and commemorated within the church would almost certainly have used the services of specialist monumental masons to make their tombs. Their grand memorials were works of art in themselves and, while they are outside the remit of this book, Sally Badham has written many authoritative books on the subject. The Church Monuments

Society is another excellent source of information and arranges many courses and day trips (**https://churchmonumentssociety.org**).

In terms of gravestones in the churchyard, the skill with which they were carved would have depended on the availability and competence of local stone masons. The most skilled monumental masons tended to accumulate in areas where there was a good source of carveable stone. In other areas, gravestones were often cut, carved and inscribed by locals whose primary occupation lay in another, perhaps totally unrelated, field. Some stones are therefore very naïve or rustic in style; some quite charmingly so. This factor has led to many local idiosyncrasies in carving, while in more remote areas, roughly hewn and crudely carved stones were a feature far longer than in areas linked by a good road network, and with better communication. Since literacy was a requirement, the carver may even have been the parson, schoolmaster or parish clerk. As the use of permanent churchyard memorials increased, a growing number of craftsmen began to take up stone carving as a business secondary to their main line of work. They produced gravestones upon request or, if their main job was seasonal, in the periods when their primary work was quiet. Blank stones could be cut and prepared in advance for future carving or inscribing. Gravestone designs were influenced by artwork from many difference sources, but notably the carver may have mimicked the symbols and images he saw represented on grander tombs within the church itself, or on earlier churchyard gravestones.

Ideas for gravestone design and imagery also came from contemporary printed books. As early as the sixteenth century, Flemish masons brought pattern books with them. Francis Quarles' *Emblems Divine and Moral Together with Hieroglyphics of the Life of Man,* a book of religious poems with accompanying woodcuts printed in 1630, was a source of inspiration for some, but more influential were the publications of craftsmen, such as furniture designers Matthias Lock and Henry Copland (*A New Book Of Ornaments With Twelve Leaves,* 1752) and Thomas Chippendale (*The Gentleman and Cabinet Maker's Directory,* 1754). Another influencer was architect and stonemason John Gibbs, who also published many books on craft designs, such as *A Series of Designs for Gothic Monuments: Churchyard Crosses, Sepulchral Slabs, and Head Crosses* in 1852 and *Designs for Memorials for Church-yards and Cemeteries* in 1864.

Newspapers and journals also spread ideas regarding memorial design, by means of advertisements placed by memorial masons, cemeteries or undertakers, and also as news items. For example, *The Illustrated London News* ran a beautifully illustrated article in November 1855, describing three newly erected memorials. One of these was in Fillingham churchyard, Lincolnshire, another in Saffron Waldron Church, Essex, but the last was overseas, in Canada. Here the citizens of London, Ontario, were erecting a memorial in St Paul's Church, to Lt-Col Chester, his officers and men who fell at the Alamo in 1854. Each of the three memorials is pictured in detail and, while many would not have had the funds to reproduce a similar memorial, the finer details of the carving could, no doubt, have served to inspire both families and masons.

By the 1850s, pattern books were increasingly used by monumental masons as the mass production of gravestones for churchyard and cemeteries became more common. These evolved into brochures for inspection by potential customers.

Style of fonts and letter-carving on stones also evolved over time. While the subject is outside the scope of this book, further recommended reading is *Tombstone Lettering in the British Isles* by Alan Bartram (Lund Humphries, London / Watson-Guptill Publication, New York).

Until the late nineteenth century it was popular for stonemasons to whitewash some stones and highlight the text in contrasting colours, perhaps in an attempt to make them look more expensive than they were. Lettering might be highlighted in gold leaf to accentuate and contrast the letters from the surrounding painted stonework. If you look closely, you may see traces of paint, sometimes several layers of paint, where the stone was repainted over the years, often when new inscriptions were added.

Towards the turn of the nineteenth and twentieth century, falling transport costs made suitable carving stone much more readily available throughout the country. This, together with the aforementioned rise in mass production and new cutting techniques, made memorials more affordable. Sadly, it also led to increased uniformity and loss of individuality in gravestone design. In the nineteenth century, many cemeteries incorporated a monumental mason's business, and there was a growing tendency for quarries to be corporately rather than individually run. These two factors encouraged importation of marble from abroad, which, in turn, ousted the use of our native stone. Many independent stonemasons found it hard to compete against this new force, and local businesses often fell by the wayside.

The number of burials in any churchyard will far outweigh the number of memorials ever erected or still standing. Even today, many people are buried with no memorial. The number of gravestones which have been lost in a typical churchyard, and to a lesser extent in cemeteries, is remarkable. Loss through natural decay, planned churchyard clearances

These comparison shots of St John's Church in Margate, Kent (above a stereocard from the 1860s and below taken in December 2019) clearly show just how many gravestones have been lost over the intervening years. (1860s photograph Anthony Lee, www.margatelocalhistory.co.uk; modern image Author's collection)

prior to building works, or simply to ease grass mowing are all primary causes. To give an idea of the extent of gravestone loss, compare the photographs of St John's Margate in Kent on page 119.

Headstones and footstones

Many graves are marked by a headstone and an accompanying footstone. The names are self-explanatory, with archaeological evidence supporting the fact that a headstone was indeed sited at the head of the corpse and a footstone at the foot. The purpose of having two stones was primarily to establish the perimeter of the gravesite for future reference. Not all headstones have footstones, however. This would have depended on what the next-of-kin specified to the stonemason and, over the years, many footstones have been lost. Conversely, some footstones survive where the headstone does not. Generally speaking, a headstone would be two to four times the height of the matching footstone, but there are many exceptions. In some cases, when stones have sunk

So-called 'body stones' do not actually contain the body of the deceased which is, of course, buried below ground. These well-known examples at Cooling, Kent, feature in the opening of Charles Dickens' novel Great Expectations. *(Author's collection)*

considerably into the ground, it is possible to mistake one for the other. Early headstones, especially those from the seventeenth century, can at first appear to be footstones, since they are often short in stature and may have sunk deeply into the ground over time.

The key point in differentiating the two is that a footstone typically bears the initials rather than the name of the deceased, often coupled with the year of death. If you are re-siting a fallen headstone or footstone, ensure the initials on the footstone correspond with the name and date on the headstone. In some churchyards, footstones have been deliberately moved to abut the headstones to make churchyard mowing easier.

A chronological guide to dating gravestones by style

This rough guide covers stones you are likely to come across in the churchyard, burial ground and cemetery, and aims to help you date external memorials, notably those which are illegible. It will help build up a picture of the churchyard or cemetery as a whole. You will spot a gamut of different symbols and designs used on gravestones. These often reflect contemporary social beliefs and attitudes towards death, and may occasionally provide an insight into the perceived qualities of the deceased, which the family particularly wished to commemorate.

Contemporary architectural styles are also found reflected in gravestone design, although the mason was not under the same pressure as the architect to follow fashion, or make a statement via his work. Fashions in gravestone style are, therefore, more fluid, covering a wider timeframe compared to equivalent styles found on church or cemetery buildings, and there are also numerous regional differences. For example, mortality symbols such as the skull, cross bones, and hourglass were very popular from the mid-seventeenth to early-eighteenth century in much of England and Wales, before yielding their place to symbols referencing resurrection or eternal life. However, in the Cotswolds, mortality symbols retained their popularity far longer.[10] Similarly, although the use of the cross on gravestones generally fell out of favour for the two centuries after the Reformation, in south-east Wales its use continued.[11]

The growth of private and municipal cemeteries in the nineteenth century encouraged the use of non-Christian symbols. Similar fashions in historic gravestone styles and symbolism can be seen across the world. Just as Britain was influenced by continental Europe, so were the British colonies and America influenced by Britain. The timeline below was written based on my own experience studying gravestones in England and (to a lesser extent) in Wales. The time brackets are simply a rough guide, and are relatively wide to account for regional variations and the time it took for new trends to creep into more remote areas. When exploring a churchyard, look at all the stones and compare dates and designs. You will often recognize the same hand at work, carving the stones of many different families (even before the days of mass manufacture) with a stonemason using his own favourite symbols and designs. Alternatively, a family might have chosen to replicate the style of an earlier relative's memorial, making the design of the gravestone look older than it actually is. By contrast, some memorials might be placed over a grave many years after the person had died, making the design look way ahead of its time.

Up to 1599
Apart from exceptional finds, such as very early chest tombs, and collections of medieval cross slabs, you are unlikely to find any memorials from this period.

1600–1650
Surviving churchyard headstones start to be found. These would typically have been for the wealthier layers of society but not necessarily gentry. Those that survive are often short, stumpy, and roughly hewn with some of discoid shape. Chest tombs start to become fashionable.

A discoid-shaped stone dated 1628 at Lower Swell, Gloucestershire. (Author's collection)

1650–1760

Simple plain shapes to many headstones, some with simple arched (hooded) tops and shoulders. At the start of this period, there is little pattern, the use of symbols is limited, and the stones are usually very thick, and often roughly hewn on the back. The frequency of symbols increases within this time frame, notably from the late seventeenth century. From the late 1600s, there is increasing use of mortality symbols, acting as reminders that time on earth is short. They typically include the skull and crossbones, hourglass, urn, scythe or dart of death, with less frequent representations of other symbols such as the coffin. The church promoted a belief that the skull and crossbones needed to be present

The skill of the mason and nature of the stone influenced the end product and naïve, rustic styles displaying crudely cut skulls, hourglasses and crossbones are common in the early eighteenth century. This one is at Milton Regis, Kent, in memory of Mary, daughter of Clement Collins, who died in 1702. (Author's collection)

Although a significant portion of this stone at St Mary's Church, Lamberhurst, Kent, now lies below ground level so that the dates are no longer visible, it can be dated by its style to the early eighteenth century. The double-headed stone with the use of a crudely carved death's head on one side and a heart surmounting crossbones are typical symbols used in the late seventeenth and early eighteenth century, while the raised border is very typical in stones found in Kent and Sussex during this period. (Author's collection)

Classic memento mori *(reminders of death) symbols, more typically associated with the early part of this century, are seen on this 1779 stone. Dedicated to John Perry, a mariner aged 24, who was 'unfortunately kill'd by a Cannon Ball by a Person unknown', at Llansallos, Cornwall, it shows how trends varied according to region and mason. On the left a finger points towards the hourglass (time running out), a winged cherub over two birds is in the centre and on the right a heart is pierced by an arrow of death. (Author's collection)*

Mortality symbols mixed with symbols denoting resurrection and eternal life can be seen on this stone at Northbourne, Kent, including (from left to right) a coffin, gravedigger's spade, skull (death's head), hourglass surmounted by a winged cherub, another skull, apick axe and the serpent swallowing its tail. (Author's collection)

for resurrection to take place and so these symbols can also suggest eternal life. Double-headed stones commemorating husband and wife are common too, divided in the middle like a book, with the husband's details on one side, his wife's on the other. Naïve portraits (heads), often in a rather crude form, depending on the skill of the local mason, are also to be found.

Towards the end of this period, we see a movement towards stones which were more highly decorated, with increased use of curves and flounces; this is often associated with the Rococo style of architecture (1730s–1760s).

1760–1830

Stones are generally much busier, and the influence of the Rococo architectural style still flourishes, outstaying the equivalent architectural period by many years. Exuberant curves and asymmetrical forms with

This delightful stone at Lamplugh, Cumbria, is to the memory of Thomas Wood of Low-Leys, who died in 1795 aged 80, Frances his wife who died 1795 aged 77, and their sons Richard, who died in 1808 aged 55 and Henry, who died in 1824 aged 37, and surely depicts an agricultural connection, represented by a wheatsheaf, plough and other farming implements. (Author's collection)

Much of the intricate detail from gravestones has been lost over the years. This pre-1939 photograph of a mid-eighteenth-century stone to John Stanford at St Michael's, East Peckham, Kent, shows the painstaking detail in the carving. The scene includes representations of the Garden of Eden (tree of life, snake eating an apple), the traditional death's head (mortality), winged cherubs and sunrays (eternal life). The central figure reads from the Book of Life (listing the names of all who were destined for Heaven). These are framed by a border of funeral drapes and flowers. (Margaret Lawrence)

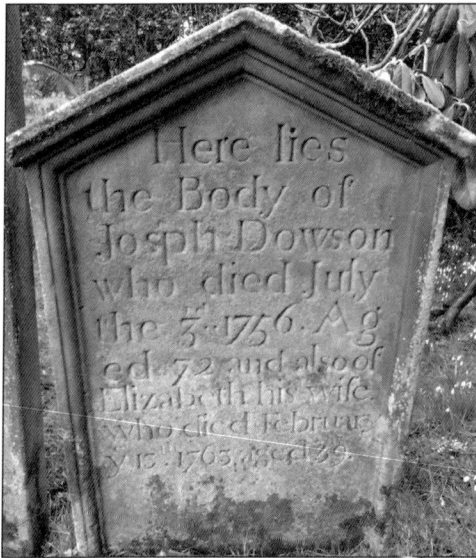

The simplicity of this mid-eighteenth-century stone at Eggleston, Co. Durham, in memory of Joseph and Elizabeth Dowson, is striking. The recessed panel surrounded by a raised border with a further raised hood molding perhaps harks back to the idea of a house in which the soul can reside.

By contrast this stone at Aldwinckle, Northamptonshire, is typical of many stones of the mid-to-late eighteenth century, showing the influence of the Rococo architectural style with exuberant curves, asymmetrical forms and elaborate ornamentation, alongside winged cherubs.

elaborate ornamentation, alongside winged cherubs and the dart of death, will be found right up to the late 1700s, with many features, such as the roundel and cartouche, also standing in isolation alongside plain text. Biblical scenes start to become more popular, including representations of the Day of Judgement, the Fall of Man in the Garden of Eden, and the Resurrection. You may also find scenes depicting apocryphal stories of a moral nature.

From the second half of the eighteenth century, and carrying on well into the nineteenth century, we see influences from the Gothic Revival movement. These are identified by headstones, chests and mausolea displaying pointed arches and decorated pinnacles, in imitation of the earlier Medieval Gothic style. Yet some stones remain surprisingly plain, notably in more remote counties, such as that shown for Eggleston, County Durham (picture above).

1830–1920

This is a long and very diverse period in terms of headstone design. It coincides with the increasing use of pattern books and catalogues, from which customers could choose their designs, and the development of mass-manufactured gravestones. Despite the continuation of the Gothic Revival movement, whose influence lingers on, many headstones start to become calmer, plainer and arguably more severe, with fewer but often larger symbols. A greater importance is given to text. You will still see the cherubs of the previous time frame, but increasingly they compete with a new range of symbols which became as popular, notably the anchor, angels, weeping figures (mourners), and the dove.

As time passes, stones reflect a variety of architectural fashions that arrive and pass within this period, not just Gothic but also Classical Revival, Egyptian Revival, Art Nouveau and Art Deco, all of which were influential on memorial design. Classical Revival harked back to Roman and Greek styles of architecture. It is identified by its symmetry, geometry and mathematical principles, with the frequent use of columns, pediments, round arches and balusters, as well as classical column capitals of all types (Tuscan, Doric, Ionic, Corinthian and Composite). The Egyptian Revival style is a feature of many cemetery monuments of the early Victorian period, coinciding with a contemporary fascination with Egyptian culture. This is stimulated by Napoleon's Egyptian campaign of 1798–99, and the discovery of Egypt's cultural wonders, notably the pyramids. It is popular with many people because it is not associated with any particular religious denomination, unlike the architecture of the Gothic Revival, which came to be associated with Roman Catholicism,

A fine representation of the tree of life on a stone in St Lawrence's Church, Appleby-in-Westmorland, Cumbria. (Author's collection)

Early Victorian stylized Neo-Classical stone at Clodock, Herefordshire, in memory of James and Ann Farr. (Author's collection)

or that of the Classical Revival, which came to be associated with Nonconformity.

By the 1850s there is a growing use of the cross (previously out of fashion since the Reformation), and the appearance of headstones which are pointed with an inset arch, much like a roof, and perhaps harking back to the idea of the house as a resting place for the soul.

Clasped hands such as those on this 1915 stone for William Lambkin and his wife Sophia at Beckermet, Cumbria, were popular from Victorian times into the twentieth century and usually represent the bond between husband and wife even after death. The decorated cuff on the left identifies it as the woman's hand. (Author's collection)

These examples illustrate the wide diversity of memorials which flourished in the nineteenth and early twentieth century cemetery environment. Shown from left to right are stones to: Frank C. Bostock, 1912 (Abney Park), Bernard Posno, 1901 (Brookwood), Garnet and Mary Mounsell 1872/1890 (Brompton) and Hannah and George Kent 1854/1890 (Brompton). The Mounsell stone shows a popular theme among more traditional stones of this era: mourners and funerary urns. (Author's collection)

From the mid-nineteenth century, the production of mass-manufactured, machine-worked stones, often made of reconstituted stone (stone dust reformed into a working material by re-bonding), starts to take hold. Lead-filled lettering becomes common and there is an increasing use of imported marble, and of different types of stone set together in one memorial.

1920 onwards

After the First World War, memorials begin to standardize and lose their individuality dramatically. Smaller stones become the norm, with the majority rarely reaching more than three feet tall, and with much less embellishment or text. This trend is no doubt influenced by Edwin Lutyens' very simple design, chosen as the prototype for the Commonwealth War Graves: its standardized simplicity, aimed at the equal commemoration of all ranks, faiths and nationalities (see Chapter 3). In the late twentieth and early twenty-first century, there is a growing trend for adding photographs of the deceased, and suggestions that QR codes be added to gravestones linking to internet-accessed data about the deceased.

Symbols on gravestones

Some of the more popular symbols are listed below.

- Anchor: hope. Could also be occupational, representing someone connected with the sea.
- Angel: messenger of God. Weeping angel: untimely death. With trumpet: the approach of God.
- Angel's head with wings: resurrection.
- Arrow: see dart.
- Axe: similar to the dart or arrow – representing death striking.
- Beehive: industry.
- Biblical scenes: often with a moral tale to tell.
- Book: representing the Book of Life, where the names of all who were destined for Heaven were written. It could also be used to represent the Bible, or a learned person.
- Butterfly: transitory life. The butterfly was thought to mate and die in a day.
- Candle: the passing of time and the fragility of life i.e., when the candle was extinguished.
- Cherubs: often with wings, representing the soul leaving the body.
- Cherub sleeping: innocence.
- Coffin: inevitability of death: mortality.

- Coins or bags of coins: paying off debts/repenting of sins; possibly paying commercial debts/gratitude for commercial success.
- Column, broken: premature death.
- Clasped hands: unity. Often used for husband and wife. The woman's sleeve, or cuff, decorated or bejewelled.
- Compass: see Tools & Masonic.
- Crossbones: often paired with the skull. The crossbones typically represent the thighbones or long bones – required for resurrection.
- Crown: eternal life.
- Dart: mortality symbol representing death striking.
- Death's Head or Skull: mortality.
- Eye: see Masonic.
- Flames: flame of eternity.
- Flowers and Plants: in Victorian times different flowers signified different qualities, e.g., the marigold represented grief and ivy depicted eternity and steadfastness.
- Heart: charity, love, or salvation.
- Hourglass: mortality symbol – time running out.
- IHC and IHS: Originally from the monograms for Jesus. IHC is derived from the Greek word IHCOYC (Jesus). Later used in a Latin form as IHS. Later the letters were sometimes used to represent the phrase 'In His Service' and used to reflect upon a life of service, for example in the Church or carrying out charitable works.
- Lamb: from the biblical refence to Jesus as the Lamb of God.
- Masonic: Freemasons chose to identify themselves using a variety of symbols which may be reflected on their gravestones, such as the all-seeing eye (pyramid with radiating light), compass (dividers) and set square.
- Oak leaves: power, authority, victory.
- Palm frond: victory over death; resurrection.
- Pickaxe and spade: mortality symbol – the tools used to dig a grave.
- Scythe or sickle: see dart
- Serpent or snake: sin or the devil. If raised up on a staff represents Jesus or healing (Reference to the Bible, John 3:14). If curled in a circle, tail in mouth, represents eternal life.
- Set-square: see Masonic.
- Shell: usually a scallop shell, these were sometimes used to pour the holy water during baptism. Can also represent pilgrimage.
- Skeleton: mortality.
- Skull: see death's head. On intramural tombs, the presence of a family member bearing a skull in their hand denoted their prior decease. If with a crown, represents triumph over death.

- Spade: see pickaxe.
- Sunrays and clouds: eternal life, resurrection.
- Tree: often represents paradise lost and depicts the Tree of Life and Knowledge from the Garden of Eden (Genesis 2.9) (See also Weeping willow and palm frond).
- Trumpet: (often carried by an angel) represents the Day of Judgement; triumph over death.
- Tools: sometimes reflect the deceased's occupation; for example a blacksmith could be represented by a hammer, anvil or tongs, a mariner by a ship or anchor. (Also see Masonic).
- Tomb, open with body rising: resurrection.
- Urn: the body turning to dust.
- Weepers: mourning.
- Wheatsheaf: full or content life.
- Weeping willow tree: sorrow or mourning.

Chronosticon gravestones

Very occasionally, you may come across a chronosticon grave. These are typically seventeenth-century memorials found within the church. A chronosticon is a sentence which incorporates roman numerals, often in lieu of letters. It is constructed so that when all the roman numerals are extracted and added together, the sum total is a relevant date or number. Latin text is often used, since this lends itself to the concept more readily. One example is in the chancel of Milford-upon-on Sea in Hampshire, dedicated to the Revd Christopher Airay who died on 18 October 1670. Sadly, this is currently almost entirely covered by a large cupboard, but research by the Milford-on-Sea Historical Record Society suggests that in this case the chronosticon spells out the year of death.

What will the stones tell you? Gravestone inscriptions

These are a key source for the genealogist, although the amount of information on gravestones varies greatly. Very early gravestones may contain only a name or initials, but later stones will typically at least give the person's name, date of death and age. Many others give far greater detail, ranging from place of death, date of birth, details of spouses, children, other relatives, causes of death and occupations. The amount of detail was, of course, the decision of the family, or whoever commissioned the gravestone, and often reflected what was important to them, or the last wishes of the deceased. It was also influenced by the family's budget. The typical cost of a gravestone in the mid-eighteenth century ran from 2s 2d to 3s 6d, per foot of stone, with a carving rate of a 'fairly standard penny a letter'.[12]

Where several family members are buried in the same grave space, you can often construct a mini family tree from the information on the gravestone. It's important to inspect neighbouring stones too, as these may turn out to be family members. This may not always be obvious if the surname is different.

There may also be a verse summing up the virtues of the deceased, sometimes hinting at the nature of the final illness, or cause of death. In Victorian and Edwardian times, these verses were often picked from catalogues offered by the undertakers, and were replicated from that chosen for the memorial card. (See *Tracing Your Ancestors Through Death Records* Chapter 7.) There was a wide range of choice and many incorporated a didactic slant on how to live a good life. Some memorial verses were clearly written directly with the deceased in mind, however, such as that for Esther Hallas. She was killed by lightning at the age of seventeen, in 1817. Her details and accompanying verse are to be found on the reverse side of a stone at All Hallows Church, Kirkburton, Yorkshire, which commemorates her parents, Amos and Ann Hallas. The stone also records that the owner of the gravestone (i.e., the person who erected it) was Esther's brother George Hallas.

Here
Lieth the Body of Esther
Daughter of Amos Hallas
Of Highburton who was
Killed by A Thunder=
Storm the 11th day of July
1817 Aged 17 Years
Death little warning to me gave
And soon did take me to the grave
As I one day was set at meat
The lightening [sic] took me from my seat
To all who hear or may be told both male and female young and
old
May this my fate a warning be
Remember God, Remember me

The Victorians loved to collect gravestone epitaphs, and published many such collections. This fascination continues into the modern day and there are numerous books and websites listing epitaphs of interest, or identifying where the rich and famous are buried. However, there is often far greater delight in reading the inscriptions and epitaphs of

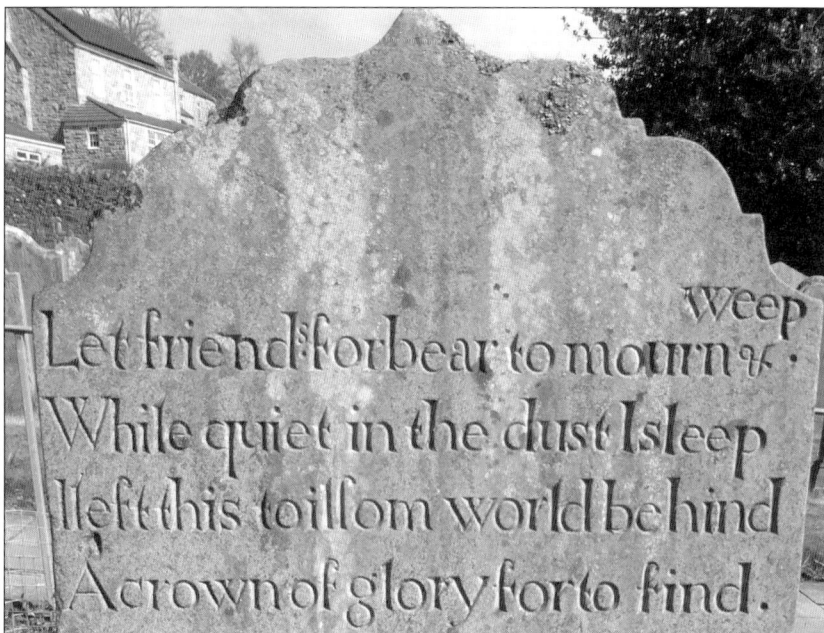

Many gravestones feature sentimental verses, often chosen from books supplied by undertakers or stonemasons, although sometimes the mason struggled to fit them neatly onto the stone, such as this charming stone in memory of Sarah Vickers, who died, aged five years, in 1787, and her parents Samuel (d.1832) and Sarah (d.1844), at Stanhope, Co. Durham. (Author's collection)

ordinary parishioners and piecing together the information gained to create a wider understanding of family connections.

While some families chose to leave a blank space on a gravestone so that later family members could be added, others had a gravestone inscribed after the demise of several family members, or once the grave space or vault was full. This may well account for the many examples where all the names fit very neatly into the space available on the stone. The amount of space in the grave may also, of course, have determined the size of the stone originally chosen.

Mistakes and recycling of gravestones

Gravestones, like any record source, can contain mistakes, especially if erected many years after a person had died, when memories of exact dates had started to fade. Equally, they could be caused by an error on the part of the mason, who miscopied the information given to him.

If you are observant, you may spot stones which have clearly been corrected, either by being overwritten, or having had new pieces of stone with the correct details inserted. There is no doubt that many mistakes were never rectified. Common errors include incorrect dates and ages, but also the spelling of surnames and totally incorrect first names. Stone was costly and, in some cases, if the mason realized he had made a mistake, he would reuse the stone, perhaps as part of a footstone, or even a headstone, but making sure that the piece he had already inscribed was underground. This can become apparent when stones are overturned or come loose. Gravestones may also be recycled to form later church fabric or to construct pathways in the churchyard or, occasionally, even outside the churchyard environment.

Gravestones in Welsh

If you are visiting Welsh graveyards, some of the gravestones will, of course, be in Welsh. There is a useful guide to Welsh vocabulary commonly used on inscriptions at **www.familysearch.org/wiki/en/ Welsh_Gravestones**.

Jewish gravestones

Jewish gravestones are similar in many ways to their Christian equivalents, potentially consisting of upright stones and chest tombs. In terms of imagery, they similarly range from plain stones through to those full of symbolism.

They are often inscribed in Hebrew, or a mixture of Hebrew and English. If there is a Hebrew inscription, it will often include the deceased's Hebrew name and also the name of their father and sometimes (especially in more modern burials) that of their mother. These can be of vital importance when you are trying to trace the origins of immigrant ancestors. The significance of the Hebrew name is that this is what they would probably have been known by prior to their arrival in England, while there could also be details of the deceased's place of origin or details of other family members in the mother country. (For more on Jewish burial records see Chapter 6.)

Durability, reading and caring for gravestones

Some gravestones survive for centuries, but many others have relatively short lives. This will partly depend on the durability of the stone used, and how exposed it is to the weather. As mentioned above, many churchyard stones have been lost or moved to facilitate grass mowing. If you visit a pre-Reformation church where there is a green expanse of grass and no gravestones, you should suspect there has been a major clearance of stones. In many cases, this will be to the side of the churchyard, where they will be propped against a wall, or even just stacked in a pile. Often, no record of their original location or their inscriptions is made before removal, but if you wish to determine the original burial site associated with a stone, it is worth checking with the PCC, or local archives, in case a burial plan exists which captured details prior to the clearance. Once resting against the church wall, many stones become overgrown with ivy, and smaller stones are more vulnerable to opportunist theft and vandalism. This was the case at Ticehurst in Sussex, where some 200 stones on the north side of the churchyard were cleared in the 1950s, to ease maintenance. A list of these was made (although not a full record), and while the intention was to re-erect them around the boundary wall, this never happened. They remain stacked in the churchyard undergrowth to this day. More recently, Ticehurst has taken great care with the recording of headstone relocations. During recent church building work, several stones had to be moved to make room for an extension, and these were all carefully relocated, and a plan made of their old and new positions. There is also now a fine plan of the churchyard and surviving memorials, together with a record of its history, which makes an admirable record for visitors.

Unfortunately, some of the measures taken by health and safety conscious burial authorities in the more recent past have been excessive,

Exploring the perimeter of the churchyard may reveal discarded gravestones such as here at Ticehurst, Sussex. (Author's collection)

resulting in the loss and premature deterioration of many precious gravestones. It can be a depressing sight to enter a churchyard or cemetery to find that gravestones appear to have been given the broad-brush treatment by the burial authority, either by means of obtrusive and insensitive staking of stones, or by lying stones down flat. This is especially upsetting if it is a memorial for members of your own family, and even more so, where the stone was unlikely to be a threat to anyone. A notorious example occurred in 2012, when over 100 graves at Anfield Cemetery in Liverpool, deemed at risk of toppling, were laid flat, causing much outcry. Such excessive behaviours were largely as a result of a very small number of, much publicized, tragic child deaths involving headstones and large compensation payments.

Technically, care and maintenance of headstones is the responsibility of the deceased's family and descendants, but local authorities in charge of graveyards and cemeteries also have a duty of care to maintain health and safety standards in relation to gravestones.

Once laid flat, the life of a stone is severely reduced, as it becomes far more vulnerable to damp, frost and mower damage. While the *Churchyards Handbook* (the Church of England's officially sanctioned guide to churchyard management) recommends that leaning stones should be straightened and repaired as soon as possible, many PCCs, local councils and cemetery authorities have historically taken a different view, and simply pushed the stones over. This is usually the simpler option, since obtaining permission from living relatives to repair stones and (in the churchyard environment) obtaining the necessary faculty from the diocese, can involve much time and effort.

Reading an illegible gravestone

A substantial number of surviving stones are frustratingly illegible, having weathered badly, or been covered with soot deposits or lichen growth. How legible a stone is does not just depend on the durability of the stone, but also how deeply the stone was incised. Even some nineteenth-century stones are now very hard to read, while, by contrast, better quality seventeenth-century stones may remain clearly legible. Some stones, which at first appear illegible, can be read with perseverance. There are several factors to be taken into account which may help you in this respect.

Angles, light and distance
Oblique light will highlight lettering, sometimes making writing that is no longer visible to the eye unaided, suddenly appear, and faint writing become clearer. A high-power torch shone diagonally towards the

writing, or revisiting the graveyard when the sun is shining obliquely onto the gravestone, will often work wonders. Experiment, shining the light from different angles. The best time to use the torch in this way is after dark, using a strong beam across the face of the stone; the raking angle of the torchlight will enhance the finer detail of the stone. You can also try using a piece of card, or even your hand, to cast a shadow over any uncertain lettering, although this is much less effective. View and take photographs of the stone from as many different angles as possible. Sometimes lettering is much easier to read from a photograph displayed on a computer screen than when on site looking at the stone. Look at the image close up, but also zoom out – this may give you a better idea of what a particular word or letter is, as it sets it into context.

Black and white

Use a photo editor on your phone or computer and turn your image into black and white, or better still, take a photo using the black and white options on your phone camera. Taking away the colour leaves a much clearer image, and often makes the stone easier to decipher.

Take prints as well as digital images

Make sure you store your images in a variety of different formats. Each will provide a backup for the other. Technology moves fast, and it's a good idea to print out your images, as well as saving shots digitally, and storing them via an online storage platform.

Water

Inscriptions often become clearer when they are wet. Visit the grave after a shower of rain, or pour plain water over the stone. There is some ill-advised advice available online regarding gravestones, one of the worst being that you should use shaving cream to make the text stand out more clearly. Most stones are very porous and quick to absorb liquids. While any form of liquid does help highlight text, shaving creams contain chemicals which can damage the surface of the stone. You should also never use bleach, or any commercial cleaners which are not specifically designed for gravestones. Some will erode the surface of the stone and make it weather even more quickly.

If you cannot fully read the inscription, hunt for an early churchyard survey which may have been made when the stone was still legible. There may also be references to inscriptions in published local or county histories. (See Chapter 6 for records related to surveys and Appendix II for how to record gravestones.)

CASE STUDY

Robert Drawbridge Chest Tomb

A large chest tomb in my home churchyard of Ivychurch was surveyed when we carried out a churchyard survey in 2014. By deduction, using an older churchyard survey from the early 1900s, the stone was almost certainly that of Robert Drawbridge who died in 1631. However, no writing could be seen on the top of the tomb or any of the sides. Then one day, as I stood in the churchyard, the sun was shining obliquely onto the front side of the tomb and the remnants of the inscription suddenly became visible again. Although not fully legible it was sufficient to see that the name was indeed Robert Drawbridge!

Cleaning and caring for gravestones

Before undertaking cleaning of any gravestone, it is advisable to seek permission from the relevant authority, typically the PCC or local council for churchyards, or the cemetery authority. Remember that some monuments may be listed, and should not be cleaned by any unauthorized person.

If you are considering cleaning a headstone, firstly ask yourself what you hope to achieve. Cleaning a gravestone in its entirety with a view to its future conservation is time consuming and needs to be done with great care. Alternatively, you may be simply clearing away overgrown ivy or floral debris over text in order to read the inscription, or prevent what you believe is potential future damage to the stone. Ivy and lichen do potentially damage stones, but clearing them carelessly can also cause damage. Assess the state of the stone before you start. Is it crumbling or laminating? If it is, pulling away plant growth may damage the stone further. Is there lead lettering? If so, this may be loosened or damaged by pulling undergrowth away from the stone. In this case, it is best to leave the stone and seek professional help.

If you have permission, and can see the stone is in good condition and is not crumbling or laminating, then gently remove any overgrowing ivy. If lichen covers the stone, assess whether it covers the whole stone and, if so, whether it is the same type of lichen. If it is, then gently cleaning it away from the area of the text you wish to read will be doing no great damage to the lichen colony. (See box on lichen growth on page 140)

Use water and a soft brush to clean the stone. An eco-friendly cleaning solution made from plant materials can be used in the water. Since most stone is porous, if you decide to use one of these cleaners for a head-to-foot total clean, then it's a good idea to start by soaking the entire stone in plain water first, and then clean it from the foot upwards, using water with the added eco-friendly cleaner in it afterwards. This is because the first dousing of water will be absorbed by the stone and the second wash of water with the cleaner in will work more effectively on the surface as a result.

Never use power tools, such as pressure washers, to clean a stone, as this removes the surface and makes the stone even more vulnerable to pollution and weathering. It's also best not to use weed killer around gravestones, as these can be absorbed by porous stones, potentially causing damage or staining the stone. Ancient parish churchyards are by their very nature relatively untainted by fertilisers or pesticides, and provide a precious, untouched environment for wildlife, which should be preserved where at all possible.

An excellent source of advice is the website of The Carved Stones Advisers Project at **https://www.scottishgraveyards.org.uk/recording. shtml**. This was a scheme which ran between 2011–2016 in Scotland and aimed to protect Scottish graveyards, but also to develop best practice in recording graveyards in general. It offers several guides covering the recording and care of churchyards and cemeteries. Its guidance sheet entitled 'Decay' clearly details the different types of weathering stones are subjected to, and how to identify various stone types. Alternatively, many stonemasons offer an aftercare service which includes periodically cleaning and resealing a gravestone, as well as re-tinting letters.

Lichen growth

Churchyards are not just the resting place of our ancestors, but in many cases also provide a natural environment for some of our endangered wildlife species. One such group of organisms that you may have noticed is lichen. These frequently find a home on church walls and gravestones. Before you start to clear lichen from the surface of any stone, bear in mind that lichen growth is a product of clean air. They are slow-growing and some will be well over 200 years old. If the lichen is not obliterating the writing on your ancestor's memorial – leave it in peace! Lichen habitats are fast diminishing and churchyards should, where at all possible, provide a sanctuary for our threatened wildlife heritage. The British Lichen Society (**www. britishlichensociety.org.uk**) is always willing to give advice on the rarity of a lichen and the best way to remove it if necessary.

Is it a gravestone?

Not everything that at first appears to be a gravestone is one. Two good examples come from my home county of Kent.

At Snave, Romney Marsh, two stones lean against the church wall, and at first glance appear to be displaced gravestones. The stones are made from Bethersden marble, a high-status stone often used for better-quality memorials. But these are not gravestones at all!

Probable boundary marker for Sir John Fagge, Snave, Kent.(Author's collection)

Closer inspection in 2018, revealed that one stone displays the text *'The Marke of Sur John Fagge'* and the other *'The Marke of Sur John Austin'*. They were actually discovered by a local farmer twenty-five years earlier, about half a mile away in a field near the Hangman's Toll Bridge. He brought them to the churchyard, where they have remained ever since. These stones are almost certainly boundary stones marking the limits of land owned respectively by Sir John Fagge and Sir John Austin, who were both members of the landed gentry. Inspection of historic OS maps reveals two 'Boundary Stones' marked in the vicinity of the field in which they were found, and corroborates this theory. The fact that they were made from Bethersden marble was probably simply due to the fact that Fagge and Austin were both men of wealth and status, and the locally-produced Bethersden marble was easily within their budget.

Of far greater importance, in terms of churchyard history, are the incised cross markers found in a significant number of Kent churchyards, and also, to a lesser extent, in some other counties. Between Ben Stocker of the Kent Archaeological Society (researching in the 1980s), myself and Andrew Linklater of Canterbury Archaeological Trust (between 2018 and 2021), a total of sixty-eight markers have been noted in Kent alone so far. These short stones all bear a cross on the front, and frequently also the reverse. Designs vary: many are lollipop-shaped, some are rectangular, but none bears any name or initial, while the style of cross varies across the range of stones recorded. While Stocker promoted the theory that they were medieval gravestones, as a result of our extensive site visits to numerous Kent churchyards, we suggest a theory he mentions in passing, but which we believe requires much more serious consideration: that they once marked the perimeters of the original churchyard, quite probably at the place where it was blessed during consecration. Very few, if any, are now in their original positions and many have been lost or recycled as a result of later building works. As news of our incised cross markers in Kent spreads, others are coming to light in other parts of the country. For a fuller account of our thoughts see Appendix I.

Gravestones today

These days, the majority of gravestones are mass manufactured and machine cut. The cost of the gravestone is often included as a package by the family's undertaker. Many cemetery stones are made of granite or marble and, as we have seen, cemeteries set their own individual regulations and fees. If you want to stand out from the crowd, however, it is possible to order a bespoke hand-crafted stone. A faculty is needed to erect a gravestone in a churchyard. These days, the undertaker, or stonemason, typically applies for this on behalf of the family. There is a fee, and each memorial is subject to strict diocesan rules regarding what is acceptable, and in keeping with the churchyard environment. These may differ slightly according to the diocese but, generally speaking, natural stones in keeping with the local area such as slate, Portland, or York stone are encouraged. Memorials with photographs, and cemetery-style gravestones with kerbs, granite chippings, and the use of artificial flowers and figurines, are considered out-of-keeping with the historic and religious nature of the site.

For details of how to record gravestones and carry out churchyard surveys see Chapter 6 and Appendix II.

Chapter 6

THE RECORDS

Studying the records detailed in this chapter will not only help you identify the resting place of the people buried in the cemeteries, graveyards and other places mentioned in this book, but enable you to learn more about their lives and the people they were connected to. It will help build a picture of each village, town, or city, and the people who lived there. This chapter largely deals with original records, explaining what they are, who created them, and where they are held. Many are now online, and online access is covered in Chapter 7, together with advice on locating missing burials, suggested recommended research practices, and tips on how to locate missing burials and identify where disinterment has taken place.

Broadly speaking, the records can be split into the following categories:

1. Records recording the act of burial.
2. Records detailing gravestones, or other memorials to the deceased.
3. Records produced in connection with funerals.
4. Peripheral sources which may help identify burial records.

Records of the parish

Parish burial registers
These relate to burials which took place in churchyards and burial grounds belonging to the Church of England (see Chapter 2). While churchyard burials were becoming the norm by the ninth century, no records were routinely kept until 1538. A new order from the king's Vicar General, Thomas Cromwell, came into force in September that year, instructing clergy to keep a record of all burials, baptisms and marriages. These records are collectively known as parish registers. Before the Dissolution of the Monasteries (1536–1541), it is highly likely that many of the high-

status burials which took place in the burial grounds attached to religious houses would have been recorded, but sadly no known records survive.

In practice, despite the order of 1538, there are relatively few surviving parish registers from this date. On average, reasonably complete coverage of burials in a typical parish begins in the early 1600s. As we have seen elsewhere, burial in the parish churchyard was most common up to the mid-nineteenth century, when lack of space increasingly led to burial in cemeteries. However, in rural areas interment in the churchyard, or adjacent parish burial ground, was the norm for far longer, as there was less demand for burial space. Parish burial registers, therefore, play a significant part in locating burials for our rural ancestors, well into the twentieth and even the twenty-first century.

Following new legislation, which first took effect in 1598 during the reign of Elizabeth I, parish register entries were written in parchment books. Prior to this, most were written in paper books or even on loose sheets of paper, and parchment (made from animal skin) was to provide a much more durable record. At the same time, it was decreed that all pre-1598 entries should be copied out into parchment books as well. You may notice the records of a parish appear to be in the same handwriting from 1538 to 1597 and this is the reason why. Copying out hundreds of register entries was a tedious task and, unfortunately, due to some ambiguity in the wording of the new legislation, many clerks took this as an opportunity to only copy out entries from 1558 (Elizabeth's year of accession). Comparing the few original paper register copies that do survive, with the later parchment copies, shows that a significant amount of the finer detail in some of the pre-1598 entries was not copied across when the parchment duplicates were made. Many copying errors also occurred, and some entries were accidentally omitted.[1]

Before 1752, England and Wales adhered to the Julian Calendar. New Year began on 25 March, and January, February and the first twenty-four days in March were, therefore, at the tail end of the year. The new-style Gregorian calendar was adopted from 1752 with New Year beginning on 1 January from this time on. When looking at pre-1752 transcriptions of entries for these months, you may see so-called 'double-dating' in operation. This records the date as it would have read according to both the Julian and Gregorian calendars respectively, for example 18 March 1653/1654. You may also see dates referred to as 'Old Style' (the date according to the Julian Calendar) or 'New Style' (Gregorian Calendar).

Throughout the centuries, many register books have been lost, stolen or damaged. Those for Harlow in Essex were stolen from the vestry of the church of St Mary and St Hugh, together with the iron chest in which they were locked, on the night of 18 August 1814. They were never seen again. They included all the parish registers up to that date, starting in the 1560s. In an attempt to mitigate this loss, Harlow's vicar, the Revd Charles Sanderson Miller, constructed a substitute register entitled *An Account of Births, Baptism, Marriages and Burials in Harlow*. This was largely compiled from the knowledge of contemporary parishioners, but also used some documentary evidence, such as accounts relating to surplice fees for 1778–1789, which also noted some burials. While the new book went nowhere near to making up for the massive loss caused by the theft, notably the information from the early registers, it was a magnificent effort and is still much appreciated by those studying Harlow families of the late-eighteenth and early-nineteenth century to this day. Sadly, few other parishes went to this trouble when registers were lost but, in some cases, you can access missing parish register information via Bishops' Transcripts (see below).

Like any source, burial registers are open to human error – incorrect names, dates, and omissions will be encountered, often unbeknown to the reader. Very few were corrected. You should be aware of this if you fail to find an entry where you strongly suspect there should be one (see Chapter 7).

Burial registers, notably between 1642 and 1660, are typically few and far between, coinciding as they do with the English Civil War and ensuing Commonwealth period. Genealogists often refer to this period as 'the Commonwealth Gap'. Initially the result of parish priests being ejected by the increasingly Puritan parliament, with no one left to record burials, in 1653 Oliver Cromwell introduced civil registration of births, deaths and marriages. All entries were to be kept in new register books, yet, frustratingly, hardly any of these books survive. Some entries did continue in the original parish registers (contrary to his orders), and some were added retrospectively from memory following the Restoration, but researchers frequently struggle to find the entries they seek at this time.

Details in parish registers: what to expect

Up to 1754, parish burial entries will often be recorded chronologically, intermingled with baptism and marriage entries. These are referred to as composite registers. Alternatively, they may be entered in the same register books as baptisms and marriages, but be allocated their own section within the book. Many parish registers were kept in a jumbled manner and it can be difficult to pinpoint the batch of burials you require, especially if searching the register on microfilm at a record office or unindexed online. From 1754, marriage entries were supposed to be kept separately in their own register books and then, in 1813, new legislation came into force which meant that entries of burial and baptism also had to be separated out in individual registers too.

Many parish registers have been digitized, making access and searching far easier, but there are many pitfalls to be aware of as you search online (see Chapter 7).

In 1645, an Act of Parliament stipulated that burial registers should include the date of death, but the legislation had little effect and, prior to 1813, it was at the discretion of whoever completed the register as to how much information was included. Burial entries tend to be fairly terse up to the early eighteenth century. There are some exceptions, but many registers simply record the person's name and date of burial. Since many families named children after parents, grandparents and siblings, it can be difficult to determine which member of a family was being buried. Occasionally a widow may simply be referred to by the epithetic 'Widow' together with her surname, or as the 'relict' of her husband.

In some cases the incumbent or parish clerk might be moved to write a lengthier entry, typically when the deceased died a shocking death, or if there was something else worthy of mention. (See *Tracing Your Ancestors Through Death Records* pp.43–47).

The examples below have been chosen from the parishes of Aldingham and Hawkshead in Cumbria (prior to the 1974 boundary changes, in Lancashire), to illustrate typical detail to be found across a range of time periods. Note the increasing detail as the years pass. Entries for women and children often include the name of the husband or father:

Aldingham

- Elin Dico[n]son [sic] buried the xixt Januarie 1558
- Eliz[abeth] Wilson of Gleaston daughter to Rich[ard] Willson [buried] 27 September 1669
- The relict of W[ilia]m Booth died in Newbigin [buried] 24 Jan 1668 Hawkshead
- Sarah wife of Peter Sorray from Hawkshead [buried] 7 September 1774
- Edward Dickinson from Green, aged 69, [buried] 10 April 1810

By contrast, below is an entry from what is often referred to as a 'Dade register'. These entries, which occur in some eighteenth and early nineteenth-century registers, will most commonly be found in

Nottinghamshire, Durham, Yorkshire and Lancashire, counties which were influenced by the beliefs of the Revd William Dade and, to a lesser extent the Revd Shute Barrington (Bishop of Durham). Both these men foresaw the importance of including detail, not just in burial entries, but also in marriage and baptism records. Apart from the basic details of name and date of burial, these entries often include the cause of death and the date of death, together with place of residence and occupation.

Ann Fieldhouse. Relict of Abraham Fieldhouse of Addingham, labourer. Died Jun. 4th. Buried June 7th of this year [1800]. 72 years. Old Age.[2]

From 1813, you should find the following in all burial entries:

• Name
• Abode
• Occupation
• Age
• Date of burial
• Officiating minister

The downside of the new legislation was that Dade-style registers ceased, although occasionally you may find secondary register copies for a parish, which continued in the pre-1813 format and ran alongside the new-style register copy. You may also encounter new-style registers where there are additional notes relating to an entry, either in the margin, or on the flyleaf of the register. A note dated 1875 in the burial register for Benenden, Kent, sets out the number of funerals that had taken place in the parish from 1813 to 1875. The Revd William John Edge was the writer, and he was clearly keen on statistics. He comments that the grand total of funerals was 1,593, 'giving a yearly average of 25¼, or about 101 funerals in 4 years.' This included the funerals of residents and non-residents in the parish, but not unbaptized children. This last is documentary evidence to corroborate the fact that, even at this relatively late date, babies who died prior to baptism were treated differently at burial, and are unlikely to have been recorded. (See also Chapter 2, pages 26–27.)

Bishops' and Archdeacon's Transcripts

If the burial registers you need do not survive, there may be surviving Bishops' Transcripts (BTs), or Archdeacons' Transcripts (ATs). These were copies of parish register entries made by the parish and were a legal requirement from 1598, although some do pre-date this. Unlike the parish registers, which were kept in a chest in the church, they were sent into the keeping of the diocese or archdeaconry. The copies were made annually or six-monthly, sometimes running from Michaelmas (29 September) to Lady Day (25 March) and from Lady Day to Michaelmas. The BTs for Ivychurch, Kent, start as early as 1564 and make a vital substitute for the first parish registers, which are missing up to 1715.

Where original parish registers do survive, these are a preferred source, since the BTs and ATs can contain copying errors and do not always include all the detail from the original entries. Conversely, however, extra details were sometimes added to the BTs and ATs as they were made, so in an ideal world you should check both. Some have been used for online 'parish register' collections, although this may not immediately be obvious. You are, therefore, advised to read the small print in the collection description.

Accessing parish burial registers and Bishops' Transcripts

Original parish registers are, with odd exceptions, held in county record offices (CROs). Prior to 1974, some county names and boundaries were very different, and you should familiarise yourself with these, as the parish registers may not be held in the CRO you expect. BTs and ATs are diocesan, rather than parish, records and may be held at a different record office again, because of the way the diocesan boundaries fell. The county/parish maps produced by the Institute of Heraldic and Genealogical Studies (now available on Ancestry) illustrate both pre-1974 county boundaries and parish and diocesan boundaries, as well as some probate jurisdictions (see also page 177). You should also check the local record office catalogue before you make a visit to ensure they have the records you want. Increasingly, parish registers are available online. See Chapter 7 for details of how to access them online and tips for searching.

Since 1978, all completed parish register books and those which contain entries over 100 years old should have been deposited in the CRO. If the registers you want are not online, you will need to visit in person, or get someone (either a volunteer or paid researcher) to go for you. Occasionally, a parish may still be using registers which date back several decades or more, and these may not be at the CRO. Some have made a special case and retain their older registers, such as All Saints at Maidstone in Kent. In that case, there may be a microfilm copy at the record office. By law, each parish must give you access to information in the register, but they also have the right to charge you for any searches made by you or by themselves on your behalf. If you are accessing parish registers at a record office you will usually view the registers via a microfilm copy, or sometimes a digitized copy. The originals are stored safely in the record office archive to preserve them. Older microfilm copies can be faded and hard to read. If the copy you are reading is illegible, staff may permit you to view the original register on request, if it is fit to be produced.

Account books of the churchwardens and overseers of the poor
Where parish burial records do not survive, check to see if there are surviving churchwardens' accounts. Among the many other entries relating to church expenses, some record not just burial fees, but also the name of the person buried, the date of burial or the date the burial fee was received. Although survival rates are not high, they can make a useful substitute for missing burial registers. Those for Kendal, Cumbria, help cover a gap in burial registers between 1631and 1679. Accounts kept by the overseers of the poor may also indirectly make mention of burials, particularly if a coffin or shroud was provided at parish cost. Any surviving churchwardens' or overseers' accounts will be at the relevant CRO and can usually be identified via the record office's online catalogue. At the time of writing there are very few online.

Burial affidavits: burials in wool
Two Acts of Parliament, in 1666 and 1678 respectively, stipulated that all corpses should be shrouded in wool, as opposed to linen or any other material. This was an attempt to boost the declining wool trade and a £5 fine could be levied if this was not done. From 1678, an affidavit had to be sworn by whoever was arranging the burial, and then signed by a Justice of the Peace or the local clergyman. Exceptions were made for paupers and plague burials. Up to about 1750, most burial registers will contain annotations to show that an affidavit had been sworn. In addition, a few parishes have surviving affidavits, sometimes referred to as certificates. As we have seen, many burial entries are terse and the affidavits provide the names of the person or people arranging each burial. While relationships are not usually recorded, in many cases these will be the deceased's next-of-kin and this information can help confirm the burial entry is the one you are looking for. The affidavits can also act as a substitute where the original burial register is missing. Use the online catalogue for the relevant CRO to see if any survive for your parish of interest.

Unique parish records
Searching the CRO catalogue by place name can turn up an unexpected record source relating to the churchyard and those buried there. A good

example is the parish of Aston Cantlow, Warwickshire, for which there is a mid-nineteenth century parish 'scrapbook' with details of each gravestone standing at the time. Although called a 'scrapbook', this term does not do this precious source justice. The information was put together in around 1847 by the vicar, the Revd Hill, and includes his own detailed sketches of each gravestone, including many which no longer stand. (See *Tracing Your Ancestors Through Death Records* pp. 80–81).

What exactly is a parish and which one am I looking for?

An understanding of how ecclesiastical parishes were organized will help you as you determine which parish registers to search for a particular burial. The parish was the smallest administrative unit of the Church of England, and should not be confused with civil parishes (see below). Angus Winchester, in his excellent book *Discovering Parish Boundaries*, defines it as 'the community which, by payment of tithes and other obligations such as Easter dues, supported a priest in a parish church, who in turn was responsible for the "cure of souls", that is the spiritual needs, of all the inhabitants within the parish community'. Parishes originally evolved as divisions of 'Great Parishes' or 'minsters', centres of local ecclesiastical administration which grew up around many of our early religious foundations from the sixth century onwards (see Chapter 2*).

There were approximately 9,000 parishes in England and Wales by the fourteenth century, and numbers remained fairly static until the booming population growth of the 1830s led to many urban parishes being sub-divided. Other parishes in heavily populated areas such as London were divided long before this.

In the north of England, parish sizes were traditionally large, reflecting the comparatively sparse population. Their geographical size presented administrative challenges, and often meant parishioners faced a long journey to attend services. Chapels of ease were frequently established to mitigate this, but few were granted burial rights until the nineteenth century, the income from this being jealously guarded by the parish, or 'mother', church. When searching for burials, it is useful to know if there were any chapels of ease for your area of interest and, if so, when they were granted the right to bury. Check record office catalogues and utilize any maps of the county which illustrate parish boundaries. These are often produced by CROs or family history societies, while *Phillimore's Atlas and Index of Parish Registers* is also a very important finding aid, with its maps now online at Ancestry (see Chapter 7). If a chapel of ease was granted burial rights, burial entries were sometimes also recorded in the registers of the mother church.

For some of our ancestors living in large parishes, the burial of a loved one might involve an arduous trek, accompanying the corpse to the distant parish churchyard along what often became well-established 'corpse routes' or 'lych wyas' (lych meaning corpse). A well-known example is that from the now extinct church at Mardale, Cumbria. The church and village were obliterated by the formation of the Haweswater Reservoir in the 1930s. Until 1736, when it acquired parish status in its own right, Mardale was in the parish of Shap. Until then, corpses were taken to Shap over a six-mile route across steep and difficult terrain via the hills of Selside Pike and Swindale Head. At Muker, Yorkshire, the corpse route was sixteen miles to the parish church at Grinton. This, no doubt, accounts for the re-establishment in 1580 of an earlier chapel of ease, but with burial rights for the first time, although burial registers only survive from 1638. Where possible, pack animals were used on corpse routes, but sometimes the coffins had to be carried by men. Therefore, wicker coffins were often used to transport the deceased, to make the journey easier. It is likely that some corpses were transported without a coffin, dressed in only a shroud, being placed into a coffin as the final approach to the church was made.

Civil parishes

New secular administrative units known as 'civil parishes' were formed from 1889. These are different to the ecclesiastical parishes we routinely deal with in our research as family and local historians, and relate to the lowest tier of administration in English secular government. It is these which are shown on modern Ordnance Survey maps. In many places in the south and Midlands of England, the boundaries of ecclesiastical and civil parishes coincide, but this is less often the case in the north of England, where they often reflect much earlier smaller administrative divisions. Civil parishes were also created in Wales but from 1974 were re-designated as 'communities'.

The *National Index of Parish Registers* (NIPR) by D.J. Steele is a comprehensive guide, which lists the location and coverage of known surviving registers for the Church of England, Nonconformists, Jewish and Catholic registers. Published in a series of volumes during the 1960s and 1970s, and arranged according to region, copies are available at genealogical archives and libraries, notably the Society of Genealogists and The National Archives, while copies are also for sale online. These days, most researchers use online finding aids such as GENUKI or the Family Search WIKI (see Chapter 7), but the NIPR still makes a useful reference source.

Nonconformist and other ex-parochial records

As we saw in Chapter 3, with the exception of the Society of Friends (see below), relatively few Nonconformist churches had their own burial grounds, until the late nineteenth century, and some never did. Separate Acts of Parliament in 1840 and 1857 required all surviving registers to be handed in to the government, and these were placed under the care of the Registrar General. All those registers handed in now form part of TNA's ex-parochial registers collection, comprising of series numbers RG4–RG8. While compliance was not comprehensive, a great number of registers were handed over, and they are an important source for family historians. They were sorted into 'authenticated' and 'unauthenticated' registers, the latter being registers which were compiled retrospectively, after the events to which they refer. (See Chapter 7 for online coverage.) The Registrar General was given authority to issue certificates of birth/baptism, marriage, and death/burial, from information in the authenticated registers (upon application by members of the public), but he was not allowed to use the unauthenticated registers for this purpose. You may find any certificates issued among family papers. Other registers which were not handed in at this time, or which post-date 1857, can sometimes be found at CROs, or may still be held by the relevant Church.

Many Nonconformist churches organized themselves on a circuit basis. Circuits covered many towns or villages, all the responsibility of one minister who travelled the circuit, holding services at different locations. Despite this, your ancestors may have had to travel some distance to attend chapel and if the chapel had a burial ground, they may be buried quite some way from where they lived. The circuit register books (which also recorded births or baptisms and from 1837 marriages) typically accompanied the minister as he travelled around his circuit, and ministers often regarded the registers as their own personal property, which is one reason that many do not survive.

Dafydd Ifans' *Nonconformist Register of Wales* (Aberystwyth: National Library of Wales and Welsh County Archivists' Group, 1994), and *Nonconformist Registers of Wales,* published by the National Library of Wales in 1994, are useful guides for Welsh Nonconformist research.

TNA holds an *Index of Places* covering RG4 which includes those registers handed in by 1840. Although incomplete, this index is fascinating in itself, as it lists many hamlets and farms mentioned in the registers. It is a useful aid for those trying to plot the history of smaller settlements, which may not feature on early OS maps, and which had perhaps been 'lost' by the time the OS introduced its large-scale 25-inch mapping (see Chapter 3). There is also a computerised list of the chapels in RG4, arranged by denomination, which quickly shows what is available for each denomination.

Two of TNA's research guides, respectively entitled *Nonconformist and non-parish births, marriages and deaths 1567–1969* and *Nonconformists,* provide further essential background on this collection.

Society of Friends (Quaker) burials

The Society was an excellent record-keeper and their burial records are some of the most detailed and are worthy of especial note. The Library of the Society of Friends in London holds many burial records, with copies also being found in CROs and at TNA (see below) and online (see Chapter 7).

The earliest Quaker burial records date to the mid-1650s, although start dates vary from place to place. Two copies of each entry were made. The first was to be kept by the local Monthly Meeting (local governing body of the church), which had charge of the relevant burial ground. The second was sent to the Quarterly Meeting. The Quarterly Meeting covered a wider geographical area, and was loosely based on county boundaries. If the deceased was not a member of the particular Meeting within whose boundaries he was buried, a copy would also be sent to the Meeting to which he belonged. In many cases, the burial entry doubled up as an instruction to the gravedigger regarding burial of the body. From 1776, records were kept in pre-printed registers and, as well as the place of burial, provide the deceased's name, date of death and burial, age, abode, and occupation. Entries relating to women and children will typically record their next-of-kin. Earlier records are not standardized but will frequently give the date of death and burial, as well as the place of burial, and sometimes the cause of death.

In addition, upon being required by the government to hand in their registers in 1840 and 1857, the Society made transcriptions of registers for their own use; these are known as 'digests'. Arranged by surname and date, they make a useful supplementary source which can act as a handy finding aid for those studying a particular surname, as well as for those seeking a particular burial. Quaker burial records at TNA are in series RG6 and go up to 1841.

The Quakers had their own system of identifying the months of the year, objecting to the fact that some standard month names evolved from words associated with pagan gods. Instead, they referred to the months by their consecutive number in the year. This can confuse researchers when dealing with dates prior to 1752, if they fail to remember that England and Wales were still using the Julian Calendar up to this point and New Year began on 25 March. For example, the Quakers would refer to September as the seventh month until 1752, when it duly became the ninth month. (See also Case Study on pages 181–182.)

Records of institutional burial grounds

TNA holds a great variety of other burial registers in its ex-parochial collections, notably those relating to burials in cemeteries attached to hospitals, gaols or workhouses.

While many inmates who died in prison were buried in the local churchyard or cemetery, some were buried in the prison grounds (see Chapter 3). There are some records at TNA in series HO324, which includes a register of prison burials, 1834–1969, and a register of graves of criminals executed in prisons in England and Wales. The latter is arranged alphabetically by name of prison and also gives the grave number, while there is also a collection of prison burial ground plans which identify the numbered plots.

Workhouse burial grounds should have burial registers, while the associated death should also be listed in its Registers of Deaths or its Admission and Discharge Registers. Not all records survive and there are no guarantees that everyone was recorded. Use Peter Higginbotham's excellent website, **www.workhouses.org.uk**, to determine where there are surviving records (see also Chapter 7). Hospital records can be identified using the Hospital Records Database at **www.nationalarchives. gov.uk/hospitalrecords**, although this has not been updated since 2012. Many long-stay asylum or hospital records will be at CROs and can be identified using the record office's online catalogue.

Armed Forces burial records

TNA holds records relating to burials in military and naval cemeteries, such as the Sandhurst Royal Military College Chapel in Surrey, the Haslar and Clayhall Royal Navy cemeteries in Gosport, Hampshire and the Sheerness Dockyards Church on the Isle of Sheppey in Kent (Series numbers ADM 6, ADM 73, ADM 305 and WO 156). These have now been digitized by the commercial burial website Deceasedonline and also include various overseas military cemeteries. The Commonwealth War Graves Commission has excellent records of those buried in the World Wars but these are only accessible online. (See Chapter 3 and 7.)

Catholic burial records

As we have seen in chapters 1 and 3, prior to 1534 England and Wales were Catholic countries, but following the establishment of the Church of England, some of our ancestors refused to accept this change and adhered to the Catholic faith. Historically they are frequently referred to as 'recusants', and since their burial was specifically officially restricted to parish churchyards until 1852, you may see the annotation 'papist' next to their entry in the parish registers. While Catholic churches were officially allowed their own burial grounds from 1852, numbers were still relatively few when compared to other Nonconformist burial grounds, and from this time you will often find Catholics buried in cemeteries, which were, of course, usually non-denominational. (See cemetery records, pp. 157–60.)

There is no central repository for historic Catholic church burial registers and the majority will be held by an individual Catholic diocese (sometimes in their own archive if they have one, but generally not available to the public), or occasionally by the actual church itself. Searches are most often made on behalf of the public by the archivist or incumbent priest, at his discretion, while some records are now coming on line (see Chapter 7).

There are also a few Catholic burial registers at TNA in series RG4. You can find all those kept at TNA by using the 'Advanced search' facility on its catalogue and searching for 'catholic' and restricting the search to record series RG4.

For further reading on Catholic ancestors see *Tracing Your Roman Catholic Ancestors* by Stuart Raymond (Pen & Sword Books, 2018).

Jewish burial and cemetery records

The Jewish Genealogical Society of Great Britain is an excellent source of information for Jewish research, and both *Tracing Your Jewish*

Ancestors by Amanda Rosemary Wenzerul (Pen & Sword, 2008) and Dr Antony Joseph's *My Ancestors Were Jewish* (4th edition, Family History Partnership, 2008) are useful guides to help track down Jewish death and burial records. If there was no Jewish cemetery in the neighbourhood, then the body may have been transported many miles to an appropriate Jewish cemetery, or the deceased may be buried in the parish churchyard.

When seeking Jewish burials, background research into a particular cemetery should tell you not only when it was first used for burials, but whether it had any bias towards burying Jews from a particular area.

Records of the cemetery and crematorium

From the foundation of the first joint stock cemeteries in the early nineteenth century, all cemeteries were legally obliged to keep records of who was buried within the cemetery. That does not necessarily mean that all records survive, or were well kept.

Records relate either to the act of burial itself, the allocation or purchase of grave spaces, or reopening of graves. While cemeteries recorded information in registers, much of this was duplicated in paperwork given to the deceased's family, and such paperwork is often found among family papers. If you are interested in the history of the cemetery itself, there may also be records relating to its establishment, administration and ongoing maintenance. These may have been deposited at the local CRO, or may still be held by the cemetery itself. The variety of records will vary from cemetery to cemetery, and each had its own system of keeping records, with larger, busier, cemeteries usually producing a greater range of records.

Records of Bunhill Fields Cemetery

Burial registers are at TNA under RG4 (see also Chapter 7). The burials cover 1713–1854. At London Metropolitan Archives there are also interment books for 1789–1854 arranged in date order (Reference: CLC/271/MS01092/1-18). These provide names, ages, dates of burial, places from which bodies were brought, undertakers' names and addresses, and the location of the grave. There is also a list of surviving gravestone inscriptions as of 1869 (Archival reference: CLC/271/MS00897/1-7), and an index to surnames (CLC/271/MS00897/8). A plan of the burial ground in 1869 (CLC/271/MS00897/9) and a set of location and section plans of the cemetery prepared in June 1973 (CLC/271/MS38987) are also available. (See also Chapter 3.)

Cemetery burial registers and day books

Burial registers are, naturally, the core source for locating cemetery burials. They are almost always ordered chronologically and provide the grave number, full name and age of the deceased, last known address, date of burial, name of officiating minister, the registration district where the death was registered, the name of the registrar and date of registration. The registration date is when the death was registered at the register office and is rarely the same as the date of death. The registers will often also record the name and address of the undertaker. Occasionally, the location of very early public graves may not be not recorded.

Since burial registers are chronological and rarely indexed, cemetery staff will be keen to obtain an exact date of death from you, if you ask them to carry out a search. If there is an Alpha Book, this will be their first port of call (see below). Remember that the majority of cemeteries buried people of all faiths, and these records are not restricted to any one particular religious group.

Some larger cemeteries also have day books, which provide a daily record of burials taking place at the cemetery. They are worth looking at even if you have seen the burial register, since they often contain greater detail. Entries may include the depth of the grave, or the size of the coffin, as well as the hour of burial and details of any stone that was later placed on the grave.

In rare cases, where the local parish had an arrangement with the cemetery to bury its dead (usually where space was running out in the parish churchyard), cemetery burials may also be recorded in parish burial registers, such as at Cullompton in Devon.

Cremation registers

Similar to burial registers, these record the date of cremation and, if the ashes were buried in the crematorium, the plot number. Cremated ashes may also be deposited in a garden of remembrance within a churchyard and an entry is usually, but not always, made within the parish burial register to this effect. Increasingly, ashes are sprinkled informally by the family at a chosen location favoured by the deceased, and there will be no formal record of this.

Alpha Books

These are a semi-alphabetical record of everyone buried in the cemetery, typically ordered by initial letter of surname. They are an important finding aid for cemetery staff to ascertain whether or not a particular individual was buried there, especially if a date of death is not known. They are usually only found in larger urban cemeteries.

Private grave registers

Private grave registers record the purchase of private grave plots, as opposed to plots reserved for public or common graves. These will tell you the name of whoever purchased the grave space, and the cost and date of purchase. It will also record the names of the people buried in that plot. Some families planned ahead and bought plots in advance. By contrast, some purchased grave space only after a family member died. After the initial interment in a family grave, the registers will note when it was reopened for any later burial. Where there was a change of ownership, records were updated where possible.

Some cemeteries kept one set of grave registers which included both private and common graves. Each entry should state if the grave was purchased, and if so by whom, or whether the grave was a common grave. Either way, there should also be details of who was buried in that grave. These registers are often organized by section and plot number, which are also recorded in the burial register, enabling easy cross-referencing between the two sets of records. By looking in the grave registers you can then see who else is buried in that grave, whether common or purchased.

Certificates of Exclusive Right of Burial

These were issued by the cemetery to the purchaser of a burial plot and may turn up among family papers. They conferred proof of the right to burial in that space and had to be produced when a grave was reopened. You will typically find details of the name and address of the purchaser, date of purchase, plot number, square number and also the dimensions of the plot. You may also see annotations (often on the reverse) recording when the grave was reopened and for whom. The ownership of burial rights could be bequeathed by a purchaser via his or her will, and from 1847 the Cemetery Clauses Act stipulated that all such bequests had to be registered by the cemetery concerned within six months of probate and before any further burial could take place. The cemetery also had the right to levy a further fee on the new owner of the grave space if they wished.

Cemetery Order for Burial

Cemetery burial orders detail the arrangements for the funeral: name, age and address of the deceased, name and address of the undertaker, details of the number of coffin bearers, and the nature of the burial – whether it was to be a new grave or the reopening of an existing private grave. They should also detail the depth of the burial and the fees paid. They will usually be discovered among family papers.

Cemetery plans

Cemeteries and crematoria will hold plans which will help you identify the location of a grave. Many cemeteries are divided firstly into large sections and then into smaller areas known as 'squares'. These are imaginary divisions and there are no formal boundary lines on the ground. Each grave plot has its own unique number, which relates to the section and square in which it lies. Some plans are online via individual cemetery websites, or other portals such as Deceasedonline (see Chapter 7). Otherwise, copies will be available at the cemetery, or sometimes in local record offices or libraries.

In some cemeteries, the proposed grave sites were drawn out neatly in advance on a plan, but in others the plans are less organized, with burial plots being drawn in only as burials occurred, and not always to scale. This can make locating the exact position of a burial plot, or even a particular row, difficult. Identifying where two rows abut or intersect, and then following a row along until you reach the grave you are looking for is often a useful method of detection.

Books of Remembrance

Intended for display in cemetery or crematoria chapels, or other public areas, these list the names of people buried in the cemetery on the anniversary of their death or burial. There was an extra charge for this, therefore relatively few people are included.

Undertakers' records and funeral papers

These include paperwork given to the family in connection with the funeral, but also records kept by the undertaker for his own reference. Funeral papers are typically found within family papers, passed down from one generation to the next. In some cases, they may be located in record offices as part of a deposited collections of solicitors' papers, if solicitors were involved with arranging the funeral. The solicitors may be mentioned in your ancestor's will as executors of the estate. Depending on the nature of the collection, and how intricately it has been indexed for cataloguing purposes, you may be able to identify the individual documents relating to your family, but more often than not you will need to search the whole collection.

Notable records found among family funeral papers are undertakers' invoices and memorial cards, and there is also a crossover here with many of the records issued by the cemetery. If the undertaker dealt with the cemetery on the family's behalf, then they might well have given the family those documents produced by the cemetery, such as burial orders and certificates of right of burial.

Undertakers' invoices often give an insight into what a particular funeral was like. They do vary depending on the date and the individual undertaker, but often include a detailed description of the coffin, the number of hearses and coffin bearers, and list any mourning items ordered, such as gloves or memorial cards. The name, date of death and age of the deceased will naturally be included, as well as any extra transport costs.

Memorial or funeral cards were small printed cards commemorating the deceased, usually organized by the undertaker on behalf of the family, and sent to family and friends after the funeral. They provide the name and age of the deceased, the burial ground and plot number, plus the date of death or burial. Most also include a short verse extolling the virtues of the deceased, or hinting at the circumstances of his or her death. They bear the undertaker's name and address and can provide a helpful lead as you move on to hunt for any surviving undertakers' records. While they are typically found among family papers, random cards are for sale online and Elizabeth Kelley Kerstens has started a database of cards at http://ancestorsatrest.com.

In Affectionate Remembrance

OF

Herbert Hemming Heritage

Who died _20th January_ 1940

Aged _54_ .

Interred at _Camberwell New_ Cemetery

Grave No. _5851_ _Sq 25_

A bitter grief, a shock severe.
To part with one we loved so dear;
Our loss is great—we'll not complain
But hope in Heaven to meet again.

J. H. Billes & Sons, Undertakers, 282, Southampton Way, Camberwell, S.E.5.

Memorial cards don't just give the date of death and place of interment, but also often provide details of the family undertaker, which could lead you to further records. (Author's collection)

CASE STUDY

Heritage family grave and funeral papers

As a curious teenager, I started rooting around our attic, looking for any records relating to my Dad's family, of which he never spoke. I found a pile of memorial cards in a box with some old photographs, and a selection of funeral papers. They provided a very useful source of information and I used them to start his side of our family tree. My grandparents Frederick Henry and Florence Heritage married in 1912 and their first child, Clarence, was born in October 1915. Sadly, he died just a few months later on 2 January 1916. He was buried at Woodgrange Park Cemetery, London, and this led to the purchase of a family grave plot. Among our family papers, we have a collection of documents received from both the cemetery and the undertakers as successive family members died. These help to build a picture of the family at the death of each person, and outline the history of the family grave space.

The first of the cemetery records is a 'Certificate of Exclusive Right of Burial'. It was issued by Woodgrange Park Cemetery to my grandfather for a grave space in the cemetery. There are also two cemetery burial orders, one for Clarence and one for his grandmother, Emily Harriet Heritage. In addition, there were several undertakers' invoices: one each for Clarence, Emily and Frederick's wife, Florence. Finally, there were papers connected with Frederick's own passing.

The documents told me the following story. At the death of his son Clarence, Frederick (by all accounts a financially astute person) invested in a grave space to accommodate other family members as they died. Purchased in perpetuity, the plot was 6ft 6in long, 2ft 6in wide. Its number was 6678 and it was located in Square 26. This grave was one coffin width and Clarence's burial order shows that his grave was dug at a depth of 14ft. Thus, there was plenty of space in the grave plot – allowing room for later burials stacked one upon the other.

The certificate of exclusive right of burial, which was issued a couple of months after Clarence's interment, records the initial burial in 1916 and on the back, cemetery staff recorded the opening of the grave each time it was opened to admit a new family member. It was opened in 1924 for Frederick's mother, Emily, and her burial order shows that she was buried at a depth of 12ft. It was then opened for his wife, Florence, in 1940, despite the fact that the family had moved to Wickford, Essex, some 30 miles away.

Although there was sufficient room in the grave plot for Frederick, when he died in 1949 he had decided he wanted to be cremated. As we saw in Chapter 4, cremation had become increasingly popular after the First World War, but it is unlikely to have been an option offered to him by the undertaker when he bought the grave space at Woodgrange in 1916. He was cremated at the South London Crematorium in Streatham Vale (opened 1936), which was about thirteen miles from where he was living at the time, and his ashes were also interred there.

Following the granting of probate for Frederick's estate, the certificate of burial rights for the plot at Woodgrange Park Cemetery records that the right to burial in the Woodgrange plot was transferred to my father on 13 February 1950.

No further burials ever took place in the Heritage plot at Woodgrange Park and, sadly, the gravestone erected to Florence and Clarence was almost certainly destroyed in the early 2000s. On this occasion, I did not find out in time to rescue the gravestone.

Extract from the certificate of right of burial for Frederick Heritage. (Author's collection)

The records kept by the undertaker for their own reference can also provide fascinating detail about the funerals they arranged and the families they dealt with. These should give an insight into the way funeral businesses were run, and what was involved in a typical funeral at different time periods. They can be used to ascertain the different levels of service provided, and to assess the contrasting wealth, and therefore the budgets, of the families concerned.

Sadly, relatively few undertakers' records survive, since there has never been any statutory legislation to preserve them. However, it is worth tracking down those that do. Typically, they consist of registers, ledgers or notebooks, although these vary greatly in format according to the undertaker and time period. You may encounter ledgers with copious details about the deceased: age, date of death, next-of-kin, funeral costs, details of the coffin, type of grave, burial place, interment fees, and a record of where the body was to be collected from. There may be details of expenses involved due to repatriation of the deceased from abroad, or transportation home from elsewhere in the UK. Some of these records are neat and fully indexed, others are messy and hard to decipher, while many use abbreviations, which can be hard to fathom. You may also find a myriad of papers relating to various funerals have been filed loose in a ledger.

By contrast, records may take the form of a plain notebook with simple lists of those buried, but sometimes including tantalisingly brief biographical details, such as those for Dray and Co. of Hythe, Kent (see below). For the family historian, these can be the most fascinating, although the meaning behind some of the remarks is often lost, leading to further questions!

There may also be records relating to the running of the business, such as cash or account books. Some of these may make reference to clients by name and help identify a funeral date, but will otherwise be of little use for family historians seeking information on a particular person. What they do provide is a rare insight into the running of an undertaker's business at any particular time, the costs of a typical funeral, and what was involved in arranging it, from lists of goods supplied, through to car hire and many other costs.

Locating undertakers' records

If you have found memorial cards, you will already have identified the relevant undertaker. Otherwise, searches in local trade directories and newspaper adverts of the time, in tandem of course with a search of the internet, should help you build a picture of which undertakers were

CASE STUDY

Contrasting undertakers' records from the 1830s and 1970s

The 1835 entry for George Colley from ledgers of Gore Brothers Undertakers, Kent. (Gore Brothers Ltd, Margate.)

Two contrasting undertaker's ledgers which provide a clear illustration of how mourning tradition all but fell out of favour in the inter-war period. The first is from Gore Brothers of Margate, Kent for the funeral of George Colley, who died aged nine in 1835 and was buried in a coffin covered in grey cloth, lined inside and fitted with a mattress, frilled sheet and pillow. Payments include those for mourning gloves

The 1973 entry for Joseph Arthur Tasker from the ledgers of James Recknall Undertakers, Hackney. (Author's collection)

and bands for the minister, clerk, and sexton, mourning cloaks, and fees for the coffin bearers, coachmen, sexton and mason. The second is from James Recknall & Co. of Hackney, London, for Joseph Arthur Tasker who died in 1973 aged 96 and concentrates on vehicle hire, names and addresses. There are many abbreviations which would only have been understood by Recknall's staff, but we also learn that Joseph had been '50 years Police Pensioner from Dalston Police Station', 'Mr Thomas Tasker of Boreham Wood' paid for the funeral, and that Joseph was buried at Abney Park Cemetery.

CASE STUDY

Dray & Son

Dray & Son was a firm of undertakers in Hythe, Kent. Records are held at the Kent History and Library Centre in Maidstone.[3] The records begin in 1814, with a notebook listing those who had died, and the date of burial. Despite the fact that they are written in a very truncated note form, they include many essential snippets of information, such as occupation, cause of death, or relationship to another person. Several examples record where a child was buried in the grave of a grandparent, while some detail the transportation of the deceased, such as 'Waggon train, Morn[ing]'. There also some interesting comments on the cost of graves and burials inside the church at Hythe. At the front of the book is a diagram showing the inhabitants of the brick-lined graves in the church porch, where families by the name of Puckle, Rogers and Wilson were buried. There is also a list of charges associated with funerals and graves as of 1814. These were as follows:

Sexton fees for a Child	£3 6d
If the Great Bell	£7 6d
Over 2 years and if under 10 years	£4 6d
If the Great Bell	£8 6d
Man or Woman	£5 6d
If the Great Bell	£9 6d
Out of Parrish [sic]. Double fees	£11
If the Great Bell	£13
Extra Digging over 4ft	£1

[Plus]: 2s for the 2nd ft, 3s for the 3rd ft, 4s for the 4th ft

An entry for 1816 tells us that the cost of a brick-lined grave for a child was £10, although, frustratingly, the cost for an adult is illegible. Below is a selection of entries from 1814–1819 which helps give a flavour of what may be learned from even such a simple listing.

- 3 soldiers buried
- 16th January Woman died in workhouse, name Jackson
- 20 March Samuel Wormall died 60 od[d] years sexton of Hythe, aged 79 years, buried 27th
- 21 Mr East Wheelwright daughter
- 23 March Mr Trivilon died March 2nd buried in church
- 11 January 1815 horse soldier son buried
- 13th February 1815 Mr Longdon the organist died
- 8th April 1815 Mr Kemp the brewer['s] daughter died, buried 15th
- May 8th Mrs Fagg died, aged 46. 12th buried in a Vault
- 13 May 1815 Mr Pilcher the brewer, child died
- May 2nd a Blind Scotch Man died at Kings Head, buried 5th
- June 9th Mr Clark, Gardener, daughter died, buried 11th
- 21 William Everden, Wife died 25th carried to Bilsington by canal
- 6th Henry Witherden, twin died
- 8th other one died, boath [sic] buried 13 December check
- 29 December 1818 Mr Pilcher the Gardener, child died 30th buried smallpox, aged 5 months
- January 20th [1819] Nurse Baker died in Hospital 24th buried aged 72 years

The later ledger books for Dray & Son include much greater detail, giving a breakdown of expenses for each funeral. They begin in the early 1900s and are indexed by name. The entries vary, depending on which aspects of the funeral the undertaker dealt with. Some include details of the coffin, and some give details of payment for organists, and the tolling of the funeral bell. Two examples are abstracted below.

Elsie Case
January 5–8th 1909
Died at the Duke of Bedford's Hospital at Woburn, Bedfordshire
Elsie Case 27 years
Cab from Hythe to Dymchurch & back to arrange funeral: 12s 6d
Various telegrams and letters to the following recipients:

- Mr Bowen, Mr Bowen, Mr Case, and Revd Bolder
- Postage on Box of flowers to Mr Woodland   15s 0d

1 Cab to Station for Mourners, then on to Dymchurch, waiting to bring back to Hythe Station   £1
1 Cab to Hythe Station for Mourners afterwards found not wanted 3s 6d
1 Waggonette from Station to Dymchurch   17s 6d
1 Car & Pair from station to Dymchurch   £3 3s 0d
Interment fees at Dymchurch   £1 1s
Gave Sexton 1s
4 Body Bearers at Station & at Dymchurch   £1 8s 0d
Attendance £40s. Allowances 9 [?d] Grave Porter   £1
18th Grave Waggoner for Carriage of Wreath received late on 12th   6d
20th Letter to Layton Bros Ditto Gerard Ltd.   9d
21st Carriage of empty to Laxton Bros Ditto to Gerard Ltd   8d

Mary Ann Wiles
1 Capel Cottages Sellindge, Hythe
January 20–27
Mary Ann Wiles, 67 years
1" Elm coffin with Nickel furniture and necessary lining   £3 10s
C.H. Dray's time getting size for coffin   2s 6d
Conveyance & men's time going to Sellindge with coffin   12s 6d
Interment fees double for non-parishioners   £1

Board fees – double for non-parishioners   5s
Ministers' fees for removal of stone   £1
Car & Pair from Sellindge to Hythe church   £2 10s
2 Flys from Sellindge to Hythe church and back to Sellindge   £1 15s
3 Bearers to Sellindge & back/3 Bearers met at end of the barracks
   £1 10s
Bell at time of funeral   1s
Attendance   20s
Gloves   7s

operating in the area when your ancestor died. The undertaker's name will also be found in cemetery records (see above). You can then search to see if there are any surviving records for the business. Start with the internet search. This may indicate that the company is still in existence and a direct approach can be made to them, regarding accessing any surviving records. Whether there are any surviving records is another matter. Many paper records have been destroyed due to lack of space, or as undertaking businesses closed, or were absorbed into larger companies. The chances of survival are not great, but it is worth looking. Some records may have been deposited at a record office, and should be included in their catalogue. Others will still be in private hands, perhaps held by descendants of the undertaker.

Monumental masons' records

This is an interesting source, especially for understanding the trade of the monumental mason and types of gravestones offered at different times. The records may also help you identify details of a particular gravestone, but many records do not survive, having been lost as the stonemason retired, or companies went out of business. You may find some records have been deposited at local record offices, while others remain in the keeping of private individuals, or as part of the records of extant businesses. In this case, it will be at the discretion of the current stonemason, or individual, as to whether they can give you access to the record or search them for you. Use TNA's Discovery catalogue to locate records which have been deposited in archives, searching on 'monumental masons'.

The amount of detail in the records will vary but they can provide a useful insight into the cost of the memorial and its design, and also the names and addresses of next-of-kin. Some will also detail the inscription, and this can be especially precious where the gravestone no longer survives, and has not been recorded as part of a monumental survey. However, you should not expect this as standard. Many stonemasons did not keep a permanent record of the inscriptions they carved, nor of the grave numbers associated with the grave plot. Entries will also include details of other work undertaken by the mason, such as cleaning and restoration, or the adding of new names when other family members died.

Records naturally follow different formats according to the individual stonemason's preference. Often taking the form of registers or ledger books, they are typically ordered chronologically, either headed with the name of each client, or by a description of each stone as it was sold, for example 'body stone 3ft 6in long' or 'Stone book on rock 15ft × 20in × 8in'. Gravestones were often cut as blanks in advance, with only the inscription needing to be added. Where registers are ordered by client, these are usually chronological and include the name of the purchaser, name of the deceased, details to be inscribed on the stone and the cost.

Identifying the name of the stonemason who carved the stone, and whether there might be any surviving records, can involve some detective work. While many stones had the mason's name carved at the foot, on the back, or sometimes on the side, this may no longer be visible above ground because the stone has sunk. In this case, and also if the stone no longer stands, research in local trade directories and local newspapers may provide the names of local monumental masons operating in the area at the time. You may also find details of gravestones among undertakers' records, if they had made the arrangements with the mason. It's important to remember, however, that many people had no memorial.

Stonemasons' records may record renovations as well as erection of gravestones. This 1946 entry from the registers of Cleverley and Spencer, Dover, relates to the renovation of a memorial to Charles Tyrell including 91 new lead letters at 7d each, all paid for by 'Mr. H.E. Frost of London Road, Dover'. (Cleverley and Spencer Monumental Stone Masons)

Newspapers and wills

Newspapers are useful for locating obituaries and notices of death, which may in turn help locate a burial place. Notices relating to the granting of probate will also help pinpoint a date and place of death, which will, in turn, potentially help identify the burial. Copies of all original newspapers are available at the British Library Newspaper Room, St Pancras, London, and copies are frequently held locally in county archives and libraries. A substantial number of newspapers have also been digitized and put online (see Chapter 7). Use the book *Local Newspapers 1750–1920* by Jeremy Gibson, Brett Langston and Brenda W. Smith (3rd edition, FFHS, 2011) to determine which papers were in print at the time you are investigating.

Although not a primary source for locating burials, wills may contain bequests of burial rights, while some testators stipulated where they wished to be buried. They are especially useful if you are researching a higher-status family prior to the nineteenth century, who were likely to have been buried in a family vault, or for earlier research into the burial history of the church itself. Prior to the Reformation, wills are one of the most useful sources for those trying to build a picture of who is buried in the church. This was an era when it was normal for those of wealth and status to donate money to the church and ask for masses to be sung after their death, to help atone for sins and speed transit through Purgatory. Such bequests and requests are often recorded in probate records, alongside a specification for burial in a certain church, or particular spot in the church. Although such requests were not always carried out, pre-Reformation wills are one of the very few sources referencing burials prior to the advent of parish registers.

In his will dated 1393, John Lynot of Ivychurch, Romney Marsh, asked 'to be buried in the chapel of the Blessed Mary in the church of Ivechurch'.[4] As well as bequests to his family, he also left money to repair one of the windows near to his burial site and for the repair of the church path which led from the door next to his resting place, towards the village. These are interesting comments on the layout of the churchyard in the late fourteenth century, and of potential interest to both local and church historian. Also in Kent, Richard de Warmyngtone, rector of the parish church of Adisham, was more precise in his will, which was proved in 1378, and stated he was to be buried in the church 'next the body of Sir Roger Dygge in the chancel'. (For further information on using newspapers and wills see Chapter 7 and also *Tracing Your Ancestors Through Death Records*.)

Memorial or monumental inscriptions, epitaphs and churchyard plans and surveys

These are all terms given to describe the recording of gravestones and other memorials; principally the written inscriptions, but in some cases also their design and form. Often they are referred to by the abbreviation 'MIs'. Some will include all memorials within the graveyard or cemetery (including those inside the church where relevant), but others will be more selective. Understanding why a survey was created is helpful, as it may reveal that not all memorials were recorded.

In recent years, there has been a growing appreciation of gravestones as a precious yet vulnerable source of genealogical data and memorial artwork. Many are fast deteriorating due to pollution, and churchyard and cemetery reordering. There are a growing number of surveys undertaken by volunteer groups and commercial companies which are going a long way to preserving a record of surviving stones, and which will also help you to identify those gravestones relevant to your research.

While your starting point should be online resources, as described in the next chapter, it's important to track down any earlier off-line surveys

This ledger stone in the churchyard at St Mary's Church, Stockbury, Kent, was uncovered during drainage works. There is no doubt that many ledger stones have similarly been covered up over the years, but relatively few are rediscovered. (Andrew Linklater)

too. Loss of gravestones due to weathering and removal is not just a modern phenomenon, and some churchyard stones had relatively short lives, or became illegible within a short space of time (see Chapter 5). Inside the church, memorials were not only frequently moved to new locations, but were also covered over by new flooring or furniture. Therefore, the older the survey the better, as long as it does not pre-date the death of someone you are looking for! Such early surveys are a great asset for tracking down details of stones which no longer survive or are illegible. There are various places you can look for these. Local historians and antiquarians have been fascinated by gravestones and memorials for centuries, often listing memorials inside and outside the church. Some of their surveys date back to the eighteenth and nineteenth century. Some were originally published as books, with others preserved in private notes but later being deposited at archives or with history societies. Many

Cemetery friends' groups

The Friends of Highgate Cemetery in London was responsible for saving the run-down Highgate cemetery after company funds ran out. Formed in 1975, its aim is 'to promote the conservation of the cemetery, its monuments and buildings, flora and fauna, for the benefit of the public as an environmental amenity'. Over the years, it has cleared a massive amount of vegetation from the overgrown cemetery, and worked to restore many of the memorials, as well as arranging major restoration of architecturally important sections of the cemetery, such as the Circle of Lebanon, the Terrace Catacombs and the chapel. The cemetery and many of its monuments have now been listed by English Heritage. While the Friends of Highgate Cemetery is well-known, there are many other groups formed by volunteers to protect and conserve our historic cemeteries, and in some cases to also care for the ecology and wildlife found within. Many organize tours, or collate information about the history of the cemetery and those buried there, and their work can be a fruitful source for the researcher. A good example of a smaller group is the lottery-funded Friends of Hastings Cemetery in Sussex, which has carried out projects to detail stories about those buried within the cemetery and to list stonemasons who operated in the area.

The National Federation of Cemetery Friends (**https://www.cemeteryfriends.com**) was formed in 1986 to help these groups and provides much advice for cemetery conservation as well as listing those groups which are members or associates of the federation.

such publications can be found at the Society of Genealogists in London, while others have been indexed and published by local and family history societies as books, CDs, or online. A good example is the Bristol and Gloucestershire Archaeological Society, which published the surveys undertaken by antiquarian Ralph Bigland in the 1750s. A local history group may have carried out a churchyard survey and occasionally these may be on display in the church, or even online (see also Chapter 7). These plans and surveys vary in accuracy and completeness and of course will only record graves which had a surviving memorial at the time the survey was made. By contrast, burial plans (made by the church or cemetery) should detail all burials which have taken place since the record began, including those with no memorials. These are rarely found on display.

CROs often hold copies of churchyard surveys, usually in paper form. These will usually be catalogued by parish, but variously described in terms of document type. When searching the record office catalogue, search under the various terms: 'Memorial Inscriptions', 'Monumental Inscriptions', 'Epitaphs' and 'Churchyard Survey'. Also search under the parish name alone. Scroll through the results with care, as a survey may form part of a parish scrapbook or other record, and may be catalogued under a less obvious heading.

Architectural and ecclesiastical histories

References to memorials, their removal or relocation, exhumations, general churchyard clearance, and vaults which have been opened, can sometimes be found in general published histories or guides relating to an individual church or parish. These may be the only surviving reference to these events. (See also Chapter 7, pages 193–196). You may also find references to tombs or burials which have been moved to the church or churchyard from other locations. Rooting about second-hand bookshops can turn up unexpected books you would never have found in an online search, while published church histories may refer to earlier, less well-known publications or record office sources, perhaps even including abstracts from them. This is incredibly useful, especially if the earlier source has since gone missing, or is difficult to get hold of. William Dugdale's book about Old St Paul's Cathedral provides a portrait of the cathedral and some of its grander tombs shortly before it was destroyed by the Great Fire of London, while the history of St Martin-in-the-Fields, mentioned in Chapter 2, was an easily accessible source of previous works on the church.

The Royal Commission on the Historical Monuments of England, and the Royal Commission on the Ancient and Historical Monuments of Wales were both established by Royal Warrant in 1908. Their aim was to make a national inventory of all buildings, structures, archaeological and other historical sites, which were deemed to best illustrate contemporary culture, civilization, or the conditions of those who lived there, to specify those most worthy of preservation. The inventories were made on a county-by-county basis. This was a mammoth task, and impossible to complete, but the work done by both commissions went on to form the basis of the graded listed building scheme later established in both countries. This, in turn, instigated the formation of localized Conservation Areas. Within the inventories were included nearly all churches, regardless of age, as well as a small sprinkling of churchyard features, and these, in turn, include a selection of gravestones and memorials. While by no means a core source for churchyards, cemeteries and gravestones, it may be of interest to some local and family historians. See **https://historicengland.org.uk** and **https://rcahmw.gov.uk**.

The Arts Society, previously known as NADFAS (**https://theartssociety. org**), was founded in 1968 and records intricate details of the interiors of churches. If they have carried out a survey for the church of your interest, it may include any memorials inside the church. A list of churches they have surveyed is available on their website and copies of each survey should be held by each church. Further copies are deposited at the diocesan record office, the Victoria & Albert Museum Art Library, Historic England Archives, and also with Church Care (**https://www. churchofengland.org/more/church-resources/churchcare**). The society currently has a project to record ledger stones in churches, and this survey can be found at **https://www.lsew.org.uk/ledgerstones**.

The Church Monuments Society was formed in 1979 to encourage the study and appreciation of church monuments. This includes medieval effigies, ledger stones, brasses, and modern gravestones. While not a key point of call for genealogists interested in memorial inscriptions, their courses and publications provide a useful background for understanding the history of memorials inside churches, especially grander monuments. They have a topographical index on their website which lists all churches covered in their publications. See **http://churchmonumentssociety.org**.

Records relating to disinterment and relocation of graves – see Chapter 7.

Chapter 7

ONLINE RECORDS AND LOCATING BURIALS: PITFALLS, CHALLENGES AND RESEARCH ADVICE

Burial and death records can be the hardest of all events to identify in an ancestor's life story. As well as considering the different places your ancestor could be buried, having a good understanding of relevant record sources is vital. Original sources are covered in Chapter 6, while this chapter will help you acquire a methodical and inclusive research technique, using online records as a starting point. Together, they will help you realize when you need sources that are not online, and help you understand why a burial cannot always be found.

Where to start

In the twenty-first century, we have a wide choice of burial place. There may be two or more different cemeteries or crematoria within easy striking distance, and also the option of a green burial site. In some cases, the parish churchyard or burial ground may still be open for burial, while many families opt for cremation and the scattering of ashes in a private, unmarked location. In the past, choices were not as great, but the time and place your ancestor died, the family's budget, and their religious affiliation could all have influenced the place of burial.

Generally speaking, rural ancestors would have been buried in local parish churchyards and burial grounds until far more recently than their urban equivalents, who would typically have been buried in the cemeteries described in Chapter 4 from the mid-nineteenth century. Where appropriate, also consider early cemeteries such as Bethlam Burial

Ground and Bunhill Fields in London and The Rosary in Norwich, as well as burial grounds attached to local Nonconformist churches, Jewish cemeteries, and institutional burial grounds.

One of the greatest challenges for the researcher is the plethora of websites providing genealogy data and local history records. It can be hard to know where to start, or which is the best choice, especially if you are deciding where to spend your money. I have tried to alleviate this confusion by providing a list of useful websites and outlining their usefulness, primarily in terms of burial (and related) records. Some of these websites are free, often collated and run by enthusiasts, but some are provided by commercial companies and will require a subscription. Some, notably Ancestry and Findmypast, can be accessed via membership of local libraries in England and Wales, or at CROs.

Parish burial registers online
Many parish registers, including burial registers, are now online, either as digitized images, or transcriptions. Without a background knowledge of ecclesiastical parishes, and an awareness of exactly which registers have, and more importantly have not, been put online, you can fail to find what you are looking for, or worse still, incorrectly attribute a burial to the wrong person.

When hunting for a parish burial, make yourself familiar with all the parish churches and chapels in the area where your ancestor lived, and therefore probably died. Some of our ancestors lived close to parish or county boundaries, so don't limit your searches to one parish or county. County maps providing a detailed breakdown of parishes, locations and start dates for surviving parish registers can be found online at family history society websites and sites such as **www.genuki.org**. As already briefly mentioned, unless you are researching records from 1974 onwards, you will need to work in pre-1974 county boundaries. Many CROs also produce helpful maps, while the Institute of Heraldic and Genealogical Studies (**www.ihgs.ac.uk**) produces a wonderful set of maps for the UK, available as standalone paper maps for each county, or as part of *Phillimores Atlas and Index of Parish Registers*. The maps are also online at Ancestry entitled, 'Great Britain Atlas and Index of Parish Registers'. The beauty of the digitized maps is that they can be downloaded and enlarged for easy study. The benefit of the book is that, in addition to the maps, it provides coverage dates of known surviving parish registers and an accompanying topographical map, which Ancestry does not. Use the two in tandem to get the best of both worlds!

All these finding aids should be part of your armoury when looking for a parish burial, and will ensure you search all potentially relevant churchyards for the burial in question. The key information is the start date of the actual *burial* registers, not just that for parish registers in general. Some churches were granted the right to baptize or marry much earlier than the right to bury. The CRO catalogue should give you all the information you need, including a breakdown of coverage dates by register type, e.g. baptism, marriage or burial. Many CRO websites will note if the records are online as well (see below). If they are not, you will need to visit the CRO or get someone to go for you.

The hardest part for the researcher is to ascertain which burial registers are *not* yet online. While digitization of parish registers has been a wonderful phenomenon, it has been piecemeal in its overall evolution, with the end result that coverage is spread over a variety of different websites, some of which require subscriptions, some of which do not. Also, some websites offer transcriptions of parish registers, but with no accompanying images.

There is no comprehensive up-to-date listing to tell you, at a glance, which parish registers are online and where, so you really do need to have your wits about you and do your homework. Many websites proudly advertise that they hold various 'county parish register collections', but these are not always complete, and there may be significant gaps in the collection's coverage. Sometimes these are just small gaps within the records of one parish because a register book is missing, or perhaps where a PCC has refused permission to film their parish registers, but sometimes the titles given to databases are euphemistic to say the least. One example is Family Search's 'England Deaths and Burials, 1538–1991'. To the uninitiated, this might sound as if they have all deaths and burials for England between these dates, but this is very far from the case.

There are several reasons why online parish register coverage has been so piecemeal. Firstly, it is the remit of the local county authority which holds the records to decide who (if anyone) will be given the contract to digitize their parish registers. The concept is put out to tender, and awarded to the bidder of their choice. Sometimes a county authority digitizes their own registers, such as Essex Record Office (ERO), which offers its images for a fee.

Some parish registers may be online with commercial companies such as Ancestry, Findmypast, TheGenealogist, or via the family history website of the Church of Jesus Christ of Latter-Day Saints (FamilySearch), others are part of small projects undertaken privately, often as part of a one-place study, or by family history societies. The Federation of

Family History Societies lists the majority of family history societies at **www.familyhistoryfederation.com**, while lists of registered one-place study projects can be found at **www.one-place-studies.org** and **www. oneplacestudy.org**. Use a search engine to locate other one-place studies which have not been registered.

One volunteer project worthy of special mention is **FreeREG.org.uk**. This is part of the Free UK Genealogy Charity, which offers several free genealogy databases. FreeREG provides transcriptions of many (but not all) parish and Nonconformist registers. Another is the free Online Parish Clerks series of databases listed below.

The above-mentioned FamilySearch website offers many collections of parish register transcriptions and images, the majority of which are freely accessible to the general public. FamilySearch now works collaboratively with both Ancestry and Findmypast, so you will find many entries collated by FamilySearch appearing on these two subscription sites.

Determining online coverage of parish registers

When accessing the online records via any website, commercial or otherwise, it is important to check any coverage lists or information about a collection. These may highlight any known gaps, or provide a list of parishes covered. Important information is sometimes tucked away, and not obvious to the casual observer, perhaps under a hyperlink at the bottom of the main collection home page. The quality of the coverage listings for each county collection is often dependent on what was supplied by the record office. It could take the form of a parish list of those parishes included, or you may have to assess coverage of a county parish collection using the browse facility on the website, and looking at the dropdown list of parishes you can search. Use one of the parish/ county maps, mentioned above, to see if any parishes are absent. Websites are very good at telling you what they have, but not so good at telling you what they do not have! It's a good idea to read the small print in the source details of any dataset, but many of these are somewhat lacking in detail. They should at least tell you who holds the original records.

As mentioned, checking the website of the CRO that holds the original registers may tell you that their registers have been digitized and the name of the relevant website, but it may also draw attention to any parishes excluded from filming, perhaps due to licencing issues, while the online catalogue will show if there are any gaps in the coverage because of missing original records. If in doubt, raise a query with archive staff.

The FamilySearch Wiki (**www.familysearch.org/wiki**) is a helpful finding aid for ascertaining coverage on an individual parish basis.

Once you have accessed the wiki page for the relevant parish, click on the hyperlink which says 'Church Records'. It will list any online registers available, coverage dates, whether they are transcriptions only, or whether there are digitized images, and which website you will find them on. Elsewhere on the page you should also find other useful information, such as start dates for original parish registers, name of the diocese in which the parish was located, and the repository where the original records are held. The wiki is not comprehensive or up-to-date, but it is a very good starting point for assessing coverage, and also acts as a useful tool for learning about genealogy record sources.

Parish registers consist of many different books (registers) of different dates and event types. Where no register books have been digitized for the parish at all, this is easy to determine. However, as mentioned elsewhere, some registers have been lost or destroyed, and this may be why there are no surviving registers for certain dates. Accidental gaps during filming are less easy to spot. A register may occasionally be omitted by mistake, or the register might be filmed but not uploaded to the website. Sometimes, collections are released in batches before digitization is complete, while in many cases registers are filmed up to a particular cut-off point, usually agreed with the record office. Occasionally, datasets can be incorrectly labelled too, with incorrect parish names or dates. Keep an eye on the parish name at the top of the original page image, or scroll to the front of the digitized register to check the parish name and register dates recorded on the cover or frontispiece, rather than relying on the label provided by the company. Rather than relying on a search engine, browsing digital records page by page can often lead to a more rewarding search experience, as well as revealing entries missed, or misinterpreted, by the indexer.

A lightly populated rural parish may still be using a burial register dating back to the early nineteenth century. If it has not been deposited at the record office, it may not have been filmed. This could account for the fact that you are unable to locate your ancestor's burial in records held by the CRO, despite the fact that they hold parish registers for the rest of the parish.

Nonconformist, Catholic and other ex-parochial burial records online

The great majority of Nonconformist and other ex-parochial registers are held at TNA in series RG4–RG8 (described in Chapter 6) and are accessible via Ancestry, Findmypast, TheGenealogist and BMDRegisters. This also includes the burial registers of Bethnal Green Protestant Dissenters

Burying Ground, Gibraltar Row (1793–1826), City of London or Golden Lane Burial Ground (1833–1853), St Thomas Square Cemetery, Hackney (1837–1876), South London Burial Ground, East Street, Walworth (1819–1837), Spa Fields (1778–1849), and Victoria Park Cemetery (1853–1876. Many Quaker burial registers and digests are also online as separate databases, notably at Ancestry and Findmypast.

Some institutional burial ground records are now online, notably those surviving records for London workhouses (whose records are held at London Metropolitan Archives), which have been digitized by Ancestry. Often you can find useful smaller projects online by using a search engine, or via CRO websites, such as the burial index for Bath Union Workhouse at **www.batharchives.co.uk/cemeteries/bath-union-workhouse**.

Similar caveats apply to the indexed digitized versions of these records as to parish registers, in terms of transcription and indexing errors, but you can be fairly certain that all known surviving Nonconformist burial registers handed to the government by 1857 are online.

Historic Catholic burial registers for England and Wales have recently started to come online, mainly at Ancestry and Findmypast, although these are currently relatively few in number, and most are subject to a 100-year closure period. The internet means it is now much easier to pinpoint the modern church which covers the area where your Catholic ancestor lived, even if you still need to access some of these records as described in Chapter 6.

CASE STUDY

Quaker registers

One of the joys of digitized records is that in-depth study and detailed scrutinizing of records is much easier. Ancestry's collection entitled 'Liverpool, England Quaker Registers 1635–1958' includes a series of different burial registers and transcripts of digests, which collectively cover various Monthly Meetings in the vicinity of Liverpool. Some of the earlier records include Quarterly Meeting burial records for Lancashire as a whole (although the latter is not currently detailed in Ancestry's description of the collection). Studying these burial entries shows what a wonderful amount of detail can be found within these records. An entry for Isaac Allen, for example, shows that he died on 14 December 1709, and was buried two days later at Penketh. He was recorded to be, 'A scholar who came from Jamaica', and belonged to the Hardshaw East Meeting.

The records frequently describe relationships: sons, daughters, widows, wives and servants. They give a far better overview of the deceased than the typical Church of England burial register. If you are looking at a digest, it will also reference the book and page number of the original registers from which it was created.

The rather damaged register page below is for Elizabeth Fletcher, a grocer of Liverpool, who was 82 when she died on 8 September 1780 and who was buried in the Liverpool burial ground the following day.

Elizabeth Fletcher, Grocer of Liverpool, aged about 82, who died the 'Eighth Day of the Ninth Month, called September 1780 and was buried the Tenth of the Ninth Month called September 1780. Witness Charles James Grave-Maker. (Ancestry.com)

Identifying and accessing cemetery burial records online

The establishment of so many cemeteries (both municipal and private) in the nineteenth century traditionally meant that locating a burial could be like looking for a needle in a haystack, especially if it did not take place in the cemetery closest to home. The growing digitization of cemetery records is making this task increasingly easy, although it can still present challenges.

Deceasedonline.com offers the most comprehensive collection of cemetery records by far. Yet, despite its growing database, there are still plenty of cemetery records which it does not include. Use an internet search engine to identify those cemeteries which were active in the area where your ancestor lived, or died, at the time he or she passed away. Check that the first burials in that cemetery do not post-date your

CASE STUDY
Gladys Barnes

The ever-growing facility to search cemetery records online means they are often a shortcut to locating details of deaths, and for locating death certificates. Together, they help to provide a picture of the family at the time of each death.

My great-aunt, Gladys Florence Barnes, died as an infant in 1906. She appears on no census return, but the 1911 census showed that her parents, Frederick and Eliza Jane, had two children who had died. I located her name via the General Register Office index of Births (**www.gro.gov.uk**), using her mother's maiden name to identify the relevant entry. I followed this with a search of Deceasedonline, which revealed cemetery burial entries in Manor Park Cemetery, East Ham, London, for her and her elder sister Jane Johannah.

From Gladys' entry, I learned that she was buried on 24 February 1906, aged eight months. Her address was given in the 'Late Abode' column as St Thomas' Hospital, Lambeth, and she was buried in square number 39, grave number 58. The officiating ministers were Revd J.P. Gray & J.W. Oliver, and the undertaker, was A.W. Simpson, of East Street, London S2.

Most hospital records are subject to a 100-year closure period, but checking the Hospital Records Database at **www.nationalarchives. gov.uk/hospitalrecords**, showed there are surviving patient records for St Thomas' Hospital for this period at London Metropolitan Archives (LMA). While this did not necessarily mean there would be a surviving record for Gladys, it is always worth following up. Frustratingly, however, records for the relevant year had not survived. The burial entry for her sister Jane, who died in 1900, showed she died at 13 Longville Road, Newington, providing me with a previously-unknown address for the family.

ancestor's death. Read the website of each individual cemetery to see if they offer their own record search facility, or advertise that the records are online elsewhere. Check Deceasedonline's coverage list, to see if all the cemeteries you have listed are covered. If not, then you may have to apply to each for a personal search (see Chapter 6).

Some cemeteries have decided to provide online access to their records on an independent basis, such as Kingston-upon-Thames Cemetery in Surrey. Others may not have records online, but are happy to answer telephone enquiries, and carry out searches from members of the public, sometimes for no charge. By contrast, others do charge a fee, or may still require postal applications before they will search their records on your behalf. It helps cemetery staff if you can provide the exact date of death, as not all cemeteries have a nominal index of those buried there (see Chapter 6).

Many cemeteries are now operated by large commercial funeral service companies, such as Dignity and Westerleigh, and this should be borne in mind when carrying out internet searches to identify cemeteries and crematoria in a particular area. Do not over-refine your search criteria. Make sure your search is broad enough to include private, municipal, borough and council-run cemeteries.

Memorial (monumental) inscriptions online

Despite the heavy losses of gravestones described elsewhere in this book, there are obviously thousands that still survive. This category of genealogical record is very well suited to the recording opportunities of the digital age, and nearly all modern-day gravestones projects include digital images of the gravestones. Many such projects encourage, or are reliant on, volunteer involvement, and provide a great opportunity for volunteers to get out and explore local churchyards and cemeteries, while helping to preserve this wonderful record source. Like any such source, hours of transcription and interpretation lie behind the final index you use to search online. As with parish registers, modern-day digitization and transcription projects have been diverse, and there is no one website which collates all recorded gravestones in one place. Use the listing of useful websites on pages 200–217 as your starting point, but, as always, use a general internet search to establish whether there are any other local projects online, carried out by individuals or family history societies. The various websites vary in quality and content, especially in terms of the geographical area they cover. Some have a bias towards American rather than British sources. As always, read the small print and any coverage charts, especially if you are going to be paying for access. Don't presume the person you are looking for has no memorial just because it is not coming up in your searches. Many of the datasets will be incomplete, either because the graveyard has not been fully recorded, or because some stones were deemed illegible. Some stones can be hard to read, despite digital enhancement, and transcriptions may be incomplete or incorrect. Depending on the depth and quality of the original carving, some numbers or letters in an inscription may have been incised less deeply than others, and it's easy to mistake one digit or letter for another. In some cases, transcriptions may not include all the information on the stone, so always look at the image if there is one.

Some eighteenth- and nineteenth-century churchyard surveys, originally published as books, or kept in private archives, have been digitized and are online for free as e-books, with initiatives such as the Internet Archive (**www.archive.org**) and Google Books (**www.books. google.com**), while many family and local history societies have put their own transcriptions of historic surveys online. Good examples are the Somerset and Dorset Family History Society, which has published an online index of Dorset parish MIs, searchable by the deceased's name, while the Kent Archaeological Society (KAS) has uploaded transcriptions of numerous surveys for the county. It's a good idea to read any accompanying notes, rather than blindly plunging in to search the listings. These can help the interpretation of the record. Many of the KAS transcriptions were carried out by the antiquarian Leland Lewis Duncan, whose work is invaluable. However, the accompanying notes (written by KAS member Frank Bampling) give important additional information, notably that Duncan rarely recorded all the details on each stone, and often omitted stones that post-dated 1900.[1]

As the number of online memorial inscription projects grows, they are an increasingly useful tool for locating missing burials, especially where the place of burial is unknown, with the caveat that many people's graves were never marked by a gravestone, or have long since disappeared.

Newspapers

As mentioned in Chapter 6, newspapers can help identify someone's burial place. The British Newspaper Archive (BNA) at **www. britishsnewspaperarchive** is a subscription site run by the British Library, and offers a wide selection of local newspapers, largely from the midnineteenth to the early twentieth century. The database is also available at Findmypast, although the search engine is inferior to the one on the BNA site. Some libraries and archives offer free access to parts of the BNA collection, via their own online reference library portal. These will typically cover newspapers relevant to their local area. While digitization has changed the process of searching in local newspapers from an arduous to a relatively easy task, not all local papers are online, and these must be accessed at the British Library itself, or via local archives and libraries (see Chapter 6). The National Library of Wales has digitized many Welsh newspapers up to about 1910, and these are free to search and view.

'The Gazette' at **www.gazettes-online.co.uk** offers free access to the London, Edinburgh and Belfast gazettes respectively. These were, and still are, the newspapers of 'official public record', where public notices, for example relating to insolvency, awards, and probate were legally required to be published. Those relating to probate may help pinpoint a date of death, and in turn a burial entry. Similarly, historic copies of *The Times* can be helpful in this respect. Access is via subscription at **www.thetimes.co.uk/archive**, but again the database is often offered free via local county library online reference collections.

Jewish records

The Jewish Genealogical Society of Great Britain has much data and background information online at **www.jgsgb.org.uk**, and both *Tracing Your Jewish Ancestors* by Amanda Rosemary Wenzerul (Pen & Sword, 2008), and Dr Antony Joseph's *My Ancestors Were Jewish* (4th edition, Family History Partnership, 2008) are useful guides to tracking down Jewish death and burial records. Some Jewish burial records are also now available online at major genealogical sites, such as those for Mile End London new cemetery, which are at Ancestry, while **www.jewishgen. org/databases/UK** lists many Jewish burials from cemeteries around the UK, and there are listings for Jewish Federation cemeteries at Edmonton and Rainham (Essex) at **www.jewishgen.org/jcr-uk**/. In addition, **www.cemeteryscribes.com** provides details of many Jewish gravestones in the UK.

Commonwealth War Grave records

These can be searched online at **www.cwgc.org** and include all those buried in Commonwealth War cemeteries or who died serving in either World War.

Each entry gives the name of the deceased (although sometimes only their first initials), place and date of death, place of burial and/or commemoration, rank, regiment, and unit. There are often also details of next-of-kin and their address. The site is free to use and should be your first searching point if trying to locate the burial place of a serviceman.

For those men who only have initials listed rather than full first names, you may first have to do some research in other sources to identify their regiment, and thus their CWGC entry, with certainty. Recommended reading is *Tracing Your Army Ancestors. A Guide for Family Historians* by Simon Fowler (Pen & Sword, 2nd Edition, 2013).

Family and Local History Society publications

As well as publishing collections of monumental inscriptions, both family and local history societies often offer a variety of other record sources online, including transcriptions of burial registers. In some cases, these will only be available to members, but membership is usually inexpensive. Some also have options to buy transcriptions on CD, and to a much lesser extent these days, in book form or on microfiche. Check their website to see what they offer for sale both on and offline. The great majority of family history societies are listed at **www.familyhistoryfederation.com**, and the British Association for Local History provides an extensive listing for local history societies.

General search methodology and problems locating burials

To successfully locate each and every burial you would like to find can be challenging. Being aware of the sources described in Chapter 6 is essential, but you can also hone your research technique to maximize your research success. You also need to be aware of any exceptional circumstances which may affect the burial, such as graveyard clearances or exhumations, which could have affected the gravesite.

Before you begin your search for a burial, memorial inscription or other record, review the information you already have about the person in question. How certain are you that it is all correct? Do you know the date and place of birth, occupation, spouse's name, and address? The last known address and, in some cases, the place of birth, are likely to have a bearing on where he or she is buried, while the other information will help determine if any record you find is likely to be the correct one. Once you have assessed and reviewed all the information, use the selection of websites in the section entitled Listing of useful websites on pages 200–217, as a starting point for your search. If you don't know any of the details outlined above, further research may be necessary.

Civil registration of deaths in England and Wales began on 1 July 1837, and a copy of the death certificate will provide the exact date and place of death, which will often aid your burial search. Certificates can be purchased direct from the General Register Office, first locating the death in their online index at **www.gro.gov.uk** or any other website providing the index. Until relatively recently, burial typically took place within a week, but might be considerably delayed if your ancestor's death was the subject of a post-mortem or coroner's inquest. (See *Tracing Your Ancestors Through Death Records* chapters 1 and 4).

Whichever website or record you are looking at, ensure you always look at the digitized image, if available. Transcriptions may contain errors and omissions, the transcriber having failed to read the handwriting correctly, or lost concentration. Professional researchers have often noticed that among some early digitized collections of parish registers, entries appear to have been routinely omitted by transcribers if they are faded or difficult to read. These 'missing' entries may be located by browsing the images or looking at the originals in the record office. If there are no accompanying images with a dataset, you should ideally arrange to view the original record, so you can check the details are correct. If you are unable to visit a record office yourself, commission a local researcher to do this for you. Lists of qualified genealogical researchers can be found at **www.agra.org.uk**.

Until relatively recently, the spelling of surnames was often inconsistent, and allowance should be made for this when searching. If there is the option to include surname variants in your searches, take advantage of it. On some websites, you will see this referred to as 'SOUNDEX'. This is a phonetic algorithm for indexing names by sound, so that all similar sounding names are produced in the list of results. Different websites use different algorithms to capture surname variants, but they are not foolproof. A name could have been recorded with an unusual variant not listed by the web company, or simply have been spelled in a very strange way by whoever recorded it. An unusual surname may be transcribed as something quite unrecognizable! Once again, browsing the records page-by-page is recommended if you fail to find an entry where you feel certain there should be one. This can usually be done with digitized parish register images, but not memorial inscriptions.

Any record source is susceptible to human error, missing entries and mistakes. This is not just when the records are indexed for digitization, but when the original information was gathered too. This can cause problems for the researcher who fails to recognize the person they are looking for, or finds the right person, but then uses incorrect detail to look for the same individual in other sources.

Occasionally, a burial will accidentally be wrongly indexed as a baptism. If you rely on a search engine only, you are unlikely to pick this up, unless you widen your search to include baptisms too. Sometimes a more general search can be beneficial, as you may recognize your ancestor's burial at about the right date and in the right place, but labelled as a baptism. Inspection of the original image should clarify this, although mistakes could also be made in original parish registers when the clerk wrote out the entries.

As we have already seen, it is essential to check coverage lists for any website, as well as any accompanying source notes, while original sources may be incomplete if entire registers or pages are missing, or individual events were not recorded. Some burials were simply not recorded due to human error, but also if the incumbent or parish clerk was ill, or had recently died and there was a gap before his replacement arrived. The Commonwealth Gap has already been mentioned in Chapter 6, but in some parishes, register entries do not recommence for several years after 1660, perhaps again awaiting the arrival of a new incumbent.

Completing the search engine boxes

Generally speaking, while this will vary depending on the surname and the database you are using, a good rule of thumb is 'less is more'. Don't over-complete the search form by filling in every search field. Start with the person's name, an estimated year of death, and expected county of death, based on what you have found in other records. Depending on the website you are using, there may be the option to search for 'exact' results. This is not usually recommended, since information will frequently be recorded in a slightly different way than expected. Unless you are certain of the exact date of death, allow a good range of years either side of your estimate. If the surname is very rare don't shy away from just entering the first name and surname. You can go back in and then refine your research further if needed.

As we have seen, search engines use different search algorithms. Each website also indexes and presents its search results in different ways. It's a worthwhile exercise to read any tips and hints for searching. Again, it can't be stressed enough that you should have an awareness of which collections and databases the website offers, so you know the actual databases you are searching.

Where appropriate, it's a good idea to target your search, selecting individual collections, rather than a more generic search which might, for example, cover 'Births, Marriages and Deaths', or 'Parish Records'. This will typically throw up a much more powerful search menu and, secondly, eliminate matches from datasets that are of no interest to you. If you know your ancestors came from Wiltshire, there is no point in including, for example, burial registers in Cheshire in your search – not to start with at least! If you are using Ancestry, you should select 'Card Catalogue', and then use a title or key word search to bring up datasets that are relevant to you. Remember to refine your search to your country of interest as Ancestry covers sources from all over the world, and many English and Welsh place names are echoed overseas. This is also a good way of locating some unexpected, little-known databases. For example, typing 'gravestone' into the title bar of the Ancestry Card Catalogue and refining your search to UK collections reveals '*Caernarfonshire, Wales, Lleyn and Eifionydd Church Registers and Gravestone Inscriptions, 1600–1902*'. Similarly, on Findmypast you should go to the search menu, select 'All record sets', and then enter a key word, for example 'Cheshire', which will bring up all relevant datasets they hold for Cheshire, and which includes Cheshire Diocese of Chester Parish Burials 1538–1911. In the light of potential indexing errors and omissions mentioned above, browsing the images in a collection can be a more powerful, if time-consuming, way of searching, rather than relying on a search engine.

Namesakes

Nearly all of our ancestors had namesakes – even those with rarer names. Do not fall into the trap of assigning a burial, or other entry, you have found from a database because it 'looks about right'. Make sure it is the correct one before you add it to your tree, or at least flag it as 'possible' if you do so. Although this sounds obvious, many modern-day researchers have an alarming propensity to attach incorrect records to their ancestors. This is especially the case where they are building a family tree online, and the host provider offers record suggestions based on computer algorithms. Although a useful mechanism, records should only be attached after careful inspection and verification. Ages on death records are notoriously inaccurate, so the actual burial record you seek may not even come up as a suggestion. Compare the details of any entry you find with what you already know about your ancestor, and also with any information about that same person you can find in datasets relating to other sources, for example monumental inscriptions. The second source may provide greater detail, which will help clarify if it is the person you are looking for. If you are still uncertain, then further research may be required in other sources to learn more about the person who is recorded in that particular burial entry.

Think outside the box

What you think you know could actually be wrong! For example, if someone appears in one census, but not the subsequent one, you may assume he or she has died, and look for a death or burial in the intervening ten years. In fact, your ancestor may miraculously reappear in the next census, simply having been omitted from the previous one for any of a number of reasons. While we should review information we have found across all sources, we must also bear in mind that the way our ancestors were recorded could vary dramatically, particularly in terms of occupations. Much was at the whim of whoever wrote the record. Furthermore, many people had more than one occupation during their lifetime, and some people had fingers in many pies! Thus, a grocer might also run a draper's or butcher's business, or perhaps all three, or a labourer might also be described as a builder. If the facts don't match, you should question but not rule out the entry, until you have carried out further research to try and clarify the discrepancies.

Although you may not know it, your ancestors may have been Nonconformists and been buried in a Nonconformist burial ground rather than the parish churchyard. Just because your ancestors married in an Anglican church, does not necessarily mean they were active members of the Church of England. Between 1754 and 1837 everyone, apart from Quakers and Jews, had by law to marry in the Church of England.

If your ancestor was in the armed forces, or served during either or the World Wars, and died during the course of his service, remember to check military cemetery records, while some people were buried in burial grounds attached to institutions, especially if they were long-term residents (see Chapter 3).

For those who were cremated, ashes were not always buried in the crematorium. Many were informally scattered in other locations and this is a growing trend. Only rarely is there any documentary evidence regarding the location. Some people's ashes remain in the funerary urn for many years before being scattered.

There are many other reasons why you may fail to find a burial. In the days before divorce was routinely available, many couples split up and formed new relationships, perhaps under new names, and some men and women simply abandoned families and changed their names because they needed a new start. If someone died while travelling, their name might have been unknown, and there are many entries in parish registers which record unnamed strangers, vagrants, or travellers. The burial of suicides frequently went unrecorded before 1823, while those drowned and washed up on the seashore are unlikely to be recorded before 1808 (see Chapter 2).

Too narrow a search perimeter

While it is generally true that most people were buried or cremated close to where they lived or to where they died, there are many exceptions. People often travelled with work, so if you are missing a burial, think about the deceased's occupation. Some jobs were overtly mobile, such as travelling salesmen (often referred to as chapmen or hawkers), soldiers, or coachmen, but other jobs involved postings or appointments to different parts of the country, such as clergymen or excisemen. Your ancestor may have moved away from the place where he or she baptized his or her children, and you could be looking in the wrong area altogether. Some people were sent away for their health, either to take the sea air, or as inmates in hospitals specializing in their particular illness, and may have died in that location. If someone died away from home, it was expensive to transport a body back home, and this accounts for many 'out-of-place' burials.

While many people died close to their place of birth, a significant number settled far from where they were born. This was the case even before the advent of the railway network in the nineteenth century, which made travel so much easier and affordable for all. Many older people moved away to live with children or other relatives in their later years and may not be buried where you expect, while the last wishes of the deceased, a strong personal connection with a particular place, or a person's religious beliefs, could also play an important part in where they were laid to rest.

While large cemeteries typically had sections reserved for different religious denominations, some tended to attract, or actively encouraged, burials of particular faiths or denominations. Streatham Park Cemetery in London buried people of all religious denominations, but particularly high numbers of Catholics.

When people died abroad, their body may have been repatriated for burial, and examples of this can be seen in undertakers' records. However, repatriation was expensive and in many cases burial would have taken place overseas. There may be a record of the death or burial in overseas church records, or those records of the Registrar General which relate to overseas deaths. (See *Tracing Your Ancestors Through Death Records,* p.31).

A reasonable understanding of geography in relation to the places your ancestors lived is very important. As already mentioned, some people lived close to county boundaries, so the burial you are looking for, while not far away, might have taken place in another county.

Graves for babies and stillborns

Before 1927, stillborn children could legally be committed to the earth without ceremony, and with no record being made of their existence. Following the Births and Deaths Registration Act of 1926, burial of a stillborn could only lawfully take place following presentation of a certificate of stillbirth. Cemeteries may have separate registers for these burials. There is also no doubt that many infant burials were not recorded. While wealthier families could afford a grave space for their child, a much more affordable option was for the child to be buried in the grave of an adult who had died about the same time. Even in the case of better-off families, children are sometimes commemorated on gravestones, but never mentioned in the burial (or baptism) register. It pays to check all available sources, while lack of any burial records may account for family stories which relate the existence of a child, but for whom no trace can be found.

Relocated burials: exhumations and reinterments

While we might know where someone was originally buried, occasionally their remains may no longer lie in the original resting place, having been disinterred and reburied elsewhere. Tracking these down, or indeed even realizing that exhumation has taken place, can be challenging. This could have taken place as part of a large-scale clearance of the cemetery, or a portion of it, or on an individual basis at the request of the family of the deceased. The former was a frequent phenomenon in London in the mid-nineteenth century, as a result of major civil engineering projects connected with the growing rail, underground, and sewerage infrastructures. For example, in 1862 the construction of Charing Cross Station and routes leading into it led to almost 8,000 bodies being removed from the burial ground of Cure's College in Southwark and being transferred (ironically by rail) to Brookwood Cemetery, where they were reburied.[2] Similarly, during excavations for the High Speed 2 Rail Link in the late 2010s, both St James' Gardens Cemetery (by then a public garden) and Park Street Cemetery in Birmingham were on land required for the project. Both cemeteries were fully excavated by archaeologists and all human remains removed. Those for St James' were reinterred in Brookwood Cemetery, Surrey, which had also received some of the St James' Garden's burials when nearby Euston Station was extended in the 1940s. At the time of writing is it unclear where the burials from the Birmingham cemetery are reinterred. (See also Chapter 2.)

For researchers hoping to identify the last resting place of a specific person, whose remains they suspect have been disinterred, there are some sources that can help, alongside the type of general historical research illustrated in the St Martin's-in-the-Fields Case Study in Chapter 2 and the suggested published sources mentioned in Chapter 6 (pages 29–38).

From 1857, there should be a record of all disinterments. The burial act of that year made it illegal to remove any burial without the issuing of a licence from the Secretary of State or a faculty granted by the local diocese. This does not mean that there are no records prior to 1857, but your chances of finding information are much lower. There are several little-known record sets held at TNA which pre-date 1857. These records may verify, or provide, the necessary missing link to confirm somebody's actual current resting place.

A useful collection to start with is TNA's 'General Register Office: Removal of Graves and Tombstones' (Series Number RG37). This covers both removal of remains and any associated memorials. However, it must be stressed that if only a gravestone was removed (not the human remains) you will *not* find it listed here. The collection includes records made by local authorities and the Church Commissioners relating to disinterments between 1923 and 2007. These coverage dates relate to the date of the removal, not the date of the initial burial. It includes burials as early as the seventeenth century, but most date from the eighteenth and nineteenth century. The collection is far from complete, and in no way represents all those burials which were exhumed and removed in this period, but it is worth looking at. The details typically replicate what was found on any accompanying memorial. If there was no surviving memorial, the entry will simply state 'unknown person'. The records for each set of removals are catalogued by location, and years covered according to the inscriptions on the gravestones. In a few cases, there are also plans of the original gravesites and notes relating to where they were reinterred. You can search TNA's Discovery catalogue by county, or place name, to see if there are any datasets which relate to your church of interest. You cannot search using the individual name of a deceased person, as the record collection is not indexed to this level. RG37 is, however, also available via Deceasedonline and you can carry out a name search there. This is the quickest way of searching this record set for a named individual.

TNA also holds Home Office Burial Books in document series HO85. The books include letters relating to burials exhumed and reinterred between 1854 and 1921, and licenses for exhumation and reinterment from 1887. There are a small number of pre-1887 exhumation licences in HO15, but these are few and far between, and seem to only relate to burials of criminals.

From 1857, if disinterment involved taking human remains from one consecrated burial ground to another, then a faculty has given sufficient authorization, this being granted by the relevant Church of England diocesan court. Records are held by the diocese, but notice of the proposed removal should have been displayed publicly beforehand.

TOWN AND COUNTRY PLANNING (CHURCHES, PLACES OF RELIGIOUS WORSHIP AND BURIAL GROUNDS) REGULATIONS, 1950.

CERTIFICATE IN ACCORDANCE WITH REGULATION 13 AS TO THE REMOVAL OF HUMAN REMAINS FROM THE PROPERTY KNOWN AS THE OLD KING STREET BAPTIST CHAPEL, OLD KING STREET, BRISTOL.

I HEREBY CERTIFY -

(1) that the human remains of 60 persons interred in the property known as The Old King Street Baptist Church, Old King Street, Bristol (hereinafter called "the property") were removed in accordance with the provisions of the Town and Country Planning (Churches, Places of Religious Worship and Burial Grounds) Regulations, 1950, during the period commencing on the 11th day of June, 1956, and ending on the 26th day of June, 1956;

(2) that the said human remains were, during the same period re-interred in accordance with the provisions of the above-quoted Regulations, in communal graves numbered "01451 Purple AA" and "01452 Purple AA", respectively, in the Avonview Cemetery, St. George, in the City and County of Bristol.

Details of the names and dates of death of the deceased persons whose remains were removed are as follows:-

Name.	Date of Death.
Rev. Thomas Roberts, M.A.	December, 1841
John Stephens	13th February, 1827
Martha Stephens	6th October, 1827
Sarah Ann Edwards	28th July, 1828
Sarah Wade	8th August, 1828
John Hart	7th May, 1829
Hester Phipps	2nd July, 1829
Thomas Phipps	23rd October, 1829
George Bowden	28th January, 1830
Catherine Bignell	28th January, 1830
Mary Hardwick	21st March, 1830
James Roberts Tratman	28th April, 1830

An extract from the RG37 entry relating to the removal of human remains of sixty individuals interred in the Old King Street Baptist Church, Bristol, removed in June 1956 and reinterred in communal graves in Avonview Cemetery. The registers vary in the amount of detail they supply; this one lists only name and date of death. By contrast the next image from St Margaret's, Rochester, Kent, records details from many accompanying memorials. (Deceasedonline.com)

```
42.  Unknown.
43.  Sarah Hills, died 25th September, 1862 aged
     70 years.
     William Hills husband of the above, died 16th
     January 1875.
     William eldest son of the above, died 16th May
     1881.
     Mary Ann Hills, daughter, died 30th August, 1891.
     aged 70 years.
44.  Unknown.
45.  Unknown.
46   Unknown.
47.  Unknown.
48.  Caroline wife of James Weeks, died 24th June 1855,
     aged 43 years.
     James Weeks ------
```

Compare the detail in this image, which is from the RG37 entry for St Margaret's Rochester, Kent, with the less detailed entries for Old King Street Baptist Chapel, Bristol on the previous page. (Deceasedonline.com)

Similarly, by law, if cemetery owners plan to clear part of a cemetery for reburial, or to clear gravestones, they have to display notices to this effect in the public domain, to inform any interested party. You will find these in newspapers or sometimes family history magazines.

THE GENERAL CEMETERY COMPANY.				
NAME.	ABODE.	Part of Cemetery.	Year.	Register No.
Wright Harriet. S.	Oxford Gardens	bon 14915	1891	June
Williams Eliza	Shepherds Bush	16819	"	"
Walker Sarah	Victoria Road	32713	"	"
Williams Eliza	Shepherds Bush	16819	"	"
Wight Catherine. H.	Torquay	9367	"	"
Ward Ann Eliza	Egerton Gardens	34 bot	"	"
Wilkins Caroline	Tufton Street	bon 21595	"	"

Page from the burial register for Kensal Green Cemetery, London, overall displaying information regarding disinterment can occasionally be found in a burial register, as shown here in a register for Kensal Green Cemetery, London. The entry for Ann Eliza Ward of Egerton Gardens has been crossed out and underneath is written 'Removed 15th October 1891 for reinterment in U.S. America, by Faculty dated 7th October 1891' (Deceasedonline.com)

Burial at sea

Those who died on long sea voyages were, historically, often buried at sea, as keeping the body on board for long periods was a health risk. These burials are understandably hard to trace. If you suspect this to be the case, search for a marine death. You are unlikely to find an actual burial record, apart from a note in the ship's log. Marine deaths on British-registered vessels were logged with the Registrar General from 1874, specifically the Registrar General of Shipping and Seamen. You can search these at most commercial genealogy sites which offer the GRO index. It is also worth checking the original registers at TNA, since not all entries from the original ship's logs were copied over. BT158 and BT159 are at TNA and online at Ancestry, The Genealogist, Findmypast, and BMD Registers, cover 1854 to 1890.

In more recent times, some people are buried at sea because they have a maritime connection. This requires a special licence from the Marine Management Organisation (MMO). There are three designated areas where body burial at sea is permitted: between Hastings and Newhaven, off the Needles to the west of the Isle of Wight, and off the north-east coast at Tynemouth, but other places can be permitted on special request to the MMO. Cremated remains can be buried at sea, or in inland waterways, with no special permission.

Searching London cemeteries

Despite the usefulness of Deceasedonline in digitizing and indexing so many cemetery records, London burials can still present a challenge. As mentioned in Chapter 4, some cemeteries, including Brookwood which was some distance from London, had special agreements to bury the dead of certain parishes. Brookwood buried a high percentage of pauper burials from London parishes, and also had agreements with various guilds, societies and other groups to bury their dead, for example the Ancient Order of Foresters. Such groups were usually buried in specially designated areas.

A really useful guide is *Greater London Cemeteries and Crematoria* by Patricia Wolfston and Cliff Webb (pub. 1994). This breaks down cemeteries by the areas they cover, and their religious denomination. It will also tell you the pre-1965 London authority and the 1984 London borough names, which can help identify the right cemetery. Thanks to this book, I have been able to locate many 'missing' cemetery burials by working steadily through the list of cemeteries for each area and checking to see whether the records were online or not. Use the book in tandem with the coverage list on Deceasedonline, noting which cemeteries you have not yet checked, particularly those in the vicinity of the place where your ancestor lived or died, or those which match his or her religious affiliation.

CASE STUDY

Two sisters: Catherine and Bridget O'Dwyer

Unfortunately, some people died alone, or away from their families, meaning there was no family member to arrange the funeral. In this case, the local authorities would have had the responsibility for arranging the funeral and burial, and also for paying for it, if there were no funds available from the deceased's estate. This was the case for two Catholic sisters Bridget and Catherine O'Dwyer, the first of whom left Limerick in the Irish Republic to find work in England in the 1940s, to be followed by her sister shortly after. Sadly, they all but lost touch with their family in Ireland. I was asked to track down where each had been laid to rest.

From her death certificate, we knew that Catherine died on 4 June 1955 at the London Hospital in Stepney, aged 52 years. Her home address was given as 1 Southfields, Park Road, Stroud, Gloucestershire. She could potentially have been buried in London or Stroud. By looking at Catherine's circumstances, and studying the death certificate more closely, I was able to put a research plan into place to locate her burial.

Catherine was unmarried and living far from any close family when she died. The person who registered the death (W.D. Carter) was described as 'Causing the body to be buried'. This nearly always indicates there were no family or friends to arrange the funeral and burial. The responsibility for this would have lain with the local council, which was obliged to bury her with decency, and according to her faith, but, of course, they would have tried to keep the costs down. Since she was known to have been Catholic, she should have been buried in a Catholic burial plot, and it was very unlikely she would have been taken back to Stroud for burial. Therefore, I was looking for a Catholic burial in London.

Initial searches were made on the Deceasedonline database and also of St Mary's Cemetery registers, a large Catholic cemetery in North London, with no trace. I then began extensive coverage checks to see which other cemeteries were not covered on Deceasedonline's database, targeting those in Stepney and checking records for Brookwood Cemetery, but again without success. Further research showed three cemeteries which specialized in Catholic burials. These were

- St Mary's Cemetery, Kensal Green
- Mortlake Catholic Cemetery, North Worple Way, London
- St Patrick's Leytonstone Cemetery

It was a telephone call to St Patrick's Leytonstone Cemetery that revealed Catherine O'Dwyer was buried there. Her age was recorded incorrectly as 58 instead of 52, but the place of death was the London Hospital and there was no doubt that this was the correct burial. She was buried on 8 June 1955 in a public grave, and the cemetery provided details of the grave row and plot number.

Catherine's sister, Bridget Ida O' Dwyer, was born in 1905. The family knew that she was living at 10 Latimer Road, Wimbledon, in 1944, and that she died between 1945 and 1947. Her death certificate took some finding, since it was registered incorrectly under the name of Beryl Ida O'Dwyer. This gave her date and place of death as 12 February 1946, at the South London Hospital. Her usual address was recorded as Merton Abbey, London, SW19.

Looking at the place of death, the South London Hospital was in the Clapham area of south London, while Merton is close to Wimbledon in west London. It was logical that she would be buried in a cemetery or crematorium in one of these areas. Both Merton and Wimbledon areas are covered by Merton Council, and I started my search with Merton cemeteries and crematoria, since all were available at Deceasedonline. Not finding her there, I took advice from Merton Local History Society who suggested that the private cemetery at Streatham Park was known to be a place where many Catholics were buried. This was confirmed by the book *Greater London Cemeteries and Crematoria* mentioned elsewhere (see the section on 'Searching London cemeteries'). A telephone call to Streatham Park Cemetery revealed that she was indeed buried there, again recorded under the first name Beryl rather than Bridget, this no doubt having been taken from the erroneous death certificate.

LISTING OF USEFUL WEBSITES

Online coverage is constantly growing, so any online listing becomes out of date relatively quickly. By the time you read this, there may be records which will provide the answers to whatever you are looking for which are not online at the time of writing. Use the listing below as a starting point and keep up-to date by following blogs and newsletters for the various subscription websites listed below, and joining family history societies and help groups. It is recommended that family historians do not limit their searches to genealogy websites. Important information relating to graveyards and cemeteries, burials and MIs can be found on local history and archaeological sites and publications. Likewise, local historians should remember to utilize what may seem to be purely family history orientated websites. The accuracy of your search will be affected by the accuracy of the transcription in the online index, since it is this which is utilized by the search engine. You may need to alter your search parameters to take this into account. See the section on 'General Search Methodology and Problems Locating Burials' above.

Commercial websites will not only require you to pay for their services, but will provide different subscription types. This will determine which datasets you can access, so do investigate this before you make your choice.

How to use the listing

I start by listing each of the major websites, with a short introduction about each, and what it offers in terms of the records covered in this book. Not every website is included in this section, just the larger ones which offer more than one type of record.

The second section takes the different types of records, as covered in this book, and lists websites to be considered when searching for the respective records types. Where they have not already been mentioned in the first section, there is a short description. This section includes some less well-known websites.

Use the listings in tandem: for example, when looking for a burial, remember to look at the listing for memorial inscriptions, as well as those for burial registers.

Website Listing Section 1 – major source providers

Ancestry (www.ancestry.co.uk)
Leading genealogy database provider Ancestry offers a wide range of digitized parish registers and transcriptions, and access to the Nonconformist registers handed in to the government in the 1840s and 1850s. It also incorporates 'Findagrave' (see below) and has some other datasets relating to memorial inscriptions. Ancestry has a UK website which sits alongside its American (**ancestry.com**), Canadian (**ancestry.ca**) and Australian (**ancestrycom.au**) counterparts. The 'co.uk' version of the website is the best one to use for English and Welsh searches, since it will automatically target searches to UK records, but (subject to your subscription level) all datasets can be accessed using any of the portals. Use the Card Catalogue to search for individual datasets, inserting relevant key words such as 'burial' or 'monumental inscriptions'. The company prefixes all its dataset titles with the name of the country, e.g. 'England & Wales, Non-Conformist and Non-Parochial Registers, 1567–1970'. Ancestry also has some special collections in the form of digital books such as *Caernarfonshire, Wales, Lleyn and Eifionydd Church Registers and Gravestone Inscriptions, 1600–1902*.

Findmypast (findmypast.co.uk)
Findmypast (FMP) is the other leader in digitized parish registers and transcriptions. Like Ancestry, this British company has different versions of the website for the UK, Ireland and America, but all datasets can be searched from each website, subject to your subscription level. FMP also provides access to Nonconformist registers mentioned above, and a selection of memorial inscription transcriptions, ordered by county.

TheGenealogist (www.thegenealogist.co.uk)
This British company provides a useful range of parish registers, including digitized images for Norfolk, Warwickshire and Wales under their 'Parish Records' heading, and access to Nonconformist registers. See their coverage list entitled 'List of all datasets' at the foot of their home page. It also has the UKIndexer Headstone Project, mentioned below, and a war memorial project, which makes a useful aid if looking for military graves.

MyHeritage (myheritage.com)
This company has some parish register and related collections for England and Wales, but is not a key provider of these records at the time of writing. It also offers access to Billion Graves, but that is available on free access via its own independent website.

FamilySearch (www.familysearch.org)
One of the worldwide leaders of genealogical online data, Family Search is run by the Church of Jesus Christ of Latter-Day Saints (LDS), and many of its databases are free to access by members of the public online, once they have registered for an account. It offers a wide range of parish register and related collections and transcriptions, and some monumental inscriptions. Go to the 'Search' menu and select 'Records'. Then either click on the world map for the country you are interested in, or select 'Find a Collection', and type your key word e.g. 'England' or 'Wales' into the search box. Either route will throw up a list of relevant datasets for you to consider, and state whether they are index only (transcriptions), images only (which you will have to browse) or images with indexes. Read the small print. For example, this will tell you that the collection entitled 'England Deaths and Burials, 1538–1991', is just an index and covers limited localities and time periods. The same applies to the Welsh equivalent collection. Not all datasets are on open access; this is usually dependent on licensing agreements with the original record office. Some can only be accessed via one of the LDS Family History Centres and a list of these can be found at **www.familysearch.org/help/fhcenters/locations**.

Website Listing Section 2 – websites listed by record source

Parish burial registers
Ancestry – see above
Findmypast – see above
TheGenealogist – see above
MyHeritage – see above
Family Search – see above

FreeReg.org.uk
This offers an impressive collection of parish and Nonconformist register transcriptions for free, and coverage is always growing. While it is tempting to plunge straight in to the 'Search' page, take time to read the page entitled 'Transcriptions' first. This explains how the project works, coverage, and how to get the most from this excellent website.

Online Parish Clerks
This is a project whereby volunteers collect, collate and transcribe records for various parishes within their respective areas. A full listing is at the UKBMD website (**www.ukbmd.org.uk**) which offers links to large collections of UK birth, marriage and death records. Select 'OPC' from the menu. There is also a listing for one-place studies under 'OPS'.

Essex Parish Registers
Digitized by Essex Record Office (ERO) and available for a fee, you can browse the registers via ERO's website, while there is an index with accompanying transcriptions at Ancestry. Use the two sites in tandem to facilitate searching and viewing.

Remember: use an internet search engine to identify local collections of parish registers. Use keywords such as 'parish registers', or the name of the particular parish or locality you are looking for. For example, a search on 'Parish Registers AND The Weald' brings up **http://theweald.org**, a collection of parish register transcriptions covering the Weald of Kent.

Nonconformist and other ex-parochial burials

Ancestry – see above

Findmypast – see above

TheGenealogist – see above

FreeREG.org.uk – see above

BMDRegisters.co.uk

This is linked to TheGenealogist but gives you the option to search all those Nonconformist registers handed in to the government in 1840 and 1857 on a pay-per-view basis.

Bunhill Fields Cemetery, London

Burial records online cover 1713–1854 and are online at Ancestry, Findmypast, TheGenealogist and BMDRegisters.

Bethlam (Bedlam) Burial Ground, London (also known as New Churchyard)

This is an online database complied as a result of a research project carried out in conjunction with Crossrail. This lists over 8,000 Londoners buried at New Churchyard. The burials were recorded in the parish registers of the deceased's home parish and entries have been collated using London burial registers. The list is not comprehensive since not all registers survive, and limited funding meant anyone buried from outside London is not included. **https://www.crossrail.co.uk/benefits/archaeology/bedlam-burial-ground-register#**

Remember: There were far fewer Nonconformist burial grounds and you should also check parish registers even if you know your ancestor was a member of a Nonconformist church (see Chapter 6).

Cemetery burial, cremation and grave records

Deceasedonline (www.deceasedonline.com) is the leading provider of cemetery burial registers. See page 183.

Individual cemetery online listings

Some cemeteries have digitized their own records and offer downloads to purchase. Prices vary. Two examples are:

• Birmingham City Council Cemeteries. Birmingham City Council has its own website where you can download copies of registers for

those cemeteries in its control. **https://birminghamburialrecords. co.uk**
- Kingston-upon-Thames offers free online access to its register images at **https://www.kingston.gov.uk/directory/20/grave_records**

Use a search engine to locate any others not online at the time of writing.

- Records of The Royal Navy and Chelsea Hospitals Cemeteries are online via TheGenealogist, BMDRegisters and Findmypast and Ancestry (see Chapter 3).

Remember: Many cemetery records have not yet been digitized, and are not online (see Chapter 6).

Monumental/memorial inscriptions, gravestones/churchyard surveys
Ancestry – see above
Findmypast – see above
MyHeritage – see above

UKIndexer Headstone Project
This project, run by the subscription site TheGenealogist, provides photographs and indexes of gravestones. It has good UK coverage. You can volunteer or contribute to the project, and earn credits towards a subscription in return.

World Burial Index
This subscription site contains gravestone images from around the world but with the highest concentration in the UK. A free basic search is available.

FindaGrave
This is part of Ancestry, but also freely available at **www.findagrave. com**. A very large database, with a strong American bias, but there are many English and Welsh entries. Its aim is to create a 'virtual cemetery' and the site is based on volunteer contributions. Visitors can also place flowers on the virtual grave, and add biographical details for the deceased. These are not always correct and any such information should be verified using other sources.

Gravestone Photographic Resource
This is part of Ancestry but freely available at **www.gravestonephotos. com**. This international database was established by Charles Sale in 1998, and includes over half a million grave monuments, and a million names for the UK. Images are supplied by volunteers. A search will supply you with details from the gravestone and relationships to other people on the monument, where known.

Billiongraves.com
A free American site, but has worldwide gravestone images and transcriptions. It is also searchable via **FamilySearch.org** and is partnered with MyHeritage. It encourages registered users to photograph and upload images of gravestones, and includes GPS locations of each gravestone.

Ancestorsatrest (www.ancestorsatrest.com)
This site is run by Canadian genealogy author Lorine McGinnis Schulze and while there is a strong Canadian/American bias, there is some UK coverage of uncertain quantity. The site is free so there is nothing to lose by searching it.

Interment.net
Run by Steve Johnson, an avid family historian and computer buff, the site provides transcriptions of gravestones (no images). While UK coverage is relatively low the site it is free to access.

The Arts Society Ledger Stone Survey (https://theartssociety.org/ what-we-do/church-recording-ledgerstone-survey-england-and-wales) (See Chapter 6.) Records ledger stones in churches.

Locally organized transcriptions and collections
Many family history societies, and private individuals, have made transcriptions of parish registers, and these may be available for sale, or online. Likewise, there are many local collections of memorial inscriptions, or published churchyard surveys, now online (and sometimes also available inside the church). Two of the best examples are at Hastingleigh in Kent **http://www.hastingleigh.com** and Kirkburton in Yorkshire **http://kirkburtonchurchyard.co.uk/ kirkburton-churchyards**. You can identify any local monumental

inscriptions held in record offices via The National Archives catalogue (**www.discovery.nationalarchives.gov.uk**), and individual CRO catalogues. Older published collections of memorial inscriptions, and parish registers, may be online via companies such as archive Internet Archive (**archive.org**) or Google Books (**www.books.google.com**).

Newspaper sources

These are of use for probate notices, obituaries etc which may help locate burials.

British Library Newspaper Archive	**www.britishnewspaperarchive.co.uk**
National Library of Wales Newspaper Archive	**https://newspapers.library.wales**
The Times Archive	**www.thetimes.co.uk/archive**

Appendix I

INCISED CROSS MARKERS OF KENT

This article was first published in my column 'Heritage Corner', in the *Kent Family History Journal*, December 2018.

In 1986, Kent Archaeological Society (KAS) member, Ben Stocker, published an article in the *Kent Archaeological Review* (1988), entitled 'Medieval Grave Markers of Kent'. In this (which he referred to as an interim report), he described research into various 'grave markers' he, and his friend Patricia Stead, had discovered in churchyards across the county. He referred to them as 'discoids', because of their discoid shape.

Stocker's research defined the boundaries of the discovered 'discoids' as '*confined to an area bounded by Stone-in-Oxney in the west and Stodmarsh in the north*', further stating they were most numerous in an area approximately six miles from Folkestone. He added that '*An arc seventeen miles long with its centre at Hythe would encompass all of them*'. Sadly, prior to his premature death, Stocker never published his later findings, but he left two large folders of research notes, currently held at the KAS archive in Maidstone. A trawl through these folders reveals his work was more extensive than his article revealed. To start with, he discovered other discoids, after the publication of the article. These were at Northbourne, Barham, Chislet, Hinxhill, Newington, Nonnington, Shepherdswell and Westenhanger Castle, and his article states that he and Patricia Stead visited about 90 percent of Kent's medieval churches, in their search for discoids. He also collected references to similar markers at several locations outside Kent; notably in Northamptonshire (Brockhall, Byfield, Preston Capes and Southwick), Derbyshire (Ashbourne), Co. Durham (Escomb), Cheshire (Chester), Pembrokeshire (St David's), Chester and Gloucestershire (Kempley), as well as in Germany, France and Spain.

His article concentrated primarily on the theory that the discoids were markers directly associated with burials within churchyards. However, ongoing research by myself and Andrew Linklater of Canterbury Archaeological Trust (CAT) is re-examining another theory (largely ignored by Stocker), that the discoids were actually churchyard boundary markers. Our research also adds a newly discovered marker to the Kent collection, consisting of a surviving discoid drum head (separated from its now lost shaft) at St Mary's Church, Lamberhurst. Its rediscovery extends the outer limit of the arc in which the markers have been found 35 miles west, to the Kent/Sussex border. It is perhaps odd that, despite Stocker's extensive expeditions, no other discoids, or similar markers, have been found to date in West Kent, or even across adjoining counties. There have, however, been further discoveries elsewhere in the country since Stocker's published article, one being during excavations in connection with the installation of mains services at St Mary's Bletsoe in Hertfordshire. Here, a very similar 'lollipop' shaped stone, with an elaborate medieval cross and floral design on both sides of its 'drum head', was found buried in the churchyard. This is probably the fate of many others and may be the reason why so few are visible today. Other markers, or fragments of them, are also to be seen within the Kent collection, reused in standing walls of later church additions, such as Adisham, Coldred, Monks Horton and Folkestone.

The main question one must ask is: Was the primary function of these stones really that of grave markers? If they were grave markers, why are relatively few recorded elsewhere across England, and why do they not regularly occur in other medieval religious institutions, such as monastic burial grounds? There are some similar markers at Strata Florida although these are not in their original site. Apparently, these were relocated from the original monastic site a mile or so up the road, but they certainly do not look like they belong to the graves to which they have been 'attached' at the present monastic site.

If they were grave markers, why does not one of them bear any personal insignia of any kind, and why do they all feature an incised cross? Stocker himself questions this in his article, but provides no explanation. Although it is true that the majority of the population at this time was illiterate, is it not odd that no personal insignia of any kind ever features on these stones? Could they instead, perhaps have marked the boundaries of the churchyard, and even been the points where the churchyard was formally blessed during the process of consecration? It is known that churchyards were consecrated in a similar manner to the church itself, and the incised crosses bear a marked similarity to consecration crosses found, both incised in the stonework, or painted on the internal faces of church walls. They may well have been used more frequently where churchyards were not already enclosed by a ditch, hedge or wall.

Stocker also recorded several other markers which, although similarly incised with crosses, were of rectangular shape. These he referred to as 'not truly a discoid' and it is perhaps unfortunate that he had chosen the term 'discoid' to describe these markers, presumably before he located the rectangular examples. Good examples of the latter are those at Ryarsh and Bonnington. Common sense would seem to suggest that all the markers – both rectangular and discoid – are likely to have served the same purpose. Churchyards have, of course, expanded over the years, meaning the original boundaries are uncertain, especially in rural locations. What should also be noted is that, while many of the markers are found loose, it is highly unlikely those still in the ground are in their original positions. It is also possible they were later recycled and used as grave markers following further formalization of the churchyard boundary. We believe it is unlikely that any of the markers has a direct relation to any contemporary burial, and suggest that it is time to give these markers a new classification and refer to them as Incised Cross Markers (ICMs) rather than 'discoids'. This designation avoids any unproven funerary association, or fixation with their shape.

Interestingly, ICMs also bear a marked similarity to wayside crosses found in counties such as Cornwall, as extensively examined by Arthur Langdon (*Old Cornish Crosses* 1896). Research is ongoing, and this article encourages you all to look out for further examples in your travels and report back to me if you find more: also to proffer your own thoughts on what they might have been. Since the one at Bletose was recovered during external excavations, one can surmise that others may lie concealed beneath the present churchyard ground surface. Many more will have been lost this way, and not be visible today, while others have no doubt disappeared among piles of discarded gravestones, or been thrown onto skips during restoration work. It must also be remembered that on rare occasions ICM fragments have turned up in secular locations. Portions of two, and possibly three, were retrieved from the foundations of the medieval Longport Farmhouse at Newington, Kent during dismantling as part of the construction of the Channel Tunnel Terminal, and an ICM drum-head was recovered from an eighteenth-century wall at Godmersham Court Lodge. The positions of both these examples lie close to ancient churches, and Godmersham formerly possessed two further ICMs in its churchyard (now lost). It may be the markers were broken and regarded as surplus to requirement, only to be seen as reusable construction rubble. So keep your eyes peeled! You never know where they may turn up.

The points raised here are to open the matter up to discussion, rather than to make a pronouncement that they are definitely churchyard boundary markers or consecration crosses. At the moment the jury is out, but all thoughts are welcomed.

Since writing this article, the discovery of another ICM at Croxton Kerrial Church, Leicestershire, has been brought to my attention. This was found by builders during work for a church extension and is similar in shape and form to lollipop-shaped Kent markers.

See pages 20 and 142 of the book and **www.chfh.co.uk/blog** for photographs and more information about ICMs.

Appendix II

CARRYING OUT A CHURCHYARD SURVEY

A comprehensive survey of the churchyard would include geometric surveying of the complete site, including its boundaries and all entry points to the graveyard, such as gates, steps or stiles, and making a record of all features within it: sundials, buildings, and natural features, such as trees. Each gravestone should be recorded in full; details of its size, stone type, inscription and GPS location.

Before you consider carrying out a survey, think about your main aims; what you hope to achieve, and what you can realistically achieve. While a full-blown survey of everything in the graveyard, together with GPS records and digital plans, would be wonderful, this is beyond the resources of most of us, in terms of time, resources and skill. Remember that *any* survey of the graveyard is better than none, especially in terms of recording the memorial inscriptions, many of which are deteriorating very quickly.

Below, I look at what you will need to complete both a low-level and a high-level survey. You will need to consider the resources you have at your disposal first. For either type, firstly check to see if any sort of survey has already been completed. If possible, look in parish archives, as well as making searches online. If there has been an earlier survey, this does not mean you should not conduct your own, but you can use the earlier survey as a starting point, double-checking the work already done. The earlier survey will help you decipher stones which are now difficult to read, and you can provide an update on the condition of the stones and details of any graves which post-date the earlier survey.

Make sure no headstones are missed because they are covered by vegetation. You may need to clear parts of the graveyard vegetation before you begin your survey, but check with the PCC or body that maintains the churchyard for prior permission, and to ensure you are not clearing an area that has been left to grow for conservation reasons. It is often easier to survey a graveyard during the winter months.

Low-level graveyard survey
This type of survey will aim to do the following:

- Produce a plan of the graveyard showing its size and shape
- Create a data entry for each headstone which pinpoints the site of each headstone on the graveyard plan

Step 1 Creating a graveyard plan
Your plan will need to be of sufficient scale to plot all the headstones. If the graveyard contains a particularly heavy concentration of stones, this is going to be essential. A scale in the region of 1:50 or 1:100 is recommended. If you struggle with such terminology, it indicates that 1cm/inch/metre (or 1 of any unit) on the paper or plan represents 50 or 100 respectively of that same unit on the ground.

It's worth checking to see if you can get hold of a plan that has already been drawn up, perhaps as a result of previous alterations to the church area. A good place to start is to approach the PCC to see if they are aware of one. Each parish church has a church architect and he or she may have produced one at some point.

Pool your resources – the local history society, archaeological group or local villagers may have surveying expertise and be happy to help. If not, a professional surveying company could be approached if there are sufficient funds, or your church may wish to become part of the Church of England's 'Burial Grounds of England Survey', if appropriate (**www.churchofengland.org/resources/churchcare/churchcare-campaigns-and-projects**). This would take much of the surveying side of things out of your hands but mean the local community could contribute to recording the gravestones.

Alternatively, you can create a plan using a large-scale Ordnance Survey map as a template. Note that Ordnance Survey maps are subject to a fifty-year copyright period, but older maps are readily available via second-hand booksellers (see Chapter 3). Use a computer scanner or photocopier to make an A3 template. Don't add any data to this template – it's a blank template from which you will be able to create new blank copies to work with. You may wish to try several different ways of arranging a churchyard plan before you start work in earnest.

You may wish to break the graveyard up into sections by drawing grid squares on the plan, which will help locate grave locations.

Step 2 Recording the headstones

The stones should be systematically allocated numbers and plotted on the plan.

A record of each stone should then be made using an individual sheet of paper or a digital page for each. You can devise your own recording template to include the points listed below. Creating a template means your records should be consistent. Also, see the downloadable headstone recording forms mentioned under the high-level survey option. Include as many of the following points as you feel able, but be consistent.

- **Allocated number on plan**
- **Full inscription**: word-for-word with any illegible sections left as dashes or question marks. If you wish, you can use a system of double slashes to denote the end of each line as carved on the gravestone.
- **Memorial type:** e.g. chest tomb, ledger slab, upright headstone, is it enclosed by railings, are there kerb stones?
- **Location:** while you will have the number of the stone on the plan, it is worth noting the position of the stone and what it is next to, especially if it could easily be missed or is unusual, e.g. if it is on the external wall of a church, or close to a major churchyard feature. If the stone has clearly been relocated (perhaps it is leaning against the church wall), this should be noted.
- **Condition:** note if the stone is damaged, losing its lettering, has sunk, is leaning or has fallen over (recumbent).
- **Photograph the stone:** (see notes on how to photograph stones in Chapter 5). While photographs will be digital, also print off a hard copy to go with individual record sheets. Black and white prints are more durable than colour, and also often produce a clearer image.
- **Other notes:** include anything unusual about the stone such as the fact it has been painted, repaired or reused. Inspection of the back of the stone might reveal another inscription, or show that an old stone has actually been recycled, or perhaps a maker's name.
- **Footstones:** record footstones as well as headstones. These should have initials on. Check these to see that they match with the headstone they face. Some get moved and attached to the wrong headstone.

High-level survey

If you have more time to spend, you can consider including the following points. You may decide to design a template that includes tick boxes to aid completion.

- **Dimensions:** width, height and depth
- **Land types and features around the stone:** these should include the following which occur within five metres of the stone: graveyard ditches, grass, flower beds, shrubs and trees, paths, gates and other memorials.
- **Inscription location:** if the stone has more than one face, note which face each inscription is on. You may wish to draw a sketch to clarify this.
- **Inscription technique**: e.g. incised, inlaid, raised
- **Artwork:** record any drawing or symbols on the stone. These may help date it if the date cannot be read. See Chapter 5 for further information on memorial artwork and symbolism.
- **Stone type/summary of materials used**: while most headstones are made of stone, others may consist of wood, iron or a mixture of materials. Recording this will help later generations identify the stone. Try to identify the type of stone. This is not always obvious, as there are many types of stone and many different local variations. There are several stone identification websites online, but Archaeology Scotland has one of the best, and it is aimed at at those carrying out churchyard surveys at **http://archaeol.wwwnlls6.a2hosted.com/wp-content/uploads/2014/01/7stone.pdf**. While the Scottish bias means it highlights stones more commonly found in Scotland, it's a very useful aid. Even if you feel unable to go into such depth regarding stone type, some are easily recognizable and worthy of note because they denote a 'high-status' headstone, e.g. Bethersden and Purbeck marble were expensive and are easily spotted since they were formed out of solid beds of crustaceous fossils.
- **Family group:** is the stone part of a family group? This may be obvious from the surname, but sometimes it will be your own local knowledge that tells you a group of stones belongs to one family, although surnames have changed at marriage.
- **Stonemason's name or mark:** check the head, foot and back of the stones for any stonemason's name or marks. These should be described, drawn and photographed.

Archaeology Scotland also has graveyard survey template forms which can be downloaded at **https://archaeologyscotland.org.uk/projects/scottish-graveyards**.

Storing and giving access to your survey

While your survey will most likely be stored on your computer or digitally online, it is a good idea to print off several paper copies. Technology and related storage methods change so quickly that, ironically, paper is still the most reliable method of preserving a record long-term. Distribute paper copies of your work in several places for safe-keeping – perhaps the local history society, library or church archive. You then need to decide whether to place the fruits of your labour online. There is insufficient room to discuss this here, but look around to see what is already on the internet to give you an idea of what looks good and is easy to use. The surveys mentioned on pages 206–207 for Kirkburton and Hastingleigh are good examples. You may wish your survey to form part of a local history, or one-place study. For more on one-place studies, read Janet Few's book *Putting Your Ancestors in Their Place: A Guide to One Place Studies* (2014).

NOTES

Chapter 1

1. Hachlili Rachel & Killebrow Ann Rachel (1983) 'Jewish Funerary Customs During the Second Temple Period, in the Light of the Excavations at the Jericho Necropolis', *Palestine Exploration Quarterly*, 115:2, 109-139, DOI: 10.1179/peq.1983.115.2.109.
2. Simmonds, Vince, '*An overview of the archeology and karst.*' Mendip Cave Registry and Archive, 2016 **www.mcra.org.uk/wiki/lib/exe/fetch.php?media=archaeology:mendip_archaeo_simmonds.pdf.** (accessed March 2021).
3. Brødholt, Ingrid 'Socialization of infants and children in Roman Britain. An analysis of burial customs with special focus on the Lankhills cemetery.' Department of Archaeology, Conservation, and History, University of Oslo, 2012.
4. Pollock, K.J. 'The Evolution and Role of Burial Practice in Roman Wales'. (BAR British Series 426. 2006)
5. 'More People May Believe in an Afterlife than Believe in God,' National Secular Society (**www.secularism.org.uk/news/2012/12/more-people-may-believe-in-an-afterlife-than-believe-in-god-according-to-a-nation-wide-survey-of-britons-born-in-1970** (accessed December 2017).

Chapter 2

1. Morris, Richard, '*The Church in British Archaeology.*' British Council for Archaeology. Research Report 47. 1983.
2. Burgess, Frederick. *English Churchyard Memorials* p.23. Lutterworth Press 1963
3. Burn, Richard, *The Ecclesiastical Law* p.344. London, S. Sweet; V.& R. Stevens & G.S. Norton, 1842.

4. Personal communication, A. Linklater 2020

5. Ibid.

6. Craig-Atkins, Elizabeth. 'Eavesdropping on short lives: Eaves-drip burial and the differential treatment of children one year of age and under in early Christian cemeteries.' Hemer, K.A. and Hadley, D.M., (eds.) *Medieval Childhood: Archaeological Approaches*. Oxbow 2014

7. Johnson, Walter, *Byways in British Archaeology*. Cambridge University Press 1912.

8. Higginbotham, Peter *The Workhouse*. (**www.workhouses.org.uk**) accessed November 2020)

9. Personal communication, A. Linklater 2019.

Chapter 3

1. 'Chapels-Merthyr Tydfil', *GENUKI*, **www.genuki.org.uk/big/wal/ GLA/MerthyrTydfil/Chapels** (accessed October 2020.)

2. Procotre, Jennifer, Gaimser, Märit & Langthorne, James Young. *A Quaker Burial Ground in North Shields. Excavations at Coach Lane, Tyne and Wear.* pp. 22-29. Pre-Construct Archaeology 2016.

3. 'Histories of Whitechapel. St George's German Lutheran Church', *Survey of London* **https://surveyoflondon.org** (accessed November 2020.

4. Hartle, Robert, *The New Churchyard: from Moorfields Marsh to Bethlem Burial Ground, Brokers Row and Liverpool Street*. Crossrail Archaeology Series 2017.

5. Harding, Vanessa, 'Burial of the plague dead in early modern London: Epidemic Disease in London', ed. J.A.I. Champion. Centre for Metropolitan History Working Papers Series, No. 1, 1993. **https:// archives.history.ac.uk/cmh/epiharding.html**; accessed November 2020.

6. Friends of East Greenwich Pleasaunce, **https://fegp.org/history/ what-is-the-pleasaunce**; (accessed January 2021).

7. Oxford Archaeology, Archaeological Excavation Report. 'The Royal Greenwich Hospital, London'. August 2007. **https://library. thehumanjourney.net/2454/1/KWK99.pdf** (accessed October 2020) and Mitchell, Piers D., & others, 'The study of anatomy in England from 1700 to the early 20th century'. *Journal of Anatomy*, first published online 18 April 2011. **https://www.ncbi.nlm.nih.gov/pmc/ articles/PMC3162231** (accessed November 2020).

8. *An archaeological watching brief in Leeds Castle grounds,* 1996; Canterbury Archaeological Trust: unpublished client report.

9. Bath Record Office Archives & Local Studies, 'Bath Union Workhouse'. **https://www.batharchives.co.uk/cemeteries/bath-union-workhouse**). (accessed November 2020).
10. Pope, Stephen, *Gresenhall Farm and Workhouse* p.65 Poppyland Publishing 2006.
11. Morris, James, 'Explorations in anatomy; the remains from Royal London Hospital' 2014. Royal London Hospital. *Anthropozoologica*, 49 (1). pp. 109-120, **http://clok.uclan.ac.uk/10707/1/08-Morris%20 corrected%20proof.pdf** (accessed November 2020).
12. Mitchell, Piers D., & others, 'The study of anatomy in England from 1700 to the early 20th century,'. *Journal of Anatomy*, – see note 11 – and James Morris, 'Explorations in anatomy: the remains from Royal London Hospital' (see note 15).
13. The National Archives, 'Asylums, psychiatric hospitals and mental health. Section 3. Mental Health and the State'. **https://www. nationalarchives.gov.uk/help-with-your-research/research-guides/ mental-health/#:~:text=Private%20'madhouses'%20were%20 licensed%20by,pauper%20lunatics%20in%20their%20county** (accessed November 2020) AND Historic England. 'The Growth of the Asylum', **https://historicengland.org.uk/research/inclusive-heritage/disability-history/1832-1914/the-growth-of-the-asylum** (accessed November 2020).
14. Chris Philo, 'Troubled proximities: asylums and cemeteries in nineteenth-century England', 2012. Downloaded from **https:// journals.sagepub.com/home/hpy** (accessed November 2020).
15. Harding, Vanessa 'Burial of the plague dead in early modern London: Epidemic Disease in London', Centre for Metropolitan History Working Papers Series, No. 1, 1993, **https://archives.history. ac.uk/cmh/epiharding.html** (accessed March 2020).
16. TUNNEL, The Archaeology of Crossrail, 'The New Churchyard'. **https://archaeology.crossrail.co.uk/exhibits/the-new-churchyard** (accessed November 2020).
17. **DOVER.uk.com** *History.* '*In Times of Peace*', **https://www.dover. uk.com/history/1916/annals-of-dover/dover-castle/in-times-of-peace** (accessed November 2020.
18. Augustine's Hospital Cemetery Kent, Geophysical Survey Report 2005/44 CA/06/1651/CHA (Unpublished client report)

Chapter 4

1. Mary Elizabeth Hotz, 'Down Among The Dead. Edwin Chadwick's Burial Reform Discourse in Mid-Nineteenth Century England'. Cambridge

University Press 2001 **https://www.jstor.org/stablc/25058537?read-now =1&refreqid=excelsior%3A615af789d87149645cb52dc11fcfae58&seq= 1#page_scan_tab_contents** (accessed May 2020) and Dr Bruce Rosen, The *Victorian History Blog*, 'To Die for Victorian Cemeteries', 20 January 2012. **http://vichist.blogspot.com/2012/01/to-die-for-victorian-london-cemeteries.html** (accessed April 2020)

2. Liverpool Necropolis-Grant Gardens **https://www.toxtethparkcemetery. co.uk/Necropolis%20Web%20Home%20Page.html** (accessed 17 May 2020).

3. Deborah Wiggins, 'The Burial Acts. Cemetery Reform in Great Britain, 1815-1914'. (1991) **https://ttu-ir.tdl.org/handle/2346/19372** (accessed 7 May 2019).

4. James Stevens Curl, *The Victorian Celebration of Death* page 60. Sutton Publishing Ltd 2000.

5. Chris Brooks, *Mortal Remains* pp. 66-76. Wheaton Publishers Ltd 1989.

6. 'Westminster cemeteries scandal', **https://en.wikipedia.org/wiki/ Westminster_cemeteries_scandal** (accessed March 2019).

7. St James' Cemetery. **http://www.stjamescemetery.co.uk/index/ category/history** (accessed February 2019).

8. The Cremation Society. *'Progress of Cremation in the British Islands 1885-2019'.* **https://www.cremation.org.uk/progress-of-cremation-united-kingdom** (accessed February 2021).

9. Ibid.

Chapter 5

1. Personal communication, A. Linklater 2021

2. Litten, Julian *The English Way of Death. The Common Funeral since 1450.* p.88 Robert Hale, London 1991.

3. Ibid p.197

4. 'An archaeological watching brief in St Nicholas' Church, The Street, Ash next Sandwich, Kent'. September 2014–March 2016 Canterbury Archaeological Trust, unpublished client report.

5. Al Garrod, *The History of the Lincoln Waites* **www.lincolnwaites.org. uk/buildings.shtml** (accessed March 2021).

6. Helen Webb and Andrew Norton, 'The Medieval and Post-medieval Graveyard, of St Peter-le-Bailey at Bonn Square, Oxford', *Oxoniensia* 22009 **http://oxoniensia.org/volumes/2009/webb.pdf** (accessed March 2021).

7. Personal communication, Prof David Austin, University of Wales, August 2019.

8. Frederick Burgess *English Churchyard Memorials* p.108, Lutterworth Press, 1963.
9. Ibid. p.147 Note 41.
10. Jonathan Taylor, 'Churchyard Chest Tombs', **https://www. buildingconservation.com/articles/chesttombs/chesttombs.htm** (accessed November 2020)
11. Dr Madeleine Gray, 'Disappearing or Overlooked Tombstones Post Medieval Cross Slabs in South-East Wales: Closet Catholics or Stubborn Traditionalists?' *The Antiquaries Journal*, Vol. 96, 2016 (accessed November 2020)
12. Burgess, Frederick *English Churchyard Memorials* p.275, Lutterworth Press 1963.

Chapter 6
1. Dr David Wright, 'The Earliest Parish Registers of the Diocese of Canterbury: some Observations, Questions and Problems', *Archaeologia Cantiana* Vol. 135 pp.159-161. 2014.
2. Addingham, St Peter parish registers, 'West Yorkshire, England, Church of England Baptisms, Marriages and Burials, 1512-1812', **Ancestry.com**. (accessed December 2020).
3. Dray & Son, Undertakers of Hythe, Kent History and Library Centre, Ref.EK/U59/B2 1814-1942.
4. Will of John Lynot, 1393 (abstract), Kent Archaeological Society, 'Medieval & Tudor Kent P.C.C. Wills - Book 57 page 16'. Original will proved at Prerogative Court of Canterbury, TNA reference PROB 11/175. Will of Richard Warmyngtone 1378, Kent Archaeological Society, 'Medieval & Tudor Kent Wills at Lambeth - Book 24 Page 447', (Original will proved at the Peculiar Court of the Archbishop of Canterbury and held at Lambeth Palace Library. Both accessed via **www.kentarchaeology.org.uk/Research/research.htm** (August 2020)

Chapter 7
1. Kent Archaeological Society **www.kentarchaeology.org.uk/Research/ Libr/MIs/MIsLLDuncan/MIsLLDuncan.htm** (accessed January 2019).
2. Clarke, John M. (2006). *The Brookwood Necropolis Railway*. Locomotion Papers 143 Oakwood Press 2006

BIBLIOGRAPHY AND FURTHER READING

General

Johnson, Walter, *Byways in British Archaeology*. (1912, Cambridge University Press)

Heritage, Celia, *Tracing Your Ancestors Through Death Records*. (2013, 2015 Pen & Sword Books).

Chapter 1: A Brief History of Death Burial

Curl, James Stevens, *The Victorian Celebration of Death*. (Sutton Publishing Ltd 2000, 2004).

Litten, Julian, *The English Way of Death. The Common Funeral since 1450*. (Robert Hale London 1991.)

Parsons, Brian, Frederick W. *Paine Funeral Directors. A History*. (Dignity 2017)

Rugg, Julie & Parsons Brian, *Funerary Practices in England and Wales*. (Emerald Publishing)

Parsons, Brian, *The Undertaker at Work: 1900-1950*. (Strange Attractor Press 2015)

Parsons, Brian, *The Evolution of the British Funeral Industry in the 20th Century*. (Emerald Publishing).

Pollock, Karen, *The evolution and role of burial practice in Roman Wales*. (**https://research.bangor.ac.uk/portal/en/theses/the-evolution-and-role-of-burial-practice-in-roman-wales(e6fe3c83-ead2-4c24-912a-741892085000).html**); accessed December 2017.

Simmonds, Andrew, Marquez-Grant, Nicholas and Loe, Louise, *Life and Death in a Roman City Excavation of a Roman Cemetery with a Mass Grave at 120-122 London Road Gloucester* (**https://library.thehumanjourney.net/378/**).

Taylor, Lou, *Mourning Dress. A Costume and Social History.* (First pub. 1983: pub. as Routledge Revival 2010).

Chapter 2: The Parish Churchyard

Bonsall, Dr Mary. *The Bickerstaffe Quakers and The Friends Graveyard at Bickerstaffe.* (2008) **www.holytrinitybickerstaffe.co.uk/wp-content/ uploads/2016/03/Bickerstaffe-New-Text-Quakers-1-PDF.pdf**)

Brødholt, Ingrid, *Socialization of infants and children in Roman Britain. An analysis of burial customs with special focus on the Lankhills cemetery.* (Department of Archaeology, Conservation, and History, University of Oslo 2012. (**www.duo.uio.no/bitstream/handle/10852/23078/ Brxdholt-master.pdf?sequence=2**);

Burn, Richard, *The Ecclesiastical Law* (London, S. Sweet; V. & R. Stevens & G.S. Norton, 1842).

Cocke, Thomas ed, *The Churchyard's Handbook* (Church House Publishing 4th Edition 2001)

Daniell, Christopher, *Death and Burial in Medieval England, 1066-1550.* (Routledge, 1997).

Morris, Richard, *Churches in the Landscape* (Phoenix House, 1997).

Rodwell, Warwick, *The Archaeology of Churches* (Amberley 2012)

Rugg, Julie, *Cemeteries, churchyards and burial grounds* (**https://webarchive. nationalarchives.gov.uk/20110118111022/ http://www.cabe.org. uk/files/cemeteries-churchyards-and-burial-grounds.pdf**).

Webb, Helen and Norton, Andrew, 'The Medieval and Post-medieval Graveyard of St Peter-le-Bailey at Bonn Square, Oxford', pp. 137-179. *Oxoniensia* 2009, (Oxfordshire Architectural and Historical Society, 2009.

White, Graeme, *The Medieval Landscape 1000–1540* (Bloomsbury Academic Collection 2012).

Chapter 3: Ex-Parochial Graveyards

Holmes, Mrs Basil [Isabella M.] (1896). *The London Burial Grounds: notes on their history from the earliest times to the present day.* (Macmillan and Co. New York 1896. Access via **https://archive.org** or **www.gutenberg. org/files/56832/56832-h/56832-h.htm**

Handlist of non-conformist, Roman Catholic, Jewish and burial ground registers. (Guildhall Library Research Guide, 1993).

Ifans, Dafydd, *Nonconformist Register of Wales* (Aberystwyth: National Library of Wales and Welsh County Archivists' Group 1994).

Powers, Anne. 'London graveyards and the Wonderful Mrs. Basil Holmes', *A Parcel of Ribbons* [Blog] (**http://aparcelofribbons. co.uk/2012/08/london-graveyards-the-wonderful-mrs-basil-holmes**

Procotre, Jennifer, Gaimser, Marit, Langthorne, James Young. *A Quaker Burial Ground in North Shields. Excavations at Coach Lane, Tyne and Wear* (Pre-Construct Archaeology Limited, Monograph No.20. 2016).

Quaker Family History Society: **https://www.qfhs.co.uk/index.html**

Susser Bernard (Ed), *The Old Jewish Cemetery on Plymouth Hoe* (The Susser Archive, **www.jewishgen.org/jcr-uk/susser/plymouthcemeteryintro.htm**).

Chapter 4: Cemeteries

Brooks, Chris, *Mortal Remains* (Wheaton Publishers Ltd 1989).

Mellor, Hugh and Parsons Brian, *London Cemeteries. An Illustrated Guide &Gazetteer.* (The History Press, 4th Edition 2008).

Clarke, John M., *The Brookwood Necropolis Railway.*, (Oakwood Press, 4th ed., 2006).

Clarke, John M., *London's Necropolis: A Guide to Brookwood Cemetery.* (Stenlake Publishing, 2018).

Fairley Nielsson, Anna, St James' Cemetery, Liverpool (**www.stjamescemetery.co.uk**)

Loudon, John Claudius, *On the Laying out, Planting, and Managing of Cemeteries: And on the Improvement of Churchyards* (1843). Available via Archive.org. https://archive.org/details/onlayingoutplan00loudgoog

Mayjonade-Christy, Kelly, *The living and the dead. Burial Reform Discourse in Victorian England (c. 1830-1880).* **https://warwick.ac.uk/fac/arts/modernlanguages/academic/kmc/burial_reform_research_proposal_-_kelly_mayjonade-christy.pdf**

Rice, Matthew, *Rice's Architectural Primer.* (Bloomsbury Publishing, 2010).

Wiggins, Deborah Elaine. *The Burial Acts: Cemetery Reform in Great Britain, 1815–1914.* (Texas Tech Universities, 1991).

Chapter 5: Gravestones and Monuments.

Badham, Sally, *Monumental Brasses* (Shire 2009).

Badham, Sally, *Medieval Church and Churchyard Monuments* (Shire Library 2011)

Badham, Sally ed, *One Thousand Years of English Church Monuments* (Ecclesiology Today 2010).

Bailey, Brian, *Churchyards of England and Wales.* (Robert Hale Ltd 1987).

Bartram, Alan, *Tombstone Lettering in the British Isles* (Lund Humphries, London/Watson-Guptill Publication, New York. 1978).

Burgess, Frederick, *English Churchyard Memorials.* (Lutterworth Press 1963)

Cramp, Rosemary, University of Durham. *The Corpus of Anglo-Saxon Stone Sculpture*. Volume I, Chapter 2, Sequence of Forms. (**http://www.ascorpus.ac.uk/1chap2.php**).

Lawrence, Margaret *For All the Saints: St. Michael's Church East Peckham, Parish and People*. (Kent Archaeological Society 2004)

Ryder, Peter *The Cross Slab Grave Covers of Cumbria* (Cumbria County Council 2001).

Taylor, Richard, *How to Read A Church* (Rider 2003).

Winchester, Angus, *Discovering Parish Boundaries* (Shire Books 2000).

Yorke, Trevor, *Gravestones & Memorials* (Countryside Books, 2010).

Chapter 6: The Records.

Herber, Mark, *Ancestral Trails* (Sutton 2004)

Humphery-Smith, Cecil R., ed. *The Phillimore Atlas and Index of Parish Registers*. (Phillimore, 1984, 1995, 2002).

Steel D.J. and Samuel, Edgar, R, *The National Index of Parish Registers Vol 3 . Sources for Roman Catholic and Jewish Genealogy and Family History*. (Phillimore 1974)

Steel D.J., *The National Index of Parish Registers Vol 5. A guide to Anglican, Roman Catholic and Nonconformist registers before 1837, together with information on marriage licenses, bishop's transcripts and modern copies*. (Phillimore 1976).

Webb, Clifford, and Wolfston, Pat, *Greater London Cemeteries and Crematoria* (3rd edition Society of Genealogists 1994).

Other resources, societies and websites

British Association for Local History
A national charity which promotes local history and serves local historians **www.balh.org.uk**

The Church Monuments Society
One of the leading educators in church monuments: **https://churchmonumentssociety.org**

The Cemetery Research Group (CRG)
Aims to expand an understanding of current and past burial culture in the UK and internationally. **www.york.ac.uk/spsw/research/cemetery-research-group**

The Cremation Society
The leading source of information on cremation. **www.cremation.org.uk**

The Ecclesiological Society
Provides events and information for those who love churches and their history. **http://ecclsoc.org**

Family Search Wiki
www.familysearch.org/wiki. Good for parish register coverage and for learning more about genealogical sources.

Library of the Society of Friends
Based at Friends House, is a unique resource and is one of the largest Quaker collections in the world: **www.quaker.org.uk/resources/library**

Institute of Heraldic & Genealogical Studies, Canterbury
Independent charitable trust dedicated to family history and heraldry education and research.

National Archive Research Guides
www.nationalarchives.gov.uk/help-with-your-research/research-guides. Search by subject, e.g. 'nonconformist'.

The National Archives
Ruskin Avenue, Kew, Surrey, England. **www.nationalarchives.gov.uk**

National Library of Wales
Penglais Rd, Aberystwyth. www.library.wales

Society of Genealogists
Leading provider of genealogical collections and education, based in London. **www.sog.org.uk**

INDEX